Daily Meditations on
Golden Texts of the Bible

Henry Gariepy

WILLIAM B. EERDMANS PUBLISHING COMPANY

GRAND RAPIDS, MICHIGAN / CAMBRIDGE, U.K.

© 2004 Wm. B. Eerdmans Publishing Co.
All rights reserved

Wm. B. Eerdmans Publishing Co.
255 Jefferson Ave. S.E., Grand Rapids, Michigan 49503 /
P.O. Box 163, Cambridge CB3 9PU U.K.
www.eerdmans.com

Printed in the United States of America

08 07 06 05 04   7 6 5 4 3 2 1

Library of Congress Cataloging-in-Publication Data

Gariepy, Henry.
Daily Meditations on Golden Texts of the Bible / Henry Gariepy.
p.   cm.
ISBN 0-8028-2755-1 (alk. paper)
1. Bible — Devotional use. 2. Devotional calenders.   I. Title.

BS617.8.G3047   2004
242'.5 — dc22
                                                    2004043328

Unless otherwise noted, Scripture quotations are from the Holy Bible:
New International Version © 1978 by the New York International
Bible Society, used by permission of Zondervan Bible Publishers.

To Marjorie
Who on this 50th year of our life journey together
Along with me lived intimately with these golden texts,
Discussing, reading, rewriting, praying through them,
And enhancing this work by her astute editing skills
And rich insights into the Word

Contents

THE NEW TESTAMENT

Introduction

I n our crisis-filled world of today, the timeless truths and guidance of the preeminent texts of the Bible are needed more than ever. This work selects 365 of the golden texts of the Bible, one for each day of the year, with all 66 books of the Bible represented. These are the crown jewels of Scripture that over time have stood out as mountain peaks on the range of Bible truth and inspiration.

Selections include classical and often-quoted biblical texts as well as some lesser-known gems of insight, instruction, and inspiration.

Other books are given for our information. The Bible is given for our transformation. The Bible presents God's love letter to human-kind, his priceless treasure to us and our guidebook for life. With the psalmist of old we affirm, "Your word is a lamp to my feet and a light for my path" (119:105).

It is important not only for us to get into the Word, but also for the Word to get into us. May the reflections on these timeless texts further lead us to declare in the words of the psalmist: "I have hidden your word in my heart that I might not sin against you" (Psalm 119:11).

The following is a suggested path for your journey through these luminous texts of God's Word:

- Read the Bible text and meditation selected for the day.
- Make a personal application of its timeless truth: What does it say to me?
- Commit to memory the Bible verse for that day.
- Use the text in some way — journaling, sharing it, calling it to mind and affirming its inspiration during the day.

The reading of and meditation upon these golden texts will intro-
duce to new readers, and reinforce for seasoned ones, the greatest texts
of the Bible — what they are, where they are located, and their message
for today. May these golden nuggets from God's Word immeasurably
enrich the lives of the readers, as they have through the years enriched
my life.

THE OLD TESTAMENT

In the beginning God created the heavens and the earth.

(Genesis 1:1)

"In the beginning God" is the seminal statement that launches the divine manuscript of the Bible. One commentator suggests that these are the most important four words ever written. This inspired quartet of words expresses faith in God as the foundation of life and the world.

They answer the riddle of the universe, affirming that the world did not come about by chance, but God is its first great Cause. They don't tell how the universe was created, but who created it, and they go on to relate, not the process, but the purpose of creation.

The verse proclaims that the universe can be understood only in the light of divine conception. Its declaration refutes atheism, contradicts pantheism, rebuts polytheism, and belies materialism.

Although it is impossible for us to comprehend fully this concept of an eternal, transcendent God, the only alternative is that of an eternal, self-existing universe, a concept that is not only incomprehensible but irrational. Eternal God or eternal matter — that is the choice.

Genesis 1:1, and its context, declares that the sovereign God created this complex, orderly universe, with intelligent and moral persons on a planet fantastically designed for their living and care. That monumental declaration of truth assures that the sovereign God also holds our future and finite lives in his mighty and loving hands.

2   A *Stupendous Announcement*

So God created man in his own image, in the image of God he created him; male and female he created them.   (Genesis 1:27)

These words may well be considered the most stupendous announcement of ancient history. It is a breathtaking thought, that on the sixth day of world history the Creator of the universe chose to mirror himself in the creation of a being with magnificent capabilities.

This declaration tells me that I am more than a cosmic accident, an animated clod, a bit of enchanted dust, a pawn in the universe, a fortuitous concourse of atoms, or the plaything of an inscrutable fate. I am something more than a series of breaths, a sequence of footsteps, a frail chain of words. I am created a two-world creature, with feet of clay to walk the earth, but with the imprint of divinity upon me. By divine fiat, God made us in his very image.

Shakespeare's Hamlet, contemplating humankind, was constrained to exclaim:

What a piece of work is man!
How noble in reason!
How infinite in faculty!
In form and moving how express and admirable!
In apprehension how like a God!

Our golden text declares that man and woman were created *imago Dei* — in likeness to God. We are a paradox of dust and divinity. "Frail children of dust," yet made in the image of the Creator, we have a holy purpose in this life and an eternal destiny in the life to come.

For this reason a man will leave his father and mother and be united to his wife, and they will become one flesh.   (Genesis 2:24)

For the first time in creation something is not good: "The LORD God said, 'It is not good for the man to be alone. I will make a helper suitable for him'" (Genesis 2:18). Without female companionship man was not complete.

God then creates woman and ordains that she and man should be as one, the words of our text providing the scriptural institution of marriage. The words have a familiar ring, of course, not only because they are usually quoted during the marriage ceremony, but also because Jesus based his own teaching on marriage on this primeval account in Genesis (Matthew 19:4-6).

In the metaphysics of marriage, one and one make one — for the two shall "become one flesh." The relationship of husband and wife is an inseparable union, the most indissoluble of all human relationships. The "leaving" and "cleaving" may sound old-fashioned — and so it is — but it is still God's societal law.

The first human institution established by God was that of marriage. In his provision for marital companionship and love, God ordained the family and home to be the basic human unit, which would provide the nurturing and training foundation for children born into the family.

This inspired passage at the very beginning of the creation account in the Bible leads us to understand afresh the divine plan for life's highest happiness and fulfillment. Only as the family is seen and understood as God's sacred institution can the life of individuals, and that of a society and nation, realize God's plan of true joy and fulfillment.

The First Gospel

"And I will put enmity between you and the woman, and between your offspring and hers; he will crush your head, and you will strike his heel." (Genesis 3:15)

This peerless promise in Genesis 3:15 has long been known as the *Protevangelium* — the "first gospel." Viewed in light of the Christian gospel, Bible scholars see a veiled reference to Christ, the earliest promise of the coming Messiah, his suffering, and final triumph over sin and Satan. Here we have the beginning and germ of all prophecy.

The "seed of the woman" (King James Version) provides the earliest hint of the Messiah's birth. It would have been traditional to write of the Lord's paternal parentage, but the prophecy speaks of "her offspring," the first intimation concerning the supernatural birth of the Savior, later prophesied by Isaiah (7:14) and ultimately fulfilled as recorded in the Gospels (Matthew 1:18; Luke 1:35).

"He will crush your head," God says to the Deceiver, predicting the ultimate defeat of Satan. "You will strike his heel" is a symbolical reference to the sufferings and death of the Savior, but this would not be a mortal wound, as Satan's wound will be. From this fountainhead the prophecy of redemption widens in Scripture as an ever-broadening stream.

This verse was to be the only star of promise for redemption on humankind's horizon until the coming of the prophets several millennia later. In humanity's darkest hour, when sin had marred the divine image, when judgment had been pronounced, in the bleak sky there appeared this scintilla of the promise of God's grace and mercy, in the coming Savior and his redemptive work.

"For dust you are and to dust you will return."   (Genesis 3:19)

How many times we have stood before the open grave and heard the words, "ashes to ashes, dust to dust." They serve as a reminder of our mortality and the ultimate consignment of life to the grave.

The great Charles H. Spurgeon in one of his sermons asked, "Why is it that I must die? The angels do not die. Why must I die? Why all this skill and wisdom to endure but for an hour?" He goes on to answer his burning question: "We die because Adam sinned. Sin is the mother of death. Sin slays the race. Adam's sin in Eden dug the graves of all his children."

The poet Henry Wadsworth Longfellow reminds us, "Our hearts, like muffled drums, are beating funeral marches to the grave." No matter how much we exercise, how much we diet, how many vitamins we take, or how many doctors we visit, someday we will die. Death is too powerful for us to fight by ourselves; we cannot face it alone. We need someone greater and stronger than death, the One who has conquered death for us!

Let us set alongside this text that given by Paul, who in his chapter on the resurrection declares: "The body that is sown is perishable, it is raised imperishable. . . . For the perishable must clothe itself with the imperishable, and the mortal with immortality" (1 Corinthians 15:42, 53).

Longfellow echoes this truth in his memorable lines from "Psalm of Life":

Life is real! Life is earnest!
And the grave is not its goal;
"Dust thou art, to dust returnest,"
was not spoken of the soul.

6 *Our Brother's Keeper*

"Am I my brother's keeper?"   (Genesis 4:9)

The context of our text shows how temptation must be mastered at the start, lest it lead us down the slippery slope to destruction. First, we find that Cain was angry and downcast with a deadly jealousy, which embittered him because of his brother Abel's more acceptable worship of God. Cain's worship was a mere formal act. Abel is commended in the New Testament for his faith (Hebrews 11:4) and Jesus himself referred to Abel as righteous (Matthew 23:35).

God sternly warned Cain about ungoverned jealousy and anger: "Sin is crouching at your door; it desires to have you, but you must master it" (Genesis 4:7). Either we master sin, or it masters us, and we can master sin only by our dependence upon God. Cain failed to heed God's warning and went on to practice deception and then to commit the first murder in God's creation (v. 8). The first man born on earth killed the second man born on earth — his own brother — and the terrifying aftermath has been the progression of violence and murder from generation to generation.

Confronted by God, Cain was called to account: "Where is your brother Abel?" He responded with an outright lie, "I don't know," and insolently disavowed responsibility: "Am I my brother's keeper?" There may have been no human witness to Cain's crime, but the eye of God had seen it. After the divine inquisition comes the divine sentence. The final consequence for his heinous sin is God's judgment upon him and his alienation from God.

John Donne reminds us: "I am involved with mankind." We cannot escape our responsibility for our brothers and sisters in our Father's world. As taught by Christ in Matthew 25, at the "Great Assize" we will be held accountable to God for our relationships with others. Our Lord calls us to be more than our brother's "keeper"; he calls us to be our brother's brother!

Enoch walked with God; then he was no more, because God took him away.
                                                                (Genesis 5:24)

The greatest thing that can be said about a person is that "He is a man of God," or "She is a woman of God." Twice in Enoch's two-verse biography it is said of him, "Enoch walked with God." If it is true that we can be judged by the company we keep, then this simple statement gives the most illuminating insight into the godly character of Enoch.

In the very next chapter of Genesis we read one of the most vivid descriptions in the Bible of humanity's depravity: "The LORD saw how great man's wickedness on the earth had become, and that every inclination of the thoughts of his heart was only evil all the time" (6:5). Then follows the account of God's judgment in sending the Great Deluge that destroyed all except Noah's family. Enoch's walk with God was going against the tide; his life was a shining light in the darkness.

To walk with God implies moral fitness and harmony with his will. A walk suggests steady progress. Enoch walked with God for over three hundred years. In that fifth chapter of Genesis no less than eight times a patriarch's genealogy concludes with the words, "and then he died." But in the cameo of Enoch we find a notable exception: "then he was no more, because God took him away." Hebrews 11:5 interprets this verse for us: "By faith Enoch was taken from this life, so that he did not experience death; he could not be found, because God had taken him away." Enoch walked with God, and one day he walked so far that he simply stepped off into heaven.

Ours is an even greater privilege than that of Enoch. We may enjoy an even closer walk with God through the grace of our Lord Jesus Christ and the indwelling presence of the Holy Spirit. May it be said of us, "He walks with God" or "She walks with God."

8　　Why Methuselah Lived So Long

Methuselah lived 969 years, and then he died.　　(Genesis 5:27)

Methuselah is known the world over for his legendary longevity, 969 years, the longest recorded life span. The most sanguine hopes of scientists today, who seek to optimize the length of life, do not approach the record in the fifth chapter of Genesis of patriarchs who averaged 912 years of life upon earth. Various theories have been advanced for such longevity, as well as speculations about the marvelous nature of the world's primeval environment, but in the end it remains a mystery.

Many embark on a rigorous quest for a long life. They consume vitamins, undertake diets, exercise on the most sophisticated equipment. But in the end, even as it was for ancient Methuselah, the epitaph is inscribed. No one escapes death.

The name given by Enoch to his son Methuselah had a sacred meaning: "When he dies, it shall be sent," or, "When he dies, judgment." A divine revelation was memorialized in his name. It was as though God said to Enoch: "Do you see that baby? The world will last as long as he lives and no longer. When that child dies, I shall deal with the world in judgment."

His name commemorated both a warning and a promise of God. As long as Methuselah lived, the day of grace was still available to humankind. What a beautiful testimony to God's grace that the longest span of life ever recorded was the measure of time God gave to humanity to repent before he would send his judgment, the Great Deluge, upon all the earth.

The stern warning of Genesis 6:3 is still true today: God said, "My Spirit will not contend with man forever." We have no Methuselah's life span today in which to repent and receive God's gift of salvation. We can be saved from the judgment of God only if we accept God's free offer of his marvelous grace and gift of life eternal.

"As long as the earth endures,
seedtime and harvest,
cold and heat,
summer and winter,
day and night
will never cease." (Genesis 8:22)

As we look about us we will find that wonders never cease as long as we never cease to wonder. The poet William Wordsworth invites us to "Let Nature be your teacher./She has a world of ready wealth,/Our minds and hearts to bless."

We live in an age more remote from nature than ever before. The difference is epitomized in the homely statement: "Grandfather had a farm, his son had a garden, and his grandson has a can opener." An urban child may suppose that breakfast comes from the supermarket, and heat from the furnace. However, our text reminds us that "seedtime and harvest," with its bountiful store of our daily bread and provisions for life, is a gift from God.

In the context of today's text, the Creator covenanted with humankind that a regular order of nature, with a fixed sequence of seasons and cycle of day and night, would prevail. These constants of nature, with the hydrologic cycle of the earth's water, marvelously provide for the maintenance of life on earth.

This golden text eloquently speaks to us of the witness and wonders of the seasons. A well-loved hymn aids our praise in extolling this faithful provision of God on our behalf:

Summer and winter, and springtime and harvest,
    Sun, moon and stars in their courses above,
Join with all nature in manifold witness
    To thy great faithfulness, mercy and love.

The Rainbow Covenant

"I have set my rainbow in the clouds, and it will be the sign of the covenant between me and the earth." (Genesis 9:13)

A popular song identifies the quests of life as "chasing pretty rainbows in the sky." The rainbow is one of the glories of nature. Its resplendent multi-hued beauty seems all the more glorious following the dark clouds of the storm. A rainbow is the union of heaven and earth, spanning the sky and reaching down to earth.

Noah's heart must have been overjoyed when, after the worst rains and most destructive flood in the history of the world, he looked up and saw the very first rainbow, and then learned that it was a token of God's covenant to all generations. Spanning the heavens after the rain, it serves as a reminder that the waters of the earth and sky will be held in check, never again to wreak their destruction upon all the earth.

The rainbow appears in the Bible again only in Ezekiel 1:28 and Revelation 4:3, where it surrounds the throne of God, and in Revelation 10:1, where it crowns a mighty angel. Rainbows in Scripture are associated with the goodness and glory of God.

George Matheson, blind preacher and poet, incorporated the glory of the rainbow into one of the devotional treasures of Christian song. Out of the crucible of his suffering he wrote:

O Joy that seekest me through pain,
   I cannot close my heart to thee;
I trace the rainbow through the rain
And feel the promise is not vain,
   That morn shall tearless be.

"May the LORD keep watch between you and me when we are away from each other."   (Genesis 31:49)

These words from the ancient book of Genesis have often been used as a benediction in parting. However, in the context of their original use, the words were in fact a malediction.

Two of the shiftiest characters in the Bible were taking leave of each other — Laban and Jacob. Laban's attitude toward his son-in-law Jacob had become increasingly unfriendly, until Jacob told his wives, "Your father's attitude toward me is not what it was before" (Genesis 31:5). What had once seemed a good working relationship between them had taken a distressing turn. Jacob's flocks were prospering; Laban's were suffering. Acrimony surfaced on the part of Laban's sons, as they accused Jacob of siphoning off their father's wealth.

Warned by God in a dream that he should move on, both to avoid Laban's wrath and to become settled in the Promised Land, Jacob obediently gathered his family and possessions and took a stealthy departure. Several days later, after he discovered the clandestine flight, Laban pursued and overtook Jacob's caravan.

A lengthy colloquy took place between the two men; then they entered into a covenant and separated. Laban invoked the name of Jacob's God, saying, "May the LORD [Yahweh] keep watch between you and me, when we are away from each other" (31:49). His words imply that Jacob needed watching, and it was his God's responsibility to keep an eye on him. This suspicious statement of Laban has often been appropriated by Christians as the so-called "Mizpah Benediction."

Separation may bring loneliness and concern for the well-being of the one held in deep affection. But there is something we can do — we can commit them to the care of our heavenly Father.

Standing on Holy Ground

"Take off your sandals, for the place where you are standing is holy ground."   (Exodus 3:5)

O ur selected text finds Moses in "the far side of the desert," caring for his father-in-law's sheep. It is hardly a setting for a life-transforming and history-making crisis. But as Edmund Burke has reminded us, "History is full of momentous trifles." Ordinary events often are fraught with extraordinary meaning.

In the desert Moses' attention was caught by a bush on fire. There was nothing unusual about that. But as he looked at it again, expecting it to crumble into ashes, he saw that the bush was ablaze, but unconsumed. He mused, "I will go over and see this strange sight — why the bush does not burn up."

As he approached, he was startled to hear the very voice of God calling his name from within the bush: "Moses! Moses!" He replied, "Here I am." Then he heard the command: "Take off your sandals, for the place where you are standing is holy ground."

God then called and commissioned a reluctant Moses to the great task of confronting Pharaoh, delivering the Hebrew slaves from the bondage of Egypt, and leading them to the Promised Land. Moses and history would be forever altered by that defining moment.

Have we not, on a much lesser scale, also been confronted with "burning bush" experiences in our lives? Has not God at times had to break through, get our attention, in order for us to know and fulfill his will for us? It may have been through a word spoken by another, or in the moment when we stood hushed beside a cradle that held the miracle of a new life, or through a tragedy that came upon us. But when God does come to us, and speaks to us by name, that place becomes holy ground.

Next time God appears to us, albeit in the most unexpected way or place, let us spiritually "remove our sandals," for we will be standing on holy ground!

"The blood will be a sign for you on the houses where you are; and when I see the blood, I will pass over you." (Exodus 12:13)

Moses had been commissioned by God to go before the most powerful man in his day and say to him, "This is what the LORD, the God of Israel, says: 'Let my people go'" (Exodus 5:1). The mighty monarch well knew what the consequences of such a release would be to Egypt's economy and the massive building projects that had become dependent upon the Hebrew slaves.

To Moses' presumptuous command Pharaoh contemptuously replied, "Who is the LORD, that I should obey him and let Israel go?" (5:2). Then came the infamous ten plagues, catastrophes that served as the instrument of God to break through Pharaoh's hardness of heart and lead the Israelites in their exodus from Egypt.

The final plague brought the angel of death at midnight to slay the firstborn of all children and cattle, except those of the Israelites who had followed God's command to sprinkle on their doorpost the blood of an unblemished lamb. This pivotal event in Jewish history became known as the Passover, one of the most vivid types in the Old Testament of redemption through the shed blood of Christ.

There was only one way for the Israelites in Egypt to be spared God's judgment. The angel of death that was moving throughout the land "passed over" any house on which was sprinkled blood of the lamb, and that household was saved. There is still only one way for us to escape God's condemnation upon sin, and that is through "Christ, our Passover Lamb" (1 Corinthians 5:7).

The blood of the Lord Jesus is available to everyone and is free to all who yield to the one whom John the Baptist designated as "the Lamb of God, who takes away the sin of the world" (John 1:29).

The Waters of Marah

When they came to Marah, they could not drink its water because it was bitter. (Exodus 15:23)

The exultant Song of Moses peals forth from the fifteenth chapter of Exodus, the *Te Deum* of Israel, celebrating God's mighty deeds and deliverance. But only three days into their journey the people's triumph turned into trouble, their praise into petulance, as they arrived at Marah and found pools of water that were bitter and undrinkable.

Marah is more than a geographical location. Marah is any place, any painful experience, to which we come on our wilderness journey through this world. It may be the loss of someone we love, or a debilitating or terminal illness, or problems our loved ones face.

Jesus never promised his followers a rose garden. He warned, "In the world you shall have tribulation." Soon or late, like the Israelites of old, we all come to the waters of Marah.

Moses' first act when confronted with the people's murmurings against him was to take the complaint to God in prayer. God has a remedy, reminding us in this passage: "I am the LORD, who heals you" (v. 26b). For every affliction of life there is a promise in the Word of God.

God chose a strange means of healing the bitter waters: "The LORD showed him a tree" (v. 25, KJV). Moses, as God instructed, cast the tree into the water, and the water was made sweet.

There was once another tree, one that suffered the axe for our sakes and now "towers o'er the wrecks of time." Our Lord, through the cross, is ever healing the bitter waters of life.

The same water that was bitter became sweet. Through the remedy of the grace of our Lord, our difficulties become doorways and our brokenness becomes blessing.

Then the LORD said to Moses, "Behold, I will rain down bread from heaven for you. The people are to go out each day and gather enough for that day." (Exodus 16:4)

Over two million Israelites required nourishing food daily, through all the varied seasons, on their long forty-year wilderness journey. Because they were constantly traveling, they could not rely on farming. The inhospitable desert offered no sustenance for the body. Only a miracle could enable them to survive. God provided that miracle, as he daily rained down "bread from heaven."

The manna came during the hours of the night, fresh as the dew each morning, described as "thin flakes like frost on the ground," and it "tasted like wafers made with honey" (vv. 14, 31).

This provision of manna was one of the most momentous events in the history of the Israelites. It was a miracle of enormous proportions — sufficient to nourish the entire company of Israel on their long wilderness journey through all seasons of the year.

But it had to be received and used on a daily basis. Today's manna could not be stored up for tomorrow. This text reminds us that God's sustaining grace to us is fresh every morning. He provides enough just for today. Jesus taught us to pray, "Give us this day our daily bread."

The whole wilderness journey of the Hebrews is a type of the Christian's pilgrimage. Our Lord himself gave a spiritual interpretation of the miracle of the manna, saying, "Our forefathers ate the manna in the desert . . . for the bread of God is he who comes down from heaven and gives life to the world" (John 6:31, 33). Then Jesus uttered one of his sublime declarations: "I am the bread of life. He who comes to me will never go hungry" (John 6:35). Praise God, for we too are abundantly sustained and satisfied by God's miraculous provision of manna — in Christ.

On Eagles' Wings

"I carried you on eagles' wings and brought you to myself."
(Exodus 19:4)

T he arrival of the Israelites at Sinai marks the climactic point of the book of Exodus. They remained there for eleven months. At the foot of Mount Sinai the Hebrews received the Law of God, covenanted with God, and were organized as a nation in the form of a theocracy.

In one of Scripture's most beautiful metaphors God reminds them of his providential care for them: "I carried you on eagles' wings and brought you to myself." That was in the past. He then calls them to future obedience and to their destiny in him: "Now if you obey me fully and keep my covenant, then out of all nations you will be my treasured possession" (v. 5).

The metaphor used by God brought to their mind the familiar image of the king of birds, the large majestic eagle abundant in Palestine, admired for its prowess and its soaring at great heights. The words of our golden text refer to the eagles carrying their young on their wings until they learn to fly. The same metaphor is used poetically in the song of Moses: "Like an eagle that stirs up its nest and hovers over its young, that spreads its wings to catch them and carries them on its pinions" (Deuteronomy 32:11). Up to this point of their maturing as a nation and as the people of God, Israel had been carried aloft by God's grace and sustained by his protective care.

What God did for Israel, he also does for us. Every believer is to him a "treasured possession." Many today sing the words of Michael Joncas, based on this lovely text:

> And God will raise you up on eagles' wings,
> Bear you on the breath of dawn,
> Make you shine like the sun,
> And hold you in the palm of his hand.

"I am the LORD your God."   (Exodus 20:2)

The twentieth chapter of Exodus enshrines one of the world's immortal documents, the Ten Commandments. The Decalogue, given by God himself, has become the basis of the jurisprudence system of much of the world. It also constitutes our blueprint for life, presenting a matchless summary of the duties and standard of moral conduct God requires of us.

These "Ten Words" from God draw a line in the sand, confronting the moral laxity of our day with the ultimate standards and disciplines of life. They make a frontal assault on the relativism of our time, stated in absolutes — "thou shalt" and "thou shalt not." If God approved of the permissiveness of our day he would have given us instead "The Ten Suggestions."

It is imperative to read the prelude to the Ten Commandments in the two short verses preceding them: "And God spoke all these words: I am the LORD your God. . . ." The Ten Commandments rest upon divine authority; there can be no appeal to escape their demands.

The Ten Commandments are not a relic from a long-gone era, but are more vital and viable today than ever before. As God delivered the Israelites out of bondage in Egypt, so he delivers us from the bondage of sin through the sacrifice of his Son. That provides both the authority and the motivation for our keeping the Ten Commandments.

The editor of a small weekly newspaper in a town in the West was having difficulty one week finding enough copy to fill his columns. So he had his compositor set up the Ten Commandments and ran them without editorial comment. Several days after the paper was published he received a letter saying: "Cancel my subscription. You're getting too personal." Indeed, the Ten Commandments are quite personal, as we shall see in the next meditations.

An Exclusive Devotion

"You shall have no other gods before me."   (Exodus 20:3)

This commandment set Israel apart from all other ancient Near East religions and shaped its monotheistic faith. In the land of Egypt the Israelites had witnessed the worship of the sun and moon and of every conceivable creature. But in this prohibition against the setting up of any mythical deities God was requiring of them a singleness of devotion.

This is the greatest of the Ten Commandments in that it invokes an exclusive and total commitment to God, which provides the motivating power for all the rest. The other commandments build on the foundation of this absolute devotion to God.

We tend to think of idolatry as the ignorant worship of man-made images, or as the worship of animals or the forces of nature. But idolatry is not just incantations to pagan deities; it is a common sin among us.

Who is on the throne of my heart? Who, or what, takes first place? Anything that replaces God in our worship and as our highest commitment violates this divine law.

The list of false gods among us is practically endless. Among them can be our hobbies, work, a person, position, power, social prestige, family, computer, money, sex, drugs, astrology, sports, ourselves, or even church. Whatever may consume us, whatever may become our obsession or object of utmost devotion, becomes a form of idolatry.

This first commandment is like a glove thrown at our feet, calling us from the world's vanities to the reality and exclusive worship of our Creator and holy and loving God.

"You shall not make for yourself an idol in the form of anything."
(Exodus 20:4)

In our day we should not think of idols as carved images or totem poles, but rather as those intangibles that we may allow to dominate our lives. Whenever anyone or anything usurps the place that God should have in our lives, we are guilty of idolatry.

Francis Bacon wrote, "Four species of idols beset the human mind: idols of the tribe, idols of the den, idols of the market, and idols of the theater." Each of these species has their modern offspring.

"Idols of the tribe" can relate to human icons, people we practically worship. We've seen it for example with the cult of Elvis Presley, which gains strength even after his untimely death.

"Idols of the den" can relate to our hobbies, pastimes, and other personal activities that may become the dominant force of our lives.

"Idols of the market" are all too common among us. Psychologists have coined a term for this disease — "affluenza." If it looks good, we must have it. The "sindrome" of the plastic credit card provides the slippery slope that leads countless people to the pit of financial disaster.

Bacon's "idols of the theater" embrace the seductive allurements of the world's entertainment, with its plethora of sleazy television shows, sex-saturated movies, gambling casinos, and a new breed — Internet pornography.

Cecil Alexander, writing in the nineteenth century, challenges us with a call to true worship:

Jesus calls us from the worship
Of the vain world's golden store,
From each idol that would keep us,
Saying: Christian, love me more.

The Sacred Name

"You shall not misuse the name of the LORD *your God."*

(Exodus 20:7)

For the Hebrew, the name of God could not be separated from God's Reality. The name had to do with the very being of God, defining the essence of the One whom it identified. It was more than nomenclature; it denoted character. To them, the name of God was of great worth, sacred.

When Moses in his first encounter with God at the burning bush asked by what name God should be known, God answered him with the two monosyllables, "I AM" (Exodus 3:14). This divine verb "to be" symbolized his self-existence, self-sufficiency.

This name of God had the Hebrew spelling *YHWH*. The lack of vowels made it unpronounceable. To render it pronounceable, its English transliteration is *Yahweh*. Before a Levite priest inscribed this word, he would clean his writing instrument out of reverence.

The sacred name of God and Jesus has been subject to profane use. Some abuse the name of God with a curse, others use the name of Jesus as an exclamation of anger. Muslims do not curse by shouting, "Mohammed," nor do Buddhists by ejaculating, "Buddha." But uniquely in our Western world, the sacred names of our Creator and Savior have become objects of human profanity. Some persons become so conditioned to profanity throughout their lives that it becomes compulsive with them. Such a careless and irreverent use of God's name violates this third commandment.

Let us heed the mandate of this third commandment and ever reverence the sacred name of our Creator and Savior.

"Remember the Sabbath day by keeping it holy."   (Exodus 20:8)

The Sabbath day was first observed by God himself: "By the seventh day God had finished the work he had been doing; so on the seventh day he rested from all his work. And God blessed the seventh day and made it holy" (Genesis 2:2-3).

Scripture implies that later the Sabbath was observed as a commemoration of the Exodus from Egypt. The Exodus account explicitly states that the Israelites observed the Sabbath by gathering a double portion of manna on the sixth day and none on the seventh day. The Sabbath as a holy day had supreme importance as a sign of the covenant: "This will be a sign between me and you for the generations to come" (Exodus 31:13; see also vv. 14-17). The Christian Sabbath was changed from the seventh to the first day of the week to commemorate the day of the resurrection of Christ.

The fourth commandment begins with the positive word "remember." The word implies that it is easy to forget and neglect the observance of God's holy day. With the secularization of the Sabbath, we need more than ever to "remember" God's commandment for the Sabbath.

The Sabbath invokes the principle that there needs to be a rhythm to life, a rhythm of work and rest. The continual expenditure of our energies requires the renewal for which the Sabbath was ordained. Under the hypnotic effect of the relentless busyness of modern life, we have lost the rhythm of action and rest. The Sabbath also reminds us of God's claim upon our lives: all our time and all our days belong to God.

William Gladstone, prime minister of England, once said, "Tell me what the young men of England are doing on Sunday, and I will tell you what the future of England will be." Let us keep holy this sacred day, and let it be a sign of our personal covenant with God.

"Honor your father and your mother."　　　　(Exodus 20:12)

The first four commandments deal with the vertical relationship of life, our responsibility to God. This fifth commandment begins the set of the final six that deal with the horizontal relationships of life, our responsibility to other people.

The family is the fundamental building block and foundation of a nation. If the foundation is not secure, the superstructure will eventually crumble.

This commandment is the only one accompanied by a promise, that of long life. Physical health is a byproduct of our spiritual health. The right thing is always the most healthful thing. This principle is not invalidated by the exception.

The story is told of a mother who found under her place one morning at breakfast a bill made out by her small son, Bradley, aged 8. "Mother owes Bradley: for running errands, 25 cents; for being good, 10 cents; for extras, 5 cents. Total, 40 cents." The mother smiled but made no comment. At lunch Bradley found the 40 cents under his plate, and another piece of paper neatly folded like the first. Opening it he read, "Bradley owes mother: for nursing him through scarlet fever, nothing; for being good to him, nothing; for clothes, shoes, and playthings, nothing; for his playroom, nothing; for his meals, nothing. Total: nothing."

This commandment challenges our culture of self-centeredness to honor those who have bestowed and nurtured the gift of life. When kept, it may not only add years to our life, but life to our years — with its fulfillment of one of life's most cherished and sacred relationships.

"You shall not murder." (Exodus 20:13)

The sixth, seventh, and eighth commandments were each expressed in the original Hebrew with just two words, simply: "No killing, no adultery, no stealing." The expanded English versions do not convey the same force of their sharp and short forbiddings.

The sixth commandment relates to the sanctity of life. It declares that an individual is more than a Social Security number, more than a pawn in society's economic structure. Each person is created with the imprint of divinity, rendering life sacred.

We need to revisit this commandment in light of ways in which society violates its mandate. The exploitation and pollution of the environment endangers the human species. Harmful drugs bring ruin and death to countless victims. Today we witness the wholesale rejection of this commandment, not only in our high homicide rates, but also with the 1.5 million abortions carried out each year in the United States, numbering over 30 million since the 1973 *Roe v. Wade* Supreme Court decision. Abortion is only a short step on the slippery slope to euthanasia; both violate the sacredness of life.

Albert Schweitzer achieved greatness as a theologian, philosopher, musician, and missionary doctor. His theme was "reverence for life," which he proposed as the solution to the world's problems. "Being good," he wrote, "is to preserve life, to promote life, to raise life to the highest level that it can attain. Being evil is to destroy life, to injure life, to suppress life which could attain a higher level." He exemplified his philosophy by becoming a doctor, and for thirty-five years he helped to preserve life at the medical center he founded in 1913 at Lambaréné in French Equatorial Africa. His memorable phrase "reverence for life" beautifully complements the sanctity of life enshrined in the sixth commandment.

Sexual Purity

"You shall not commit adultery." (Exodus 20:14)

I n a day when marriage and the family are under siege, this commandment upholds the sanctity of family life. The sacred institution of marriage and the family is an endangered species today. Historians consistently warn that the strength and stability of society are dependent upon the stability of the marriage relationship. The rampant permissiveness and moral laxity of our day threaten the very foundation of our nation.

The keeping of this commandment requires respect for the sanctity of the marriage covenant. It calls God's people to an inviolable commitment as it relates to expression of our sexuality. Jesus amplified the keeping of this commandment by saying that even lustful desires violate God's commandment for purity. The sex-saturated and sex-satiated culture of our society induces the shattering of this commandment.

In 1623 the so-called Wicked Bible was published in England. It was so named because the little word "not" was omitted in the seventh commandment. The printers were heavily fined by the High Commission, and the entire edition was destroyed.

It seems that many have left that all-important word "not" out of the seventh commandment. They are living by their own standards, a situation ethics, and reaping the consequences of failed marriages, broken homes, and broken lives. When sex is in the saddle it will ride life into ruin and regret. But when sex is harnessed to its ordained life ends, it sublimates into creative fulfillment.

"You shall not steal."   (Exodus 20:15)

This eighth commandment is a foundation of our economic system and addresses the issue of property. Theft is the taking or keeping of what is not ours.

This commandment can be broken in many ways, both blatant and subtle. One of the most common infractions of this law is that of shoplifting. The U.S. Commerce Department reports that about four million people are caught shoplifting each year; but for every one caught, it is estimated that thirty-five go undetected, resulting in over 140 million shoplifting incidents a year. The average consumer pays the penalty with the increased costs of goods to cover the losses.

Unjust wages and dishonest gains have often taken from the poor the dignity of an adequate livelihood and lifestyle. Embezzlement and fraud have stolen that which belonged to others. We have also seen the rich and the powerful brought to court for their dishonest manipulations, often at the high cost of honest investors and the working class. Most burglaries are petty theft compared to the thievery on a massive scale that too often comes to light in the world of business.

There are also subtle ways in which we may break this commandment. Plagiarism and cribbing steals other people's ideas. Employees who fail to give a full day's work in return for a full day's pay steal from their employers. Shakespeare, in *Othello*, reminds us that even gossip and careless talk can be an infraction of this rule, in stealing from a person his or her good name.

Let us be on our guard, lest all too casually, or even inadvertently, we fail in the keeping of this sacred commandment.

"You shall not give false testimony against your neighbor."
(Exodus 20:16)

The ninth commandment is a prohibition against untruthfulness of any kind. It includes hypocrisy, exaggeration, false excuses, insincerity, half-truths, and outright lying. Falsehood, of any kind, always compromises a relationship as well as poisoning one's own soul.

In our "postmodern" world, we have witnessed a propensity for lying. More than one former U.S. President has demonstrated the art of duplicity. In their company of deceit have been politicians, professors, diplomats, journalists, sports figures, and Pulitzer Prize-winners. In *The Day America Told the Truth*, authors James Patterson and Peter Kim estimate that 91 percent of Americans regularly embroider the truth. They state that people lie and don't even think that it is a lie.

Allan Bloom, author of the best-selling critique of American higher education, *The Closing of the American Mind*, states, "There is one thing a professor can be absolutely certain of: almost every student entering the university believes, or says he believes, that truth is relative."

Ever since Adam and Eve sewed their fig-leaf cover-ups, we have been disguising the truth about ourselves. Self-deception and personal dishonesty are insidious diseases, building up layers of deceit, so that the true self may never become known.

The "Father of Lies" will tempt us to subtle falsehoods, to become masters of the masquerade. The secret to keeping the ninth commandment is our total commitment to the One who declared, "I am the truth." Then honesty will reign over falsehood and deceit.

"You shall not covet."   (Exodus 20:17)

Rebellion against God's law begins in the heart, and this commandment relates to the inner desires that prompt disobedience to God's laws. The commandment applies not just to deeds but also to attitude, desires, and motive.

"To covet" means to jealously desire what someone else has that we have no right to possess. Covetousness breeds a host of carnal desires, including the lust for position, money, fame, selfish aims, and pleasures. It has within it seeds of disillusion, despair, defeat, and death. Happiness comes not from external material things but from those attributes that are within the heart.

In Tolstoy's story "How Much Land Does a Man Need?" Fortune the hero is told he can have the right to all the land around which he can plow a furrow from sunrise to sunset. The man started off with great vigor, intending to encompass only that which he could easily care for. But as the day progressed he desired more and more land. He plowed and plowed and greedily pushed himself to such exhaustion that, just as the sun went down, he collapsed in death. The only right he secured was the right to the eighteen square feet of land in which he was buried.

The well-known legend of Midas tells that when Midas was offered his choice of gifts, he asked that whatever he might touch should change into gold. Granted his request, he quickly put his newly acquired power to the test. He touched a twig of an oak and it became gold in his hand. He took up a stone and it changed to gold. And so it was with everything he touched. Upon his return home he ordered a great feast to celebrate. But when he touched bread, it hardened into gold. Most tragically, he found that not only his food, but even his loved ones were destroyed by "the Midas touch."

Jesus sternly warned: "Watch out! Be on your guard against all kinds of greed; a man's life does not consist in the abundance of his possessions" (Luke 12:15).

Then Moses said, "Now show me your glory."   (Exodus 33:18)

The book of Exodus makes this stunning statement: "The LORD would speak to Moses face to face, as a man speaks with his friend" (33:11). Following such intimate communion with God, Moses was emboldened to make perhaps the most momentous request in the Bible, if not in all spiritual history: "Now show me your glory." He could not have asked for anything greater. It is the loftiest human ambition expressed in the Bible.

On Mount Sinai he had encountered something of the awesome majesty of God, the blaze of whose splendor glowed like the fire of a volcano and enveloped the mountain in smoke. The glory of God surpasses human comprehension. Flesh and blood cannot apprehend God. Yet the great lawgiver dared to think that, as God's friend, the Creator might somehow reveal himself to him. Mortals have limitations. No human being could look upon the ineffable glory of the infinite God and live (Exodus 33:20). So God graciously shielded his friend, putting him in the cleft of a rock. He covered Moses with his hand until his glory passed by, allowing Moses to glimpse the afterglow of the One before whom suns are but as candles and stars are as jewels in his diadem.

We of the Christian era have been privileged to see the revelation of God's glory as never seen by Moses. The sacred record declares that God in Christ was made flesh and "we have seen his glory" (John 1:14). Moses' bold prayer, through God's amazing grace, has been answered for each child of God. The perfect life of Christ reveals the glory of God in terms perceivable to human understanding, for Jesus is to us the radiance of God's glory.

"Be holy, because I am holy." (Leviticus 11:44)

The book of Leviticus served as a worship manual for the priests and Israelites. Its theme and key word is "holiness"; the word occurs more than eighty times. It denotes the purity and perfection of God and applies to whatever is set apart and dedicated to him. Leviticus teaches that holiness is the supreme requirement in our worship, as well as for all the practical conduct and relationships of life.

Holiness is highly important to God; the word is found no fewer than 650 times in the Bible. This clarion call to holiness in our text is repeated in verse 45, and again in Leviticus 19:2 and 20:7. We find this call of God resonating once again in Peter's epistle: "But just as he who called you is holy, so be holy in all you do; for it is written: 'Be holy, because I am holy'" (1 Peter 1:15-16).

The foundation of holiness is the nature of God — "because I am holy." In the Bible, the attribute of God's holiness is stressed more than any other. It is the only attribute thrice repeated: "Holy, holy, holy is the LORD Almighty" (Isaiah 6:3; Revelation 4:8).

Some are called to the field of medicine, others to teaching, music, art, or the ministry. These callings relate to the endowed aptitudes of those so called. But to every child of God comes the call found in our text, "Be holy." This is a call to living a life in the Spirit, with a renewal of our disposition and motivations, a renunciation of all that is wrong, and an unreserved commitment to Christ. Holiness is a lifelong process of becoming conformed to Christ.

When we come to God, he accepts us just as we are, but he does not leave us there. He calls us to holiness so that we may know his power and purity, and his broken image may be restored in us.

"It is the blood that makes atonement for one's life."

(Leviticus 17:11)

Physiology echoes the Bible teaching that "life is in the blood." The heart pumps the body's entire blood supply through the vascular system in less than a minute, and by this means the body is nourished and kept alive. Blood sustains life. Blood transfusions are given to save life.

The penalty for sin was death, but in the Old Testament system of sacrifices the death of an animal could be substituted for the death required by the judgment of a righteous and holy God. The animal became the ransom price, and its sacrifice pointed toward the blood of the Lamb of God that would be shed for the redemption of the world.

The Bible is a living book; its message imparts life. This principle of blood runs like a scarlet thread throughout its pages, starting with the sacrifice of Abel, then the Passover lamb, and here in Leviticus the tabernacle sacrifices. We follow this line until we see on Calvary God's perfect Lamb for which all other sacrifices were but a type.

Christian hymns are replete with references to this theology of atonement by the blood of Christ. Isaac Watts, almost three centuries ago, penned this truth in a memorable song:

Not all the blood of beasts
On Jewish altars slain,
Could give the guilty conscience peace,
Or wash away our stain.
But Christ, the heavenly Lamb,
Takes all our sins away,
A sacrifice of nobler name
And richer blood than they.

"The LORD bless you and keep you."   (Numbers 6:24)

The apostle Paul reminds us, "For everything that was written in the past was written to teach us" (Romans 15:4). This is true of the book of Numbers, which some readers may think to be merely a muster roll of the armies of Israel. Its opening words, "The LORD spoke to Moses," are repeated in various forms more than 150 times in the book, emphasizing its divine authorship and authority.

The book could appropriately, and perhaps more invitingly, be titled "Wilderness Wanderings" or "Pilgrimage." As wayfarers on a wilderness journey, we can learn from this book "written to teach us."

In the account of the Israelites' wilderness journey, we come upon one of the most beautiful and poetic benedictions found in all Scripture. Given by God, it served as a formula for priests in the consecration of the people.

Each of its three rhythmical clauses begins with the sacred name YHWH (Yahweh — "the LORD"). The nature of the blessing is three-fold.

First, it invokes divine blessing and protection — "The LORD bless you and keep you." John Calvin said, "The blessing of God is the goodness of God in action."

Second, in warm imagery it petitions the Lord's favor and grace — "the LORD make his face shine upon you and be gracious to you."

The benediction rises in a grand crescendo, culminating with the third and highest gift God can bestow — "the LORD turn his face toward you and give you peace." The Hebrew word for "peace" is *shalom*, denoting highest and total well-being.

Through the grace of our Lord, blessings invoked by this classic benediction can be ours.

"You may be sure that your sin will find you out."

(Numbers 32:23)

A superficial reading of this text may lead one to think that it says, "Be sure your sin will be found out." But that is not what it says. Rather, it warns, "Your sin will find you out."

Augustine wrote long ago, "The punishment of sin is sin." Sin blights the life. It is an infestation in the soul. We absorb its consequences in ourselves. Sin robs us of a clear conscience, of peace within. It stains and can ultimately destroy our character. We cannot sin with impunity; one way or another sin will find us out and register its fatal disease within us.

Jesus said, "The kingdom of God is within you" (Luke 17:21). It is in our nerves, our very makeup. Even the common lie-detector tests bear scientific witness that human nature has a moral set, otherwise a lie would register no slant of the needle away from basic moral nature. God's moral law of the universe is written into our tissues as well as the texts of his Word.

David thought kings could get by with cover-ups until the bony finger of the prophet Nathan pointed in his direction, saying, "You are the man," leaving David prostrate and penitent before God (2 Samuel 12).

The word "evil" is the word "live" spelled backwards. Sin is life lived backwards; it is sand in the machinery of life. God's moral law of the universe does not tolerate sin, but rejects it as a virus in the soul.

But God has provided a cure. "If we walk in the light . . . the blood of Jesus, his Son, purifies us from all sin" (1 John 1:7).

"Man does not live on bread alone but on every word that comes from the mouth of the LORD." (Deuteronomy 8:3)

During the Israelites' thirty-eight years of sojourn in the wilderness, the older generation had perished. Now, a new generation of Israelites is about to enter the Land of Promise. At this crossroads, Moses admonishes the people to remember God's providence. He calls them to obedience to the God who had brought them through their trials and testings.

In particular, he reminds them of the miraculous provision of daily manna that had sustained them in the arid desert all those years. However, he emphasizes, "Man does not live on bread alone but on every word that comes from the mouth of the LORD." There is not only a body, but also a soul to sustain, and that sustenance comes from the words of God. The soul, like the body, lives by what it feeds on.

The human body, with all its organic functions, requires food for physical nourishment, lest it die. This law of the physical world is extended into the metaphysical realm in that the soul requires spiritual food for its life and preservation.

The words of this text were the first of three quotations that our Lord employed in his conflict with the tempter (Matthew 4:4; Luke 4:4). In his own wilderness temptation, Jesus repudiated the tempter's lure to make earthly bread dominant, declaring that the Word and the will of God should be our motivating force and priority for our soul's health.

With John Wesley we say: "I am a creature of a day, passing through life as an arrow through the air. I want to know one thing — the way to heaven; how to land safe on that happy shore. God Himself has condescended to teach the way. He has written it down in a book. O give me that book. At any price, give me the book of God."

Strength for the Day

"Your strength will equal your days."   (Deuteronomy 33:25)

In claiming this promise we acknowledge our own weakness and dependence upon God. We need his grace, guidance, and strength for each new day and the tasks, challenges, and opportunities it brings.

Yesterday's provision of strength does not carry over into today. God does not give us Tuesday's grace on Monday. We need the Lord's daily provision of strength when we go through suffering and trial. We need his enablement for spiritual tasks that are beyond our human resources. We need his daily strength for victory in the hour of testing and temptation.

We can, with total assurance, rely on this promise of God. The boundless reservoir of God's grace can never be exhausted. The same God who created the world out of nothing, who guides the stars in their unerring courses, and who directs the earth in its orbit has promised to give us strength sufficient for the day.

It is an all-sufficient promise. Some days are "little days," with no great task or test. But some days are "big days," with major needs. God gives strength sufficient for the need of each day. If we should have a day such as we had never had before, God would send us strength such as we had never known before.

As the King James Version renders it, "As thy days, so shall thy strength be." God's provision of strength adapts itself to all the changes and exigencies of our lives. Because of this promise, nothing can happen to us today that we and God cannot handle together.

"But as for me and my household, we will serve the LORD."

(Joshua 24:15)

With the leaders of the Israelites assembled, Joshua delivers his farewell address. His words take on a greater urgency as he tells his people, "Now I am about to go the way of all the earth" (Joshua 23:14). His oration calls to mind the mighty acts of God on behalf of the people, emphasizing God's faithfulness and calling the nation to remain faithful to God, to be obedient to his law, and to separate themselves from the pagan culture around them.

In one of the classic biblical texts the 110-year-old warrior throws down the gauntlet: "Choose for yourselves this day whom you will serve." Today there are "multitudes in the valley of decision" who need to choose their life's loyalty, whether it be to God or to things outside the faith. For Joshua himself, there was no equivocation: "But as for me and my household, we will serve the LORD."

When Joshua first appeared on the biblical scene, he was selected as one of the twelve spies sent to survey the Promised Land (Numbers 13–14). He, with Caleb, returned with a minority report that, although the opposition was formidable, God would give them conquest over their enemies. His faith in God never faltered, as he ultimately succeeded Moses and led the Israelites across Jordan to conquests over their enemies.

Joshua's was not a solitary faith. It extended to all his family. Nothing brings greater peace and joy to a family than a shared faith in God. Centuries later the apostle John wrote, "I have no greater joy than to hear that my children are walking in the truth" (3 John 4).

Let us also affirm our uncompromising stand for God and assure that our loved ones, for whom we are responsible, share our heritage of faith.

Everyone did as he saw fit.   (Judges 21:25)

This final verse in the book of Judges presents a devastating summary of the moral situation during the premonarchic period in Israel. The full verse, repeated in 17:6, 18:1, and 19:1, reads: "In those days Israel had no king; everyone did as he saw fit." There was no civic and moral authority for the guarding of the nation's covenant with God.

The story of this period was a sad tale of gloom and doom, of violence and intrigue, a depressing catalog of unfaithfulness to God on the part of Israel. We all too often see its counterpart on the nightly newscast, with parallels to our day.

Today many fear cancer, budget deficits, nuclear arsenals, and terrorists. But the fear of and reverence for God are all too often missing. One atheist can obtain a court ruling to delete the words "under God" from the pledge of allegiance to our flag. Occurrences such as this are symptomatic of modern humanity's infection with the myth of autonomy and self-sufficiency. As Israel had no king, so we want no absolute authority to which we are accountable. We anesthetize the conscience by saying, "If it feels good, it must be all right." We want to be the captains of our own fate.

Although scientific advances have created a veneer of prosperity and progress, our nation's moral values and convictions have been crumbling. "The terrible danger of our time consists in the fact that ours is a cut-flower civilization," prophesied Elton Trueblood a half century ago. When a nation or an individual is severed from its roots, the end result is withering and decay. May we care for the roots, both for our nation and ourselves.

"Where you go I will go, and where you stay I will stay. Your people will be my people and your God my God." (Ruth 1:16)

All the world loves a love story, and the biblical story of Ruth presents a literary jewel of a romantic drama that outshines the TV soap operas of our time. It is the only book of the Bible besides Esther that bears the name of a woman. Its pastoral setting is the backdrop for this story of the selfless devotion of a daughter-in-law who accompanies her mother-in-law to a foreign land, marries into the community of Israel, and becomes a convert to its faith.

After the death of her husband and two sons, Naomi begins her journey from Moab homeward to her native Bethlehem. As she takes leave of her daughters-in-law Ruth and Orpah, she urges them to remain in Moab rather than go as strangers to a foreign land. Orpah yields to her persuasion, but Ruth persists with her classic expression of love and devotion, which has graced many wedding ceremonies and bonded lives in marriage.

Ruth's devotion to her widowed mother-in-law led to her marriage to Boaz, who, according to Israelite custom, paid the price of her redemption and took her as his wife. Ruth abandoned the gods of Moab and became a believer in the God of Israel. Hers was a choice not only of family and friendship but also of faith. It led to the high honor of becoming the great-grandmother of David and an ancestress of Jesus (Matthew 1:1, 5).

For each of us, our choices decide our destiny. Let us, at every crossroads of life, choose the path that leads to life abundant here, and to life eternal in the world to come.

"Speak, LORD, for your servant is listening."   (1 Samuel 3:9)

It was a dark and difficult period in the history of the young nation of Israel. The two-hundred-year period of the judges was now coming to a close with Eli, the last of the twelve. A repetitive cycle of faithlessness led the historian to record: "In those days the word of the LORD was rare" (1 Samuel 3:1).

But the account also says, "The lamp of God had not yet gone out" (v. 3). Although Israel had been unfaithful, God remained faithful, and he still had a destiny for Israel to fulfill.

One night, a voice calling "Samuel!" awakened the young acolyte, who according to the Jewish historian Josephus was 12 years of age. He ran to the old priest, thinking it was he who called. Eli disclaimed having called him and instructed him to return to bed. Twice more, "Samuel!" sounded in the still of the night, and the lad ran to the priest. The third time, Eli discerned that it must be the Lord calling, and he told Samuel if he heard the voice again to answer, "Speak, LORD, for your servant is listening."

Once more the silence of the night was broken, as the Lord called, "Samuel! Samuel!" This time Samuel answered, "Speak, for your servant is listening." Samuel's listening obedience launched him on his historic role as one of the most prominent figures and spiritual leaders in the Old Testament.

God still calls today. He calls us by name, and if we will listen and respond, he will use even us to help build his kingdom upon earth. But listening is an art. If we are intent upon our own will and whim, there is the danger that we may paraphrase Samuel's "Speak, Lord, for your servant is listening," to "Hear, Lord, for your servant speaks."

"How the mighty have fallen!" (2 Samuel 1:19)

When he received the news that Saul and Jonathan had been slain in battle, David composed one of the most eloquent elegies in Scripture (2 Samuel 1:17-27). No fewer than three times in his dirge (vv. 19, 25, 27) he laments, "How the mighty have fallen!" All the loss that Israel suffered on one day is gathered up into this one haunting phrase.

The friendship of David and Jonathan was a classic friendship of the Bible and of history. In verse 26 David exclaims, "I grieve for you, Jonathan my brother; you were very dear to me." Israel's first king and its crown prince lay fallen.

"How are the mighty fallen!" (RSV). The "how" in life's failures is all-important. Saul was slain not so much by the Philistines as by his own pride and forgetfulness of God. Self-defeat all too easily comes in the wake of self-confidence and compromise in our spiritual lives.

The text calls to mind the story of Samson, known as the strongest man in the Bible, who was slain, not on the battlefield against an overpowering foe, but through the wiles of a woman. Let us also not forget that David himself, one of the mightiest heroes of Scripture, also became a victim of lust.

The scandals of our own day all too vividly illustrate the truth of this text. Indeed, the mighty continue to fall around us.

This text has become a byword that serves as a warning. As Paul reminds us, "So, if you think you are standing firm, be careful that you don't fall!" (1 Corinthians 10:12).

"Not one word has failed of all the good promises he gave."

(1 Kings 8:56)

These words were spoken in a climactic moment in Israel's history by King Solomon at the dedication of the resplendent temple. He looked back on the long road from Sinai and the wilderness and summed up Israel's history in one sentence describing the faithfulness of God: "Not one word has failed of all the good promises he gave."

The Word of God is filled with promises throughout its pages. Someone has counted them — an astounding 8,810 promises! This should lead us to stand on tiptoe as we come to the Scriptures, to discover and appropriate this lavish treasure trove of blessings.

A young man leafing through his grandmother's Bible questioned the T's and P's penned in the margins of the pages. "Tried and Proven," she responded, "each a promise of God to me that I have proven to be true." The promises of God are ours for the asking, waiting to be "tried and proven" by the children of God.

In these perilous times, the reply that Adoniram Judson gave to his mission board when they inquired about the prospects for the future in Burma, with all its dangers and difficulties, is still true: "The future is as bright as the promises of God."

With the songwriter Russell Carter, we confidently affirm:

Standing on the promises that cannot fail,
    When the howling storms of doubt and fear assail;
By the living Word of God I shall prevail,
    Standing on the promises of God.

"Indeed, not even half was told me."   (1 Kings 10:7)

One of the most enchanting stories in the Bible is that of the visit of the queen of Sheba to Solomon (1 Kings 10:1-13). She traveled fifteen hundred miles each way with a caravan of camels to see for herself the legendary wisdom and wealth of the king of Israel and to bring him costly gifts.

The queen plied Solomon with her most difficult questions and riddles. Upon seeing for herself his wisdom, opulence, and religious practice, she exclaimed, "Indeed, not even half was told me; in wisdom and wealth you have far exceeded the report I heard." The historian records, "she was overwhelmed" (v. 5). A modern rendition might read, "It took her breath away."

It may well be that she traveled so far and brought such costly gifts for more than just to satisfy curiosity about rumors she heard. She may have been a seeker after deeper truth, for the record states that she had "heard about the fame of Solomon and his relation to the name of the LORD" (v. 1). Her response to what she found was, "Praise be to the LORD your God" as she acknowledged that Solomon's greatness was due to "the LORD's eternal love" (v. 9).

Jesus cited this story in a response to the Pharisees who asked for a sign: "The Queen of the South will rise at the judgment with this generation and condemn it; for she came from the ends of the earth to listen to Solomon's wisdom, and now one greater than Solomon is here" (Matthew 12:42). Indeed, Christ's wisdom is infinitely greater than that of Solomon (Colossians 2:2-3). Every question has its ultimate answer in him. And when we meet him, we too find that the half has not been told, that he far exceeds our greatest expectations. He "takes our breath away."

Elijah's Chariot of Fire

Suddenly a chariot of fire and horses of fire appeared . . . and Elijah went up to heaven in a whirlwind. (2 Kings 2:11)

This verse gives us the familiar and dramatic rapture of Elijah, God's rugged prophet, known for his spectacular miracles and fearless pronouncements of God's wrath.

God had revealed to Elijah that he would be taken home in a whirlwind. He headed for Bethel and Jericho for one last visit, followed by his fellow prophets. At each stop along the way Elijah tried to leave them behind. Perhaps he wanted to spare them the pain of his final departure from them, or perhaps he did not want this final event to become a spectacle. This giant of the Lord in Old Testament history, with his close friend Elisha, and with their fifty young colleagues left behind, came to the Jordan for the dramatic closing of his life.

In this climactic moment, Elijah asked of Elisha, "What can I do for you before I am taken from you?" Elisha boldly replied, "Let me inherit a double portion of your spirit." Elijah responded, "If you see me when I am taken from you, it will be yours" (vv. 9-10). Elisha remained close to his mentor, and he did see Elijah's spectacular translation on a chariot and horses of fire. No end could have been more in keeping with the fiery prophet's life, who himself was like a whirlwind. Elisha went on to do great miracles for God and Israel.

None of us will have as dramatic an entrance into heaven as Elijah, but we do lay claim to the great promise of our Lord to his followers, "I am going there to prepare a place for you. And if I go and prepare a place for you, I will come back and take you to be with me that you also may be where I am" (John 14:2-3).

"Oh, that you would bless me and enlarge my territory!"

(1 Chronicles 4:10)

This vignette, describing Jabez as an honorable man and recording his now-famous prayer, is like a window amid the monotonous genealogical lists in one of the least-read sections of the Bible. His very name, meaning "pain," commemorating the hard time his mother had in giving him birth, was an ill-omen that could have made him a born loser.

But the chronicler lists him as a notable exception and achiever, "more honorable than his brothers." What was his secret? The secret was his prayer and God's answer to it.

He knew where to turn for the resources for overcoming obstacles. He "cried out to the God of Israel, 'Oh, that you would bless me and enlarge my territory! Let your hand be with me, and keep me from harm so that I will be free from pain.' And God granted his request."

This text has become famous because of the best-seller *The Prayer of Jabez* by Bruce Wilkinson. In it he writes, "This petition has radically changed what I expect from God and what I experience every day by his power. In fact, thousands of believers who are applying its truths are seeing miracles happen on a regular basis."

This model prayer reminds us that God's bounty of blessing is limited only by our sincere asking. With Jabez, we would pray for God to "enlarge our territory." This was not a request for more real estate, but rather for expanded opportunities for service to God. "Let your hand be with me," Jabez prayed. The hand of God in the Bible symbolizes God's power and presence in our lives.

"And God granted his request" is the final word in this brief biography. When we pray with sincerity for God's richest blessings, he will grant our request as well.

"If my people, who are called by my name, will humble themselves and pray and seek my face and turn from their wicked ways, then will I hear from heaven and will forgive their sin and will heal their land."

(2 Chronicles 7:14)

This text has often been cited as what our nation needs to do to receive God's forgiveness and healing for blatant disobedience to his commands.

America was founded upon the principles of our Christian faith. After four weeks of failure by the Constitutional Convention to write one word for the Constitution, Benjamin Franklin called for prayer. From that moment progress was made. The Bible was the cornerstone for the early educational institutions of our country. For example, in 1642 the guidelines that would govern Harvard University, our nation's first college, read, in part, "Let every student be plainly instructed, and earnestly pressed to consider well, the main end of his life and studies is, to know God and Jesus Christ which is eternal life." The motto of Harvard was *Christi Gloriam* (Christ be glorified).

In our day, George Barna, a well-known Christian researcher, reports that regular churchgoers are shockingly similar to the populace at large in any number of ways. Consider these statistics: those who buy a lottery ticket: non-Christians 27 percent, Christians 23 percent; those who watch a PG-13 or R-rated movie: non-Christians 87 percent, Christians 76 percent; those who have been divorced: non-Christians 23 percent, Christians 27 percent.

Our nation's flagrant sins — such as our silent holocaust of abortion, the epidemic of pornography, crime, and violence — should lead us to take to heart this call to repentance for our nation's forgiveness and healing.

Because the hand of the LORD my God was on me, I took courage.

(Ezra 7:28)

The book of Ezra records the return of the Jews to Jerusalem, under the edict of Cyrus the king of Persia, to rebuild their temple. Those undertaking the task of restoration found their work beset with obstacles and strong opposition. Their sacred task could be accomplished only by setting priorities that would lead the people back to God.

The first item of business undertaken by the returned exiles was to build the altar to reestablish their worship of God (Ezra 3:2). The next task was the rebuilding of the temple (3:7-9). The record also reads: "Ezra had devoted himself to the study and observance of the Law of the LORD, and to teaching its decrees and laws in Israel" (7:10).

Their action reminds us that when our relationship with God is broken, we need to rebuild the altar of our life, that place where we meet with divine presence, reestablish our worship and devotion to God, and know and observe the commands of God's Word.

Ezra acknowledged that the opportunity they had received to become a united people again was from the Lord: "Praise be to the LORD, the God of our fathers, who has put it into the king's heart to bring honor to the house of the LORD in Jerusalem. . . . Because the hand of the LORD my God was on me, I took courage" (7:27-28).

In virtually every area of life we may confront the need for restoration and renewal. Busyness or neglect takes its toll, relationships become broken, zeal grows cold, we yearn for a fresh and closer walk with God. Ezra provides a recipe for restoration and renewal, both personal and corporate, reminding us that devotion to God is our first priority. Then, we too may take courage and find that the hand of the Lord is upon us.

A Resolute Commitment

"I am carrying on a great project and cannot go down."
(Nehemiah 6:3)

The daunting task of Nehemiah and his coworkers to rebuild the walls of Jerusalem did not go unchallenged. It met with vigorous opposition. They had a threefold formula for success: a heart to pray (4:4), a heart to work (4:6), and an eye to watch (4:9). Prayer, hard work, and vigilance are still secrets of success in doing the work of God.

The enemies of Nehemiah invited him to meet alone with them in a distant place. He recognized the invitation as a trap and refused to be distracted or to divert his energies from rebuilding Jerusalem's wall. His famous reply was: "I am doing a great work and cannot come down" (RSV). To their persistent proposals, no fewer than four times Nehemiah unflinchingly gave this stirring reaffirmation of the urgency of his God-appointed task.

Walls around us are in disrepair. Immorality, violence, and secularism have in some places reduced our nation's walls to rubble. The walls of defense for many individuals have tumbled down upon them. Ours is the enormous task to help rebuild those walls, to help establish defenses of society, of individuals, and perhaps even of ourselves, from our enemies.

Nehemiah's answer to his detractors reminds us how we should respond when we face distractions that would divert our energies from the work God calls us to do. We may find it difficult to remain focused when faced with the imposing agendas others may seek to set for us. Let us echo Nehemiah's resolute commitment: "I am doing a great work and cannot go down." It is always "down," a downward course, when we neglect the priorities God has for our lives. God calls each of us to "a great work," requiring our resolute allegiance.

"The joy of the LORD is your strength."   (Nehemiah 8:10)

The eighth chapter of Nehemiah records a great revival styled by J. Sidlow Baxter as "a back to the Bible movement." Ezra's reading of God's Word launched an awakening and reform among the people. Before all the gathered people, Ezra read the Law of Moses from daybreak to noon. "All the people listened attentively" (v. 3) to the reading and exposition of the Scriptures. As they remembered God's mercies of the past, the assembly was overcome with conviction and began "weeping as they listened to the words of the Law" (v. 9).

Nehemiah urged his hearers, "Do not grieve, for the joy of the LORD is your strength" (v. 10). These words have come down as a golden text for the people of God. They preach a timeless truth that we derive strength and victory from the joy of the Lord in our hearts.

The joy of the Lord, unlike happiness, is not dependent on circumstances. It is not dictated by happenstance. It is an abiding quality that surmounts trial and tragedy.

Our text of joy comes to us from a context of grief. When the people were weeping, they were told instead to celebrate. Joy is the Christian's antidote for depression, discouragement, and defeat. May God's revelation and promises in Scripture fill our souls with joy, and from that joy bring strength and victory.

"Who knows but that you have come to royal position for such a time as this?" (Esther 4:14)

E sther's name means "star," and she suddenly appears on the scene in one of the darkest moments in the history of the Jewish people. Xerxes, king of the Persian empire, ordered a "Miss Persia" contest to select the new queen when Queen Vashti fell into disfavor. Esther won the beauty pageant, and thus a Jewess became queen of the most powerful empire of that day.

But a dark and threatening cloud appeared in the sky when Haman, prime minister and great Jew-hater, plotted for the extermination of the Jews. In the midst of the great mourning and fasting by the Jews, Mordecai, cousin and foster father of Esther, urged Esther to intercede with the king for her people. But the custom was that if anyone approached the king without being summoned, that person would be put to death, unless the king extended his gold scepter. When Esther hesitated to go to the king, since she hadn't been summoned, Mordecai challenged her with the famous words of our text: "And who knows but that you have come to royal position for such a time as this?"

The well-known story relates Esther's courage and rare resourcefulness, which exposed Haman's planned treachery and saved the Jewish people. In remembrance of that deliverance, there was instituted the Feast of Purim, a celebration observed to this day by the Jews.

God has a plan and purpose for each of us. He calls us to vulnerable involvement and courageous faith, to be his star in a world of darkness. Shine, for you may be the only light in someone's darkness.

"Man is born to trouble as surely as sparks fly upward." (Job 5:7)

Some of the most profound truths in the book of Job come from the lips of his contestants. Though Job's friends were flawed in their theology, the universal truths that they uttered merit consideration, such as the one by Eliphaz: "Man is born to trouble as surely as sparks fly upward."

Dr. M. Scott Peck, in the opening sentence of his seminal bestseller *The Road Less Traveled*, echoes this text in Job: "Life is difficult." He explains: "This is one of the greatest truths. Life is a series of problems." He reminds his readers that to live successfully we must accept this truth and be prepared to cope with its meaning.

Throughout history, believers have not been immune from suffering and the consequences of living in a depraved world. The disciples of our Lord were called to a cross, and in the end they paid the ultimate cost of discipleship. The apostle Paul three times took a crash course on "How to survive shipwreck." Another lesson he mastered was "How to escape when held hostage" as he was let down over the city wall in a basket. In his catalog of sufferings, he refers to stonings, floggings, imprisonments, and other trials that would have turned back any but the totally committed. In the end, he was beheaded in Rome.

This ancient text from the book of Job reminds us that trouble is the common lot of our humanity. But as that book, and the rest of the Bible reminds us, we are not without resources that will enable us to cope. A good prayer for all of us is, "Lord, help me to remember that nothing can happen today that you and I cannot handle together."

"Though he slay me, yet will I hope in him." (Job 13:15)

From the depths of his torment, Job vows: "Though he slay me, yet will I hope in him." This vow has all the greater meaning because of the night-enshrouded setting in which it was uttered.

Job seemingly had lost everything. Even his wife told him to "curse God and die" (2:9). With friends assailing his integrity, he maintained his trust in God, even if God should slay him. It is one of the high points of trust recorded in the annals of human history.

From his ash heap, Job uttered a testimony that can keep believers triumphant amid the worst that life can throw at them. Joni Eareckson Tada remarkably illustrates this truth, testifying: "My paralysis has drawn me close to God and given a spiritual healing which I wouldn't trade for a hundred active years on my feet."

When everything else in life may be shattered, we can still hold on to that which is most valuable — God himself. Our trust in him is not subject to life's trials. May we, with Job, have an unflinching faith that affirms in the words of Ella Wheeler Wilcox:

> I will not doubt, though all my ships at sea
> Come drifting home with broken masts and sails;
> I shall believe the hand that never fails,
> From seeming evil worketh good for me.
> And though I weep because those sails are battered,
> Still will I cry, while my best hopes are shattered,
>   I trust in Thee.

"If a man dies, will he live again?" (Job 14:14)

J ob here poses the universal question. There was no doctrine of immortality in Old Testament times. But Job dared to go beyond the strict limits of the traditional theology of his accusers and boldly asked: "If a man dies, will he live again?" For Job to ask this very question was a leap of faith.

It is an ancient question, the central question of history and life echoing across the centuries. Inscriptions on tombs of tribes extinct for centuries and remarkably preserved mummies offer mute testimony to humankind's ancient quest for immortality.

It is an anxious question. Job himself referred to death as "the king of terrors" (18:14) and "the journey of no return" (16:22). Shakespeare's Hamlet echoed Job's sentiment in describing death as "the undiscovered country from whose bourn no traveler returns." Death raises fear and anxiety in many.

It is an argued question. Mind you, people do not argue with death, but about death. There have been endless speculations on its meaning and mystery.

Job's question has been the riddle of the universe throughout the ages. He put into words the yearning sigh of all humanity. It is a question that the schools of philosophy cannot answer and that is beyond the reach of science and technology.

This ancient, anxious, and argued question finds its answer in Christ. Our risen Lord alone could declare with ultimate authority: "He who believes in me will live, even though he dies" (John 11:25). Jesus Christ's triumph over death transforms the grave into a passage to immortality.

"I know that my Redeemer lives."   (Job 19:25)

J ob rose from his pit of despair to his pinnacle of faith in the best-known and most-loved passage of his book. A shaft of brilliant sunlight broke through the storm clouds and he exclaimed: "I know that my Redeemer lives, and that in the end he will stand upon the earth. And after my skin has been destroyed, yet in my flesh I will see God" (19:25-26).

Job's testimony is one of the rare texts on immortality in the Old Testament, and it is the most radiant. His staunch affirmation has been appropriated by Christians as we listen to the stirring strains of Handel's *Messiah:* "I know that my Redeemer liveth."

Suffering never leaves us where it finds us; it is a passage, not a cul-de-sac. Job's suffering led him to one of the loftiest affirmations found in the Bible. For each of us, our trials and sorrows can become a passage to a deeper trust, a more steadfast faith, and a closer relationship with God. Through the resurrection power of Christ our Redeemer, we too can be lifted from pit to pinnacle, from depths to height, from being a victim to a victor amid life's struggles and sorrows.

This golden text is animated with three vital concepts of our faith — immortality, resurrection, and the return of Christ. They proclaim the message most needed in our world today: Christ is vibrantly alive and will someday make his reentry into our troubled and tortured world when "he will stand upon the earth."

"But he knows the way that I take." (Job 23:10)

J ob testified that, though he could not find God by searching, God knew him and the way he was going. In one of the most affirming verses in this book, Job testifies, "He knows the way that I take."

God knows the storms that buffet our lives. He knows the trials that we must endure. He knows the afflictions that come into our lives. He knows the cross we are called to carry. He knows the path we must travel. He knows, and he understands, and he will be by our side to help and sustain.

How incredible it is that the Creator and Governor of the universe knows me and the way that I take. How comforting it is that the One who holds the stars on their unerring courses holds my finite life in his mighty hands.

When Job's faith was tested to its limits, he was able to say, "When he has tested me, I will come forth as gold" (23:10b). Just as gold, tested by fire, comes out pure and shines all the brighter, so Job came through his furnace of affliction with a radiant and purified faith.

God brings forth good from the suffering of his people, causing our trials to work for us, not against us, building character into our lives. He can grow a mushroom overnight, but it takes many years — and many storms — to build a mighty oak.

An anonymous composer has embraced the essence of this text in the chorus:

> He knows, he knows,
> The storms that would my way oppose;
> He knows, he knows,
> And tempers every wind that blows.

Songs in the Night

"God . . . gives songs in the night." (Job 35:10)

S tately passages in the book of Job often come from the lips of Job's accusers. In his long oration, Elihu gives us the radiant statement: "God . . . gives songs in the night."

When the black curtain of catastrophe fell over his soul, in his darkest hour Job gave the centuries the celebrated song, "I know that my Redeemer lives." Job's song in the night, given him by God, has sung its way through the centuries into our living rooms and hearts as we thrill to it anew each Advent and Easter season. From one of the Old Testament's greatest tragedies God brought forth the song of grand triumph.

Job was a forerunner of the great company to whom God would give songs in the night. Many of our favorite hymns were composed in night seasons of the soul. Fanny Crosby was incredibly prolific, composing over six thousand hymns, many of which have immeasurably enriched us. Fanny Crosby did her composing in a dark room — total darkness — for she was blind. But God lit a light in her mind and soul that enabled her to see and share "rivers of pleasure" and "visions of rapture." God gave her songs that will sing on through eternity.

When the night seasons of our life are turned over to God, he turns our adversities into anthems, our problems into praises, and our sorrows into symphonies.

"Stop and consider God's wonders." (Job 37:14)

From the book of Job comes good counsel to all of us: "Stop and consider God's wonders."

Our fast-paced culture makes it difficult to stop. We are hyperactive people, traveling in the express lane, and we don't want to slow down, let alone stop. Our culture conditions us to quickness with its sun tanning parlors, frozen dinners, fast-food restaurants, overnight delivery, digital cameras, microwaves, and instant coffee.

Life in the fast-forward mode can keep us from an encounter with the wonders of God all around us. Like the sound of a distant bell comes God's call to humankind: "Be still, and know that I am God" (Psalm 46:10).

The ancient text of Job sounds a note that needs to be heard above the fury and frenzy of our time. We need to "stop and consider God's wonders," which are all about us. Let us make ample room on our calendars to gaze at sunsets and stars, to ponder the tapestry of a tree and the delicate beauty and fragrance of a flower, to hear the carol of the birds, to walk through redolent pines after a rain, to gaze out on the vastness of an ocean, to feel the clasp of a friend's hand, and to see the quiet trust and love of a child's eyes.

God has fabulously endowed our world with wonders all around us. Let us not go through life so fast that we miss them.

Two Ways of Life

Blessed is the man who walks not in the counsel of the ungodly.
(Psalm 1:1)

For many people, Psalms is the best-loved and most-quoted book of the Bible. This keynote psalm defines the two ways of life, and thus its teaching is a foundation for the whole book. It first describes the righteous man as "blessed." The Hebrew word for "blessed" is plural, in keeping with the innumerable and incredibly diverse blessings from God.

The psalmist says of the man of God, "But his delight is in the law of the LORD" (v. 2). If he took delight in such a fragmentary record in his day, just the first five books of Moses, how much more should be our keenness for the inspired Old and New Testaments.

The godly man is "like a tree planted" (v. 3). His life is fixed, stable, and can withstand the winds and storms that will surely come. He is like a fruitful tree. Every life is a fresh thought from the mind of God. No two stars, no two snowflakes, no two fingerprints, no two lives are the same. Each of us has a purpose no other can fulfill.

The psalmist cites the three steps in the downward spiral to destruction. First, the ungodly man *walks* in the way of sin. Sin gets his attention. Next, he *stands* in sin, a more settled posture, a settling in. Finally, he *sits.* He becomes habituated to evil. Augustine, writing of his bondage to sin prior to conversion, warns of this downward spiral: "A perverse will produces lust. Lust yielded to becomes a habit. A habit not resisted becomes a necessity. These links of a chain bound me hand and foot."

The psalm concludes, "the way of the wicked will perish" (v. 6). Charles H. Spurgeon put it memorably: "The righteous carves his name upon the rock, but the wicked writes his remembrance in the sand." For the sinner, Psalm 1 serves as a call to repentance. For the Christian, it is a call to renewal on the path that leads to life eternal.

O LORD, our Lord, how majestic is your name in all the earth!

(Psalm 8:1)

Psalm 8, a masterpiece among the psalms, proclaims in elegant language the inexpressible theme of the glory of God.

Do you recall some moment of awe and wonder when you beheld the majesty of a star-spangled sky? One such moment is enshrined in our family archives of memory. On a camping trip in northern Canada, after the evening campfire had died down, we strolled down to the lakeside, sat on some large rocks, and gazed up at the star-studded canopy of the heavens. Our son, about 7 years of age, said reverently, "I never knew there were so many stars!" It was a moment of discovery.

On one dark, clear night, a shepherd looked up at the star-bejeweled sky. His spirit overflowed with awe and wonder. A burning of the poet kindled within him: "Where is my pen? I must write." A surge of music stirred in his soul: "Where is my harp? I must play." The moment seemed inexpressible. He began with an exclamation addressed to God himself. David's hillside song of praise that night became a classic of devotion for the ages.

What would the psalmist have said if he could have peered out into fathomless space through one of our giant telescopes and discovered that the universe is made up of billions of galaxies, each containing on average a hundred billion stars! If he was struck with awe at the beauty and immensity of what he could see, how much more should we marvel in light of what modern astronomy reveals?

The psalmist terms the cosmos *"Your* heavens." He saw beyond nature's grandeur to nature's Author. Eugene Peterson renders Psalm 66:5 this way: "Take a good look at God's wonders — they'll take your breath away." The mind-boggling wonders of the cosmos lead us to praise and adoration for the grandeur and glory of God.

What is man that you are mindful of him? (Psalm 8:4)

Awed at the incalculable grandeur of God as revealed in the heavens, the psalmist is moved to exclaim, "What is man that you are mindful of him?" We might well ask, is it credible that the Creator of this unthinkable universe with its hundreds of billions of stars really knows and cares for me, such an infinitesimal speck in the scheme of things?

The psalmist leads us to ponder our true identity. How do I fit into God's plan of creation? Why should the God of the universe be mindful of me? His contemplation issues forth in his probing, pertinent, and provocative question: "Who and what are we, really?"

Human curiosity about the meaning of life has bred endless speculations and controversies. Bertrand Russell has called man "a curious accident." H. L. Mencken denigrates the human species: "Man is a parasite infecting the epidermis of a midget planet." Shakespeare's Macbeth declared: "Life's but a walking shadow."

The psalmist portrays man as the crown of God's creation: "You made him a little lower than the heavenly beings and crowned him with glory and honor" (v. 5). William Barclay describes this text as "The paradox of man. Frail, puny, transient, insignificant, mortal, but God has appointed him his viceroy on earth."

You and I are Somebody in the plan and purpose of God. We are more than a restless protoplasm, enchanted dust, a fortuitous concourse of atoms, the plaything of an inscrutable fate, a pawn in the universe. "Our dignity is that we are children of God," writes William Temple, "and destined for eternal fellowship with God."

The heavens declare the glory of God;
the skies proclaim the work of his hands. (Psalm 19:1)

I n this eloquent lyric, the psalmist rhapsodizes about God's glory in the heavens. God has written his autograph across the velvet scroll of the night sky. The resplendent pageantry of the heavens proclaims "the work of his hands." William Barclay observed: "Approached with reverence, nature gives a glimpse into the interior of God's workshop."

If we found a watch ticking on a desert island, we would know that somewhere there had to be a watchmaker to make an instrument of such complexity. The universe transcends the design and precision of the world's finest watch. Such a marvelous world must have a world-maker. Behind such an intelligent universe must be a Cosmic Intelligence, a Master Engineer.

What if the psalmist knew that the earth, which seemed to him to be the center of things, was only a pygmy islet in a fathomless sea of intergalactic space? What if he knew that the light sparkling from a star actually left the star two million years ago to travel through space at its phantom speed of 186,000 miles a second?

"Day after day they pour forth speech" (v. 2). The verb for "pour forth" means "to bubble up." Creation effervesces with its witness to the glory of God.

Sir Christopher Wren lies buried in London's St. Paul's Cathedral, the great church that his genius planned and built. On his tombstone is a simple Latin inscription that reads, "If you wish to see his monument, look around you." The psalmist, too, invites us, if we want to see the glory of God, to look about us.

Words and Thoughts

May the words of my mouth and the meditation of my heart
be pleasing in your sight,
O LORD, my Rock and my Redeemer. (Psalm 19:14)

This psalm closes with one of the memorable short prayers of the Bible, which has become a permanent part of Christian worship, both private and public.

The prayer concerns two vital areas of life; it asks that both our words and our thoughts will be pleasing to God. Our thoughts give birth to our words, so that when the source is pure then that which comes forth will be acceptable to God.

Socrates said, "Speak that I may see thee." We might have expected him to say, "Speak that I may hear thee." But the wise philosopher knew that our words reveal who we are. Every time we speak, the world "sees" us.

Words are always moral, for they reveal the heart and soul of the one who utters them, and they leave their impact on other lives. Our Lord has said that we shall be held accountable for every idle word. We are responsible for our words.

Mother Teresa was the most revered woman in the world during her time. She saw the dying, the crippled, the unwanted, and the un-loved as "Jesus in disguise." Her work among the dying on the streets of Calcutta became legendary. Awarded the Nobel Peace Prize, she was described as a "burning light in a dark time." What was the secret of her saintliness? Perhaps it is found in the response she gave one day to a reporter: "I am like a pencil in the hand of God. That is all. He does the writing. The pencil has only to be allowed to be used." We too can be "a pencil in the hand of God," with our words and deeds as instruments of his love and grace.

The LORD is my shepherd. (Psalm 23:1)

For nearly three thousand years, Psalm 23 has been among the best-known and best-loved texts of the Bible. Jesus applied its imagery to himself in saying, "I am the good shepherd" (John 10:11).

The venerable phrasing and imagery remain timely and timeless. "The Lord" — he who is the Lord of the whole creation has become my shepherd. I, a mere mortal, have become a cherished object of divine care. The common clay of my humanity becomes linked with divine destiny in Christ.

"My shepherd" — the psalmist doesn't refer to the Lord as the shepherd of the world, but he is confident of the Lord's personal relationship and care as his very own shepherd. "The sweetest word of the whole psalm is that monosyllable *my*," writes Charles H. Spurgeon.

Being a shepherd is hardly a romantic vocation. Rather, it is fatiguing, with long hours and isolation, dealing with creatures prone to stray, being assaulted by storms, and fighting wild beasts and robbers. Our Shepherd came to dwell among us and lay down his life for us.

The story is told of two men who once repeated Psalm 23 to a large audience. One was a polished orator, who quoted the psalm in an eloquent fashion. When he finished, the audience gave a prolonged applause. Then the other man, somewhat older, repeated the same words. But when he finished, no sound at all came from the audience. Instead, the people were hushed, as though in a spirit of prayer. The polished orator stood up and said, "Friends, I wish to make an explanation of what has happened here tonight. You gave to me your applause, but when my friend had finished, you remained reverently silent. The difference is, I know the psalm, but he knows the Shepherd."

The Shadow of Death

Even though I walk through the valley of the shadow of death,
I will fear no evil, for you are with me.   (Psalm 23:4)

The Shepherd's presence is with us, not only all through life, but even when we come to its termination.

"Walk" indicates the steady advance of a soul. Death is not the end, but a continued progress in the plan of God. The believer approaches the end of life, not flurried or frantic, but calm and composed. There is no need for alarm, because we are in the company of the Good Shepherd. Fear is eclipsed by his presence.

We do not stay in death; we walk *through* its valley. Death is but a thoroughfare to the new, bright, shining world to which the Chief Shepherd leads us. This psalm eloquently declares that death is not a dead end but a pathway to the house of the Lord. William Barclay writes: "The last step of life is the step which leads into the presence of God."

The psalmist likens death to a valley. Valleys need not be forbidding places. They are most often well watered, with rich feed and forage along the route. As we come to this valley, we will find even there provision to sustain us, enabling us to pass through.

This radiant psalm reminds us that death is not substance, but shadow. It is not the valley of death, but the valley of the *shadow* of death. Where there is a shadow, there must be light. Let us look beyond the shadow of death to the Light of the World.

When we come to this consummating experience of our lives, may our confident testimony ring out with the psalmist, "I will fear no evil, for you are with me." The sense of Christ's presence is real to the Christian, in life, at death, and beyond the grave.

Who may stand in his holy place?
He who has clean hands and a pure heart. (Psalm 24:3-4)

The highest ambition of our soul should be to reach the holy place of God's presence, to enjoy constant fellowship with him. But who can enjoy such unspeakable blessedness? Who can ascend to such heights? Who can know the secret of his presence? Is such an Everest of attainment possible for us finite, frail, and faltering human beings?

This psalm invites us to those heights, to the very presence of God. The psalmist does not leave us without an answer to the question he poses: "Who may stand in his holy place? He who has clean hands and a pure heart, who does not lift up his soul to an idol or swear by what is false." The sacred privilege carries its responsibilities. Our hands, the outward practical life, must be clean. Our hearts, the inward life with its motivations and innermost thoughts, must be pure.

Such communion with God is attained by an upward path, for we "ascend" this height of holy and divine fellowship. This pilgrimage of the soul has its required disciplines, renunciations, and dedications. The work of the cleansing of our soul will be a lifetime process. Our perfection consists of struggling against our imperfection.

William Pennick has expressed for us in song the longing inspired by this text:

There is a holy hill of God,
Its heights by faith I see;
Now to ascend my soul aspires,
To leave earth's vanity.
Lord, cleanse my hands and cleanse my heart,
All selfish aims I flee;
My faith reward, thy love impart,
And let me dwell with thee.

Our Light and Salvation

The LORD *is my light and my salvation.* (Psalm 27:1)

This verse has long been a favorite quotation for Christian witness. The psalmist does not say that the Lord gives light, but that he *is* our light; not that he gives salvation, but that he *is* our salvation.

The world without Christ is one of darkness, groping and lost. Jesus is the Light that dispels the world's spiritual darkness. He is the Light of the World who came to be the Light of every life. As our Light, no clouds can obscure him, and no night can eclipse him from shining upon and within us.

Inscribed in Latin at that great seat of learning, Oxford University, is its motto: *Dominus illuminatio mea* — "The Lord is my Light." May these words be inscribed upon our hearts as the theme of our life. Let our prayer ever be that of John Newman:

> Lead, kindly Light, amid the encircling gloom.
> Lead thou me on!
> The night is dark, and I am far from home;
> Lead thou me on!
> Keep thou my feet; I do not ask to see
> The distant scene: one step enough for me.

"The LORD is my salvation" is the joyful witness of the psalmist. What a comprehensive blessing salvation bestows. It brings deliverance from the guilt of sin, from its dominion, its curse, its punishment, and ultimately from the very existence of sin.

Worship the LORD *in the splendor of his holiness.*   (Psalm 29:2)

God's holiness exceeds the bounds of human vocabulary in any attempt to define it. The psalmist provides an appropriate matching word when he speaks of the *splendor* of God's holiness. The dictionary defines "splendor" as "dazzling brightness, magnificence, grandeur." A traditional hymn speaks of God as "pavilioned in splendor." Thus the terms "splendor" and "holiness" are compatibly yoked together in this psalm of David.

We do not find frequent references to God's sovereign name, his loving name, or his powerful name, but time and again God reminds us of his holy name. It is the only attribute thrice repeated: "Holy, holy, holy is the LORD Almighty" (Isaiah 6:3; Revelation 4:8).

There are many calls to vocation — some are called to medicine, some to teaching, some to music, some to writing, some to art, some to ministry. But God calls every believer to the life of holiness. The call to be holy is not a call to vocation but a call to character, a call to soul health. No fewer than three times in the Bible the people of God are called to "Worship the LORD in the splendor of his holiness" (1 Chronicles 16:29; Psalms 29:2; 96:9).

Our petition for this blessing has been expressed in Charles Wesley's hymn:

He wills that I should holy be;
    That holiness I long to feel,
That full divine conformity
    To all my Savior's righteous will.

Blessed is he whose transgressions are forgiven, whose sins are covered.   (Psalm 32:1)

Psalm 32 is a joyful beatitude of the pardoned sinner. Augustine had this psalm written on the wall opposite his bed during his last sickness. His early life of wanton indulgence and licentious living had been forgiven. The joy of liberation from sin and the reality of forgiveness was his comfort as he was to depart this life.

Most people judge by the outward appearances. Many in the world measure a person's "blessings" by their portfolio of assets, their success in their profession, the education they have acquired, or their uninterrupted good health. But one may possess all these things and still have an emptiness within one's life. The psalmist sees through the masquerade of outward appearance and pronounces that person blessed who has received God's forgiveness.

In human jurisprudence, there is what is known as "double jeopardy," which rules that a person cannot be tried twice for the same offense. If he is tried once and acquitted, he cannot be tried again. This same principle is true on a much higher scale in divine jurisprudence. Christ paid the penalty for our sins. When we accept his forgiveness, there can be no further penalty for that which he has forgiven. Our sin is "covered," never again to be brought up against us.

He lifted me out of the slimy pit,
out of the mud and mire;
he set my feet on a rock
and gave me a firm place to stand.   (Psalm 40:2)

Psalm 40 is a ballad, a song of human experience. Its theme has inspired the composing of songs through the years. Black slaves in America paraphrased its words as they identified with its expression of hope for spiritual and social salvation:

He took my feet from the miry clay.
   Yes, He did.
And placed them on the rock to stay.
   Yes, He did.

"He lifted me out of the slimy pit" is an apt description of the situation of a person in the grip of sin. The familiar "miry clay" of the King James Version conveys the moral suggestion of the clinging quality of clay. The psalmist's metaphors of "slimy pit," "mud and mire," speak of our condition before "he set my feet on a rock, and gave me a firm place to stand" (v. 2). There could not be a greater contrast between mud and rock, or between "a slimy pit" and "a firm place to stand," just as there cannot be a greater contrast between our condition of sin and of salvation.

Sin was a horrible pit and miry clay for each of us. We were trapped, held in its power, helpless and unable to escape. But God delivered us. He brought us up and out of sin's entrapment. Indeed, he has given to us a jubilant song of deliverance.

As the deer pants for streams of water,
so my soul pants for you, O God.   (Psalm 42:1)

The psalmist, who lived close to the outdoors and its wild creatures, would have seen deer panting for the clear water of the mountain brook. The animal's compelling thirst formed a picture for him that symbolized his intense longing and need for God: "My soul thirsts for God, for the living God" (v. 2).

This longing is the elemental need of the soul. Jesus promised: "Blessed are those who hunger and thirst for righteousness, for they will be filled" (Matthew 5:6).

Augustine gave this longing memorable expression in his prayer: "O God, our hearts are restless until they find their rest in you." There is a deep thirst of the soul that no earthly spring can slake. There are hungers that no earthly bread can satisfy. God alone can fulfill the deepest longings and needs of the spirit. He alone can still the restlessness of the soul. Without him we are as fish out of water, birds without sky.

Christ is to our souls what water is to our bodies — an absolute necessity for life and sustenance, and the satisfaction of our most intense longings. Jesus declared that he is the Living Water: "Whoever drinks the water I give him will never thirst. Indeed, the water I give him will become in him a spring of water welling up to eternal life" (John 4:14). The final invitation in the Word of God is: "Whoever is thirsty, let him come; and whoever wishes, let him take the free gift of the water of life" (Revelation 22:17).

God is our refuge and strength. (Psalm 46:1)

In times of great danger, Martin Luther would say to his friend Philipp Melanchthon, "Come, Philipp, let us sing the forty-sixth psalm." It is called "Luther's Psalm," not because he staked any proprietary claims to it, but because he fashioned from the bright gold of its truth his great Reformation hymn, "A Mighty Fortress Is Our God." This sixteenth-century hymn became the battle song of the Reformation. Succeeding generations of believers would ever afterward sing:

> A mighty fortress is our God,
>   A bulwark never failing;
> Our helper He, amid the flood
>   Of mortal ills prevailing.

When we come yieldingly into God's presence, we discover his power and peace. We too will find that "God is our refuge and strength, an ever-present help in trouble. Therefore we will not fear" (vv. 1-2). There are times and troubles that even our closest loved ones and friends are not able to enter into. But God is always "an ever-present help in trouble." The word "ever" gives a reassuring emphasis.

When the forecast calls for storms, ships need a sure anchor; buildings need a sure foundation; trees need deep roots. In each case, their survival through the storm depends upon a strong link to that which cannot be moved. The divine Refuge and Strength of Psalm 46 is that for the Christian.

The Power of Stillness

Be still, and know that I am God. (Psalm 46:10)

This psalm became a major source of comfort and courage in the aftermath of the terrorist attack on America on September 11, 2001. Things that had once seemed so secure came tumbling down upon us. Since that day of unspeakable atrocity we have needed more than ever the assuring word that God is an ever-present help in the time of trouble, and because he is with us we need not fear.

What can we do when potentially shattering experiences come upon us? "Be still, and know that I am God" is the assuring word from this psalm. To "be still" is often the opposite of what we tend to do when hit by stress. We react, become exercised, and get caught up in hurry and worry.

There is a mighty power in silence. Gravity is a silent force, yet it holds stars and galaxies in their orbits. Sunbeams make their long journey to earth, unheard by human ear, yet they bear an incomputable energy. Dew falls silently, yet it brings refreshment and beauty. Nature's mighty miracles are wrought in silence. Noise and confusion come from humankind.

John Oxenham's hymn speaks to us of this silent source of serenity and strength:

> 'Mid all the traffic of the ways,
> Turmoils without, within,
> Make in my heart a quiet place,
> And come and dwell therein.
> Come occupy my silent place,
> And make thy dwelling there!
> More grace is wrought in quietness,
> Than any is aware.

Create in me a pure heart, O God.   (Psalm 51:10)

"Create in me a pure heart" is the cry of David as he is confronted with his sin against a holy God. He does not pray to have his nature improved, or amended, but recreated. Eugene Peterson paraphrases this prayer of David: "Give me a clean bill of health. God, make a fresh start in me, shape a Genesis week from the chaos of my life."

Purity has become a major concern. We want pure water, free of pollutants. We want pure food, free of poisons. We want pure air, free of toxicants. We pass legislation and spend great sums to assure purity. We prefer purity to impurity, health to sickness, perfection to imperfection, flawlessness to faultiness, the authentic to the artificial. However, when it comes to the spiritual life, many settle for less. But God calls us to purity.

William Law in his enduring work, *A Serious Call to a Devout and Holy Life*, reminds us, "Our lives should be as holy and heavenly as our prayers. It is as great an absurdity to offer up holy prayers without a holy life as it is to live a holy life without prayer." David's prayer of confession revealed his need for purity as well as pardon.

Søren Kierkegaard, in his classic work two centuries ago, wrote: "Purity of heart is to will one thing." To those who pray the prayer of David in this psalm as their one dominant desire, God will give the blessing of a pure heart.

Tennyson's Sir Galahad said, "My strength is as the strength of ten because my heart is pure." Spiritual power becomes the byproduct of purity of heart.

I had rather be a doorkeeper in the house of my God than dwell in the tents of the wicked.   (Psalm 84:10)

There is an old saying, "If I had my druthers," meaning if I had my choice. The psalmist, expressing his "druthers," says: "I had rather be a doorkeeper in the house of my God than dwell in the tents of the wicked."

C. H. Spurgeon writes on this text: "God's worst is better than the devil's best. God's doorstep is a happier rest than downy couches within the pavilions of royal sinners, though we might lie there for a lifetime of luxury."

A doorkeeper fulfills an important function in the house of the Lord. He is the first one in, and the last one out, seeing the worshipers safely on their way. He also has the high privilege of ushering others over the threshold to the One who said, "I am the door." In this sense, we are all called to be doorkeepers in the house of the Lord, encouraging and helping others to come into our Father's home.

The doorkeeper in the Lord's house, by a friendly smile, a warm handshake, and a genuine "God bless you," may on occasion preach an even more effective sermon than the preacher. No service rendered to God is menial, but rather our modest offerings of loaves and fishes in the Lord's hands become multiplied blessings to the lives of others.

Brother Lawrence (1611–1691) bequeathed to us his classic memoir, *The Practice of the Presence of God.* He referred to himself as "the lord of all pots and pans" in honor of his employment in the kitchen of the monastery until his death. For him no task was too trivial, as he transformed mundane chores of the kitchen into "the sacrament of the present moment." So with us, when each task however menial is rendered as service to the Lord.

LORD, *you have been our dwelling place throughout all genera-tions.*
(Psalm 90:1)

This oldest composition in the Psalter, composed by Moses, speaks eloquently of God's eternity, "From everlasting to everlasting you are God," and of man's transience, whose span is but as "a watch in the night."

Moses did not write our text from the palace of Pharaoh, but from the barren wilderness through which he wandered with the Israelites for forty years. He, with his people, had no dwelling place on earth, only a moving tent as they pressed on. They could not plant a garden, or plan and build a home; nor could they become attached to a place and settle down. They must be always journeying, ever moving on-ward, from place to place, never settled.

But as Moses contemplated their situation, he realized that though he and his people lived in tents, they had something better than an earthly abode: "Lord, you have been our dwelling place throughout all generations." In the eternal God he found a home for himself and his people that would never change or pass away. The God who inhabits the heavens also deigns to dwell with us, to be our helper, our friend, our heavenly Father.

May we, with the psalmist, know the comforting assurance of hav-ing God as our dwelling place, for which he has given us an eternal lease. The apostle John caught the wonder of this experience for us in Christ when he recorded: "We know that we live in him and he in us, because he has given us of his Spirit" (1 John 4:13).

Precious Death

Precious in the sight of the LORD is the death of his saints.
(Psalm 116:15)

When God created the world he looked upon the work of his hands and pronounced it "good." But none of that handiwork was called "precious in his sight." The death of the saints, however, is called "precious in his sight." The people of God are of far greater worth to him than all the planets and stars of his creation.

Why is the death of the believer singled out as precious to God? It is the moment in which the believer is received into the eternal embrace of the heavenly Father. It is the moment the soul goes from the toil of the world to the rewards of eternity, from the sorrows of this world to the eternal joys of heaven, from the temporal fellowship of earth to eternal fellowship with God and the people of God.

Death, considered a calamity by many, becomes a celebration for the believer; considered a terror by many, it becomes a triumph for the child of God. Death for the saint is the last step of life that leads into the presence of God forever.

When Catherine Marshall's husband Peter, the noted Scottish preacher, was felled by a heart attack, he whispered to his wife as he was carried from the house, "See you in the morning, darling." Those last words later took on a transcendent meaning. Indeed, after our night in this world, the morning dawns.

In a London cemetery stands a headstone with an unusual epitaph, erected by the famous pastor, Joseph Parker, for his beloved wife. He could not bring himself to write the word "died." Instead, he had inscribed the word "Ascended." The believer at death does not leave the land of the living to go into the land of the dying. Rather, he leaves the land of the dying to go into the land of the living.

This is the day the LORD has made; let us rejoice and be glad in it.

(Psalm 118:24)

Each new day is a gift from God. Time is life, and when we run out of time we will have run out of life.

Ours is the choice either to waste or to invest wisely the priceless gift of each new twenty-four shining hours. We can spend this account any way that we desire, but then we must accept the results or consequences.

The psalmist reminds us that each new day is a cause for rejoicing. Today is the most important day of our lives. Yesterday is forever gone. Tomorrow may never come. But today is ours to live, to laugh, to learn, to labor, to love. An unknown poet has eloquently expressed this theme in "Salutation to the Dawn":

> Look to this day!
> In its brief course
> Lie all the verities and realities of your existence:
> The bliss of growth,
> The glory of action,
> The splendor of achievement.
> For yesterday is but a dream,
> And tomorrow is only a vision.
> But today well lived makes every yesterday a dream of happiness
> and every tomorrow a vision of hope.
> Look well, therefore, to this day!
> Such is the salutation to the dawn.

Your word I have hidden in my heart that I might not sin against you.   (Psalm 119:11 NKJV)

The wonders of God's Word fill the 176 verses of Psalm 119 — the longest song in the Psalter and the longest chapter in the Bible. Its verses comprise the single most complete treatise and testimony in the Bible on the subject of God's Word.

This great 119th psalm opens, as does the entire Psalter, with a beatitude: "Blessed are they . . . who walk according to the law of the LORD" (v. 1). The word "blessed" is plural, speaking of the multiplicity of blessing that comes from heeding the Word of God.

Our memorable golden text can be simply summarized and outlined as follows:

The best possession — "your Word"
The best place — "I have hidden in my heart"
The best purpose — "That I might not sin against you"

With the psalmist, let us have the Word of God in our heart, as an integral part of our life. One of the ways to do that is the old-fashioned practice of memorization of Scripture. Memory is said to be "the sheath in which the sword of the Lord is kept."

John Burton's words have been sung for over a century by Christians who acknowledge the Bible as God's treasure for the believer:

Holy Bible, book divine,
Precious treasure, thou art mine;
Mine to tell me whence I came;
Mine to teach me what I am.

Your word is a lamp to my feet and a light for my path.
(Psalm 119:105)

God has no eraser on the end of his pencil, or an "undo" on his computer. What he writes never needs to be changed. Such a basic document as the U.S. Constitution had to be amended almost before the ink was dry, with the Bill of Rights and the first ten amendments added. Isaiah proclaimed: "The word of our God will stand for ever."

This psalm reminds us that its enduring truth has the most practical application to our everyday lives. It is our constant companion — "for [your commands] are ever with me" (v. 98). It is our most cherished possession — "a joy beyond all wealth" (v. 14 JB). It is our unfailing guide — "your statutes are . . . my counselors" (v. 24).

"According to your word" recurs throughout this psalm. The Word of God sets the standards in our age of "situation ethics." It provides the absolutes amid the sea of relativities on which many flounder. Jesus prayed for his disciples, "Sanctify them by your truth. Your word is truth" (John 17:17). Such is the cleansing power of the Word of God.

Our golden text, no doubt well marked in many Bibles, affirms that God's Word "is a lamp to my feet and a light for my path." Those words were penned before the day of electric lights, when people had to make their way often in inky darkness and over rough terrain. The lamp would not illumine the distance ahead, but would light the way for the immediate step to be taken. God's Word gives guidance for each moment, each hour, each day. May we follow faithfully its light upon our path of life.

The Traveler's Hymn

I lift up my eyes to the hills. (Psalm 121:1)

Psalm 121 is a traveler's hymn. Before the Israelite families would start out on their pilgrimages, they would sing these words as an affirmation of their trust in God.

The first word and statement of this psalm makes it very personal: "I lift up my eyes to the hills." It speaks of the personal pilgrimage of each life. The word "pilgrim" has, for the most part, dropped out of religious speech. We are only "passing through" this life. It is but a brief moment of our eternal existence.

John Bunyan's *Pilgrim's Progress* is popular, not only for its literary genius, but because Christian's perilous journey parallels our own pilgrimage. Our own soul makes the journey, through crisis after crisis, struggling through the Slough of Despond, walking through Vanity Fair, with the need to continually press on. As pilgrims, we too need to affirm and pray this traveler's hymn of trust in the One who will "preserve our soul."

On his journey, the psalmist asks, "Where does my help come from?" With confidence he replies, "My help comes from the LORD, the Maker of heaven and earth" (v. 2).

For some years our family owned acreage with a cabin on top of a mountain in the Catskills of New York State. It often sheltered us from the busyness and the daily duties and deadlines back in the city. Amid its sylvan hills and vistas of distant valleys, and in its quiet solitude, our bodies, minds, and souls were renewed. From the heights, we returned to the busy routines of life with a clearer perspective.

As the psalmist affirms, to lift our spiritual sights toward heaven brings assurance that God is our helper who enables us to safely pass through our brief pilgrimage of life.

The LORD shall preserve you from all evil; He shall preserve your soul.
                                                    (Psalm 121:7 NKJV)

Human beings are the most helpless creatures of all, cradled, coddled, and cared for a whole year before we can walk. Throughout our life we are vulnerable and dependent. "The LORD is your keeper," affirms the psalmist (v. 5 NKJV). What condescension, and what a supreme provision, for the Almighty, the Creator of the cosmos, to be our keeper!

This psalm does not promise that we will be spared difficulties, danger, or death. History is all too instructive for any such unrealistic concept. But the valid promise of this psalm is: "The LORD shall preserve you from all evil; He shall preserve your soul." God may not protect us from danger, but he will preserve us from evil and will even bring blessing out of the brokenness of our lives.

Now and again we cross a threshold, passing from one environment to another. It may be a son or daughter going off to college, from the home with its intimacies and security, to new associations and challenges. Another goes out into the world to live and work, leaving the home with its tenderness to face a world that is often callous and competitive. Or we pass over the threshold of marriage, the birth of a child, the loss of a loved one, new directions in our life. Major changes occur that represent a "going out," a transition.

The beautiful promise concluding this psalm is that, for God's people, the last part of life's journey is not a "going out" but a "coming in": "The LORD shall preserve your going out and your coming in from this time forth, and even forevermore" (v. 8 NKJV).

Unless the LORD *builds the house, its builders labor in vain.*

(Psalm 127:1)

Agood carpenter can build a house, but only the Lord can build a home. The psalmist states the timeless truth that the Lord alone gives the needed foundation for harmonious living.

Today family breakdown has reached epidemic proportions. More than a thousand times every day, somewhere in the U.S., a judge's gavel falls and with two words, "Divorce granted!," somebody's love story comes to an end. "Happily ever after" has been quantified by the census to about seven years. The family in America has become an endangered species.

But when Christ is the head of the home, there is love, peace, positive communication, affirmation, empathy, compassion, forgiveness, honesty, loyalty, prayer, and unselfish sharing. Christ makes the difference.

The Living Bible paraphrases verse 3: "Children are a gift from God." Our children are the richest treasures of our lives. No material goods or gain compares with their worth. During a visit to see our beautiful new granddaughter, our son told us that her name, Lauren, means "gift from God." Every child is a priceless gift from God to the parents.

Children are also our most sacred responsibility, the first priorities of our lives. The Lord holds us accountable for their spiritual nurture by training and example. A parent has about eighteen years to raise a child, amid the external pressures of our world today. In that short space of time there are two lasting bequests we can give — roots and wings.

Search me, O God, and know my heart. (Psalm 139:23)

The psalmist tells us God is not only the God of creation, but he is also the God of re-creation. The omnipotent God who flaunts his power in orbiting spheres also displays his creative power in our individual lives. A loving, divine craftsman fashioned the genes, the chromosomes, the RNA and DNA into the marvel of life beyond our comprehension. And where our strength ends, there God's omnipotence begins.

He is the God who will search our hearts and make them anew, that we may have life everlasting. The poet of the psalms would lead us to pray with him:

Search me, O God, and know my heart;
    test me and know my anxious thoughts.
See if there is any offensive way in me,
    and lead me in the way everlasting. (vv. 23-24)

Self-examination is painfully difficult. Christian psychologist James Dolby says that "some people would rather die than be known. To be honest with ourselves is not natural." How courageous was the psalmist in asking God to search him.

We have been reminded by this majestic psalm that we have an omniscient God who gives us wisdom, an omnipresent God who is always with us, an omnipotent God who gives us power, and an all-loving God who leads us in the way everlasting. Praise him!

He heals the brokenhearted. (Psalm 147:3)

A sign in an old-fashioned tinker shop read, "We can mend anything except a broken heart." But the assuring announcement posted in the Bible says of our heavenly Father, "He heals the brokenhearted and binds up their wounds" (Psalm 147:3).

Sorrows and troubles come in a thousand guises. A heart may be broken by loneliness, anxiety, misunderstanding, a fractured relationship, a dear one struck down, shattered dreams, the unfaithfulness of a trusted loved one. It may strike from the outside, as with the trauma of 9/11. Increased longevity has brought the indescribable brokenheartedness of many who stand by a loved one ravaged by Alzheimer's or other debilitating diseases.

But praise God — a remedy has been provided. God intervenes on our behalf; he comes to us in our despair and he heals the brokenhearted.

For twenty years Mrs. Doolittle had been confined to bed as an invalid. Her husband, a partial invalid, managed his business from a wheelchair. One day, the evangelist Dr. W. Stillman Martin and his wife came to visit them. Deeply impressed with the joyful spirit the Doolittles maintained in spite of severe adversity, they asked, "What is the secret of your joy?" Mrs. Doolittle replied, "His eye is on the sparrow, and I know he watches me." That reply lodged in the Martins' mind and soul, and inspired them to write:

> "Let not your heart be troubled,"
> His tender word I heard,
> And resting on his goodness,
> I lose my doubts and fears;
> Tho' by the path He leadeth,
> But one step I may see;
> His eye is on the sparrow,
> And I know He watches me.

Praise the LORD.   (Psalm 150:1)

The flow of the broad river of the book of Psalms ends in a cataract of praise and unbounded exultation. The word "praise" is repeated thirteen times in the six verses of the concluding psalm. Each elevenfold exhortation is framed by "Praise the Lord," or its equivalent, "hallelujah," which has become the universal word of praise and worship.

We are prone to chronicle our complaints, but too often neglect to sound forth praises for what God has done for us. Many occasions call us to praise — the glory of a sunrise, the majesty of a star-filled sky, the beauty of a garden, the refrain of a melody, the touch of a loved one. But, of course, we praise God most of all for his infinite love bestowed upon us. He is the Sovereign who became our Savior.

Francis of Assisi was called "God's Troubadour," his life marked by an exuberant abandonment to God. He tramped the villages, joyfully announcing the kingdom of God, preaching even to the birds along the way. His life was a paean of praise to his Creator, and for almost a millennium his song invites God's children to join with him in praise:

> All creatures of our God and King,
> Lift up your voice and with us sing
>   Alleluia, alleluia!
> Thou burning sun with golden beam,
> Thou silver moon with softer gleam:
>   O praise him, O praise him,
>   Alleluia, alleluia, alleluia!

The fear of the LORD is the beginning of knowledge.

(Proverbs 1:7)

Today we are drowning in a sea of information but starving for wisdom. The media overload of the outer world incessantly impinges upon us while the inner world all too often remains unexplored and unknown. Everywhere uncertainties abound, and like the dove after the Deluge, we seem to find no solid ground for the soles of our feet.

In this era, married to atomic energy for better or worse till death do us part, true wisdom is no longer an option. It is a life-or-death matter. We run the risk of becoming technical giants but ethical infants. Our survival as a society and as a planet, and our adequacy for daily living, require a wisdom that transcends mere human understanding.

"Reverence" is perhaps a more helpful translation than "fear." This verse could be a synopsis of the book of Proverbs, and a motto for life. "Fear of the Lord," like the four notes that present the theme of Beethoven's Fifth Symphony, appear at the beginning, as well as recurringly throughout the book. Its repetition underscores that fear or reverence for the Lord is the only foundation for wisdom.

We urgently need wisdom, wisdom for life's choices and directions, wisdom for life's testings and challenges, wisdom for adequacy in daily life. True wisdom begins with a reverence for God. Let us be among the wise.

Trust in the LORD with all your heart.   (Proverbs 3:5)

W hat is there in life to which we can safely commit our trust? We
cannot rely fully on ourselves: we are frail and finite. We cannot rely on nature: it is sometimes beautiful and sometimes fickle,
even savage. Others we trust may fail us. Organizations, even churches
and governments, betray their "feet of clay."

But the Lord is always faithful, ever dependable. He is immutable:
"I the LORD do not change" (Malachi 3:6). The royal sage of Proverbs directs us to the only and ultimate One to whom we can commit our
lives.

His counsel begins with the commitment of nothing less than "all
your heart." There can be no reservations in our consecration. The
trust of which the text speaks invokes all of life. It calls us to "lean not
on your own understanding." He climaxes his mighty maxim: "In all
your ways acknowledge him, and he will make your paths straight."

The Greek mathematician Archimedes sought only for one fixed
and immovable point in order to move the whole earth from its place
— "if I find even the least thing that is unshakably certain." This proverb reveals that Archimedean point for living — the basis of all certainty — the Lord. He alone can sustain the whole structure of human
knowledge and experience.

This is a text I have often inscribed inside a book cover, or in a note
to the grandchildren. Its deep wisdom should be inscribed on the heart
of every believer.

There is a way that seems right to a man, but in the end it leads to
death. (Proverbs 14:12)

This is such an important truth that God repeats it in 16:25. It warns
of self-deception in the way of sin. The person going down the
road of moral destruction is often blind to its peril. He rationalizes,
justifies, excuses himself. The path he travels "seems right" to him.
"But" — and that is always a word to reckon with in the Bible — "in the
end it leads to death."

John Newton, early in his life, ran headlong down that road. He op-
erated slave ships from Africa and lived a profligate life. But in the
depth of his sin and despair, he turned to Christ and was transformed.
From that experience he gave to Christendom one of its greatest songs,
"Amazing Grace." His self-written epitaph reads:

> John Newton, clerk,
> Once an infidel and libertine,
> A servant of slaves in Africa,
> Was, by the rich mercy of our Lord and Savior, Jesus Christ
> Preserved, restored, pardoned
> And appointed to preach the faith he
> Had long labored to destroy.

Paul, the great professor of Christian theology, once was going
down the road to Damascus, a way that seemed right to him. But it was
leading to death. On that road he met Christ, was turned in the opposite direction, and life was never the same.

The only way to life and liberty is to follow the One who declared,
"I am the way."

Righteousness exalts a nation.   (Proverbs 14:34)

What makes a nation great? Not military might, scientific advance, or great prosperity. But as our text reminds us, righteousness exalts and makes a nation great.

In the 1830s the French statesman and author Alexis de Tocqueville came to America, traveled throughout our land, and wrote a report that stands as a monument to his perspicacity. He said: "I sought for the greatness and genius of America in her commodious harbors and ample rivers, and it was not there; in her fertile fields and boundless forests, and it was not there; in her rich mines and vast world commerce, and it was not there; in her democratic Congress and her matchless Constitution, and it was not there. Not until I went into the churches of America and heard their pulpits aflame with righteousness did I understand the secret of her genius and power. America is great because she is good. And if America ever ceases to be good, America will cease to be great."

The conflict we witness today between church and state has far-reaching implications for the moral standards of our nation and its people, as secular forces aggressively work to obliterate all religious influence from society. We have seen in recent days the banning in schools and public buildings of the Ten Commandments, and the complaint of one atheist that led to a court ruling that would cause the Pledge of Allegiance to be removed from every school classroom because of its phrase, "one nation under God."

Let us be among the company of the committed who work towards making America a righteous nation, a "nation under God," which alone will make it a truly great nation.

Children's children are a crown to the aged, and parents are the pride of their children.   (Proverbs 17:6)

James Herriot, every reader's favorite veterinarian, reflects a special insight with children as well as with animals: "I'm into a lower gear now. Life's passing by and I'm getting into the last lap. I missed my children's childhood, and I don't want to miss my grandchildren's childhood" (from *The Lord God Made Them All*).

God gives a special blessing after our children are grown and flown, in the joy of relationship with children all over again. It adds great joy and blessing to the "last lap" of life. Grandchildren are indeed "a crown to the aged." With typical bias as a grandparent, I often refer to our twelve very special gifts as our "crown jewels."

Grandparents provide a living link between yesteryear and the present. The grandmother's stories and photos of the child's parents provide a bridge of understanding with his or her roots and family, not readily revealed in day-to-day relations within the family. It is always an exciting observation to see children discover the childhood of their parents.

Indeed, "Children's children are a crown to the aged." But that's only one side of the coin of this golden text. The other is that "parents are the pride of their children." If we are faithful, we end up doubly blessed — the joy of our children's children, and the pride of our children. What a tragedy when children cannot be proud of their parents. May God help us to be faithful to this, life's most sacred trust. Then the rich blessings of this text will be our heritage.

A cheerful heart is good medicine. (Proverbs 17:22)

He was given a one-in-five-hundred chance of survival upon diagnosis of his disease. The prognosis: a degenerative spinal condition; time to finalize his will. That was in 1964. Instead, Norman Cousins turned to an unorthodox therapy. He took massive doses of laughter. He secured and watched Marx brothers movies and "Candid Camera" reruns and found that laughter gave him pain-free sleep. He continued laughing. As he describes in his well-known book, *Anatomy of an Illness,* his symptoms disappeared and he was cured.

Medical science has been finding that laughter is good medicine. "Bring in the clowns" may become a reality in medical units of the future!

Cousins merely put into practice what the sage of Proverbs wrote almost three thousand years earlier. He and others have discovered that "There ain't much fun in medicine, but there's a lot of medicine in fun."

Laughter is good for body and soul. God made us to laugh, as surely as he made us to breathe and to cry. Stern, dour, gloomy personalities are a far cry from the life and teachings of the One who said, "I have come that they may have life, and have it to the full" (John 10:10). God calls us to reflect and pass on the unspeakable joy he has given us.

God, whose humor is revealed in the design of a camel and the playfulness of a kitten, would teach us the art of not taking ourselves too seriously, to laugh heartily, and to be a winsome witness. So, go ahead, laugh!

A Good Name

A good name is more desirable than great riches; to be esteemed is better than silver or gold. (Proverbs 22:1)

R eputation is a priceless treasure. It is of far greater value than any earthly possession, to be safeguarded by uncompromising integrity and character.

In his *Othello*, Shakespeare puts this truth in perspective:

Good name in man and woman, dear my Lord,
Is the immediate jewel of their souls;
Who steals my purse steals trash; 'tis something, nothing;
'Twas mine, 'tis his, and has been slave to thousands;
But he that filches from me my good name
Robs me of that which not enriches him,
And makes me poor indeed.

We live in a day that is highly image-conscious. Public relations firms are paid large sums to polish, protect, and project the best images for their clients. Many Christians get caught up in the image syndrome. We cultivate and nurture our image to make a good impression that shows us to be good, gracious, and sometimes, great.

Reputation is but the external, the print of what we really are, the outward growth of the inner reality. A good name, one's reputation, is one of the greatest assets and should be the hallmark of a Christian. It gives credibility, bestows confidence, and gains acceptance.

*Train a child in the way he should go, and when he is old he will not
turn from it.* (Proverbs 22:6)

The Jesuits have their own proverb on this topic: "Give me your
child until he is twelve, and I care not who has charge of him after-
wards." The tree follows the bent of its early years and so do our sons
and daughters, as this proverb preaches.

There is a "way" we should all go. It is the way of life, the direction
of our true destiny. Many miss it. All other ways lead to death.

But we do not go the way of life as a natural course. We need encouragement, guidance, and training. God has given parents that most
sacred trust of all — the training of children so they will go in his way.
Their training is life's highest honor and most sacred trust. It needs the
reinforcement of example, for children will be most influenced, not by
what we say, as much as by what they see in us.

May we who are parents dedicate ourselves to giving the quantity
and the quality time merited for the training of our children. They may
depart for a time from that training, but God promises if we are faithful, and "train a child in the way he should go, . . . when he is old he will
not turn from it."

Billy and Ruth Graham's son, Franklin, is a classic example of this
promise. In his early life he strayed far from God and was a major concern to his parents. But they continued to pray and believe God's
promise. Today he has emerged as one of the great Christian leaders of
our time and heir apparent to lead the Billy Graham Evangelistic Association.

There is no higher claim on our time and energy than the training
of our children, no activity that brings greater reward.

A Word Aptly Spoken

A word aptly spoken is like apples of gold in settings of silver.
(Proverbs 25:11)

For those of us who have fallen captive to the charm and magic of words, this proverb has become a "golden rule" to strive for in speech and writing.

Conjure up in your imagination the beautiful picture of this striking simile — "apples of gold in settings of silver." It delights "the mind's eye" and pays a high compliment to "a word aptly spoken." A picturesque presentation of well-chosen words may be celebrated as an exquisite work of art.

Shakespeare, writing with a whittled quill by the light of a tallow candle, produced lines that will be read until the end of time. A commonplace writer would have said that a certain thing would "be superfluous, like trying to improve the perfect." In his *King John*, Shakespeare expressed the same thought with a picture-phrase that is immortal: "To gild refined gold, to paint the lily, to throw perfume on the violet." Such writing and speech is an art of the highest form.

The Bible itself is the greatest example of our proverb. Its memorable phrases have been engraved on the hearts and minds of people through the millennia — memorized, quoted, and lived out. God adorned his message to us in exquisite beauty. No literature rivals the Bible's picturesque and simple beauty, its immortal lines of timeless truth.

This proverb speaks to us of the impulse to move beyond necessities toward beauty. God delights in beauty as evidenced by the way he shaped and colored fish, birds, insects, flowers, and plants with such incredible variety. As we witness to eternal truths, let us learn from the Divine Connoisseur of beauty the art of the aptly spoken word.

A wife of noble character who can find? She is worth far more than rubies. (Proverbs 31:10)

The book of Proverbs climaxes with its immortal tribute to the virtuous wife, and the praiseworthy character of her life and deeds. After many words said about contentious, adulterous, and sinful women, it presents a beautiful portrait of wifely excellence.

This eulogy of a noble wife was written in the form of an acrostic in the original Hebrew language. The first letter of each of its twenty-two couplets follows the order of the Hebrew alphabet. That device aided memorization and suggests that the writer had to summon the entire alphabet to describe the virtuous wife, leading the chapter to be called the "golden ABCs of the perfect wife."

The virtuous wife is portrayed in her various roles. She models the faithful wife, the diligent mother, the believer known for her reverence of the Lord, and her industry and prudence in looking after the needs of her household. Her works are known beyond her own home as she "extends her hands to the needy."

Her crowning characteristics are strength, honor, dignity, wisdom, kindness, and faith. Comeliness of soul and mind excel even the beauty of her face and form. The highest praise proceeds from those who know her best — "her children arise and call her blessed," and her husband exclaims, "You surpass them all."

The book of Proverbs, which puts religion in working clothes and relates it to our world of practical relationships and realities, could not end on a higher note.

"Meaningless! Meaningless!" says the Teacher. " . . . Everything is meaningless!"   (Ecclesiastes 1:2)

These words may be the most despondent and pessimistic opening of any piece of literature ever. With this expression, history's eminent sage, Solomon, describes the sum of life.

Who would expect a preacher to commence with such a declaration of futility? It creates a shock effect. The word translated as "meaningless" appears thirty-three times in this brief book. The author is not being redundant, but underscoring his finding that life is meaningless.

"The mass of men lead lives of quiet desperation," observed Henry David Thoreau of his own generation. The son of David found it so in his lifetime. Many today still find life to be a grinding boredom, futility, and purposelessness.

His famous phrase "under the sun" (1:3) occurs thirty times, reminding us that the writer is dealing from an earthbound horizon. His observations originate from ground level. His famous phrase "nothing new under the sun" (1:9) reveals that his statements are limited to the seen world. The vertical perspective is not found until the end, and is not complete until we come to the New Testament.

Is life merely a vicious circle? A treadmill? Or "a chasing after the wind" in the repeated metaphor of the Teacher (1:17; 2:11, 18, 26)? Or have we found life's true meaning as in the valedictory at the conclusion of this provocative book. Solomon's search for meaning in the endless halls of humanism now over, the solution to life's riddle he reserved to the end: "Here is the conclusion of the matter: Fear God and keep his commandments, for this is the whole duty of man" (12:13).

There is a time for everything, and a season for every activity under heaven. (Ecclesiastes 3:1)

The Teacher of Ecclesiastes has given us one of the better-known poetic portions of Scripture, fourteen couplets that cover the range of human activity:

a time to be born and a time to die,
a time to plant and a time to uproot,
a time to kill and a time to heal,
a time to tear down and a time to build,
a time to weep and a time to laugh,
a time to mourn and a time to dance,
a time to scatter stones and a time to gather them,
a time to embrace and a time to refrain,
a time to search and a time to give up,
a time to keep and a time to throw away,
a time to tear and a time to mend,
a time to be silent and a time to speak,
a time to love and a time to hate,
a time for war and a time for peace. (3:2-8)

He starts with the most momentous events of birth and death, the two parameters that surround our lives. "A time to plant and . . . uproot" reminds us we must cooperate with the seasons of life. Each time or experience has its antithesis, its opposite — kill and heal, tear down and build, weep and laugh, mourn and dance, etc. The tapestry of life is woven from such contrasts, and these contrasts give it meaning and beauty.

Thomas Chalmers once said, "Mathematician that I was, I had forgotten two magnitudes — the shortness of time and the vastness of eternity." May we ever have that kind of binocular perception of God's gift to us of time.

He has made everything beautiful in its time.

(Ecclesiastes 3:11)

The Teacher in this text gives us one of the loveliest statements of the Bible about God's creative handiwork: "He has made everything beautiful in its time."

It is mind-boggling to contemplate the beauty and majesty of God's creation. Just think of some wonders he has endowed us with in such abandonment: star-strewn skies, majestic mountains, fragrant flowers, exquisite birds, fertile fields and forests, boundless oceans, sunsets wrapped in gold.

Our world manifests a marvelous design wedded to its extravagant beauty. Birds are designed to fly, fish to swim, clouds to water the earth. Our bodies give witness to the great Designer — with eyes to see, ears to hear, hands to touch, feet to walk, minds to know, hearts to feel, and capacity to grow and reproduce. Our very clocks are set and corrected by astronomy; we cannot know what time it is except by the stars.

God is the Cosmic Connoisseur. Anywhere we turn in nature we see the demonstration of this, from the lowliest roadside flower to iridescent seashells like the chambered nautilus, from the radiant beauty of the male cardinal to the flashing brilliance of the tiny hummingbird. "Beauty is God's handwriting," wrote Emerson, and indeed we see God's signature all about us.

We pray that the God who touches earth with such indescribable beauty would also touch our lives, and make them a reflection of his love and grace.

He has also set eternity in the hearts of men.

(Ecclesiastes 3:11)

This text stands as a sovereign mountain peak of truth that dominates the landscape of life. It beckons us to our true destiny in our pilgrimage of life.

All around us God has put intimations of our immortality. He has planted within us an unrelenting intuition to see beyond temporal horizons and press beyond the limits of the finite. A sense of destiny haunts us. Eternal forces ripple in our blood. Immortal cadences echo in our ears. Sublime visions flash upon the screen of our imagination. Eternity beckons as deep calls unto the depths that God has put in our souls.

With Francis Thompson, from his haunting "The Hound of Heaven" written almost a century ago, we hear the sound of a distant trumpet:

> Yet ever and anon a trumpet sounds
> From the hid battlements of Eternity.

Augustine summarized this longing and homesickness of the soul: "O God, You have made us for Yourself and our hearts are restless until they find their rest in You."

"Eternity is at our hearts," wrote Thomas Kelly, "pressing upon our time-torn lives, warming us with intimations of an astounding destiny, calling us home unto Itself. Yielding to the Light Within is the beginning of true life."

May we yield to this Light Within who brings radiance and joy and fulfillment.

The spirit returns to God who gave it.   (Ecclesiastes 12:7)

The penman of this classic earlier wrote, "All come from dust, and to dust all return" (3:20). Here he repeats that thought but adds a vital new dimension: "And the dust returns to the ground it came from, and the spirit returns to God who gave it." The body will perish and decay, but the immortal soul will return to the God who created us.

"Dust to dust" has become a requiem as old as mortality, commonly intoned at the interment of the dead. The Greek writer Euripides called death "the debt we all must pay." But this melancholy teacher in a breakthrough for the Old Testament affirms that a person's spirit will survive death and decay and will return to the God who created it.

In one of the most poignant passages in the Bible he writes: "Remember him — before the silver cord is severed, or the golden bowl is broken" (12:6). He likens life and death to a golden bowl suspended by a silver cord, with the cord finally becoming frayed and it breaks and the bowl is shattered. But before that happens, he warns us to remember God and to do his will.

The Teacher has here surmounted his pessimistic memoirs and declares that man goes from dust to destiny with God. In that context he reminds us to prepare for that ultimate destiny of our soul by remembering God.

Two are better than one. (Ecclesiastes 4:9)

"There was a man all alone" (4:8) speaks of the worst of all human afflictions — loneliness. "Loneliness" has been called the most desolate word in the English language. In our lonely society old-fashioned neighborliness has given way to urban high-rises and private lifestyles.

This brings us to one of the serendipities in Ecclesiastes, as the author moves from the despair of loneliness to the blessing of companionship. "Two are better than one," he records in his journal. He cites three circumstances of life to illustrate his point: "If one falls down, his friend can help him up. But pity the man who falls and has no one to help him up! Also, if two lie down together, they will keep warm. But how can one keep warm alone? Though one may be overpowered, two can defend themselves" (4:10-12).

Who of us does not have moments of weakness, those times when we stumble and fall, when we need a friend? What of those "cold" moments in our lives, when sunshine is obscured by some dark night of distress and we crave the warmth of a friend's presence? Neither are we exempt from hostile attacks — the fierce onslaughts of Satan, the assaults of circumstances. In such moments, friendship is sustenance, perhaps even survival.

Our text summarizes this discourse with its powerful metaphor: "A cord of three strands is not quickly broken" (4:12). The strength of the three-ply cord was proverbial in the ancient world. One cord can easily be broken. Two cords are difficult to break. But three cords cannot be pulled apart. When two friends, or a husband and wife, take the Lord as their third and chief strand, their union becomes unbreakable amid the stresses of life.

Sharing Our Bread

Cast your bread upon the waters, for after many days you will find it again. (Ecclesiastes 11:1)

Our contemporary culture is obsessed with the passion to possess. The clever G. K. Chesterton noted that there are two ways to get enough: one is to continue to accumulate more and more; the other is to desire less. The word from the Teacher of Ecclesiastes is not a casual suggestion, but a caveat against hoarding and a mandate for unselfish giving.

This text takes on a new urgency in our day. Never in history has there been such a need to share our bread. Millions across the waters are starving. Our suffering world calls for our compassion and action. "The road to holiness necessarily passes through the world of action," wrote Dag Hammarskjold in his diary.

We will be the poorer, for our souls will be impoverished, if we do not respond to the cries and heartaches of our world. As our text reminds us, what we send into the lives of others ultimately comes back into our own.

Those who will pay the price of caring are desperately needed today. May we be God's instrument of compassion to the hungry, the hurting, and all to whom we may give the cup of cold water or the sustaining bread, in his name.

An anonymous poet helps us express our response to Solomon's text:

The bread that brings strength I want to give,
The water pure that bids the thirsty live:
I want to help the fainting day by day;
I'm sure I shall not pass again this way.

Of making many books there is no end.   (Ecclesiastes 12:12)

"Reading maketh a full man," wrote Francis Bacon in the seventeenth century. Over two centuries later, Thoreau stated, "Many a man has dated a new era in his life from the reading of a book."

John Bunyan was a pagan when he married. His wife's dowry was just two books. Bunyan read them, they changed his life, and he gave to the world his immortal *Pilgrim's Progress*. Books have had an inestimable impact upon human history.

When the old warrior Paul was in a damp jail cell, what was his request? He asked his friend to bring a cloak for his body and books for his mind. C. S. Lewis, who has left a peerless legacy of Christian literature, said that it was through the reading of the works of George MacDonald that he was influenced to Christ.

How bereft we would be without the friends on our bookshelves. They instruct and inspire us as they share struggles and triumphs and encounters with God. In his best-selling and seminal book, *The Closing of the American Mind*, Allan Bloom laments: "The failure to read good books both enfeebles the vision and strengthens our most fatal tendency — the belief that the here and now is all there is." Bloom's statement challenges us to read those books that illumine the meaning and destiny of life.

We are grateful that "of making many books there is no end," when those books are wholesome and contributive to our growth. "A good book is the best of friends." Let us therefore enrich our lives by a goodly company of them.

I am a rose of Sharon, a lily of the valleys.   (Song of Songs 2:1)

From this lyrical love song of the Bible, we have the companion titles that have been ascribed to Christ — *Rose of Sharon* and *Lily of the Valley*. They are set in the context of an exuberant expression of love, an allegory of the relationship between the Lord and the Christian. It is a nuptial anthem with a dialogue of love in the most intimate and endearing language.

These beautiful titles for our Lord have become part of our devotional language. Among our hymns are the well-loved "Jesus, Rose of Sharon" and "He's the Lily of the Valley." Our Lord is as the exquisite flower that thrives in the cool countryside or in the quiet field. We discover his beauty when we enter into solitary communion with the Lover of our soul. Then, with the lyricist of this book, we will joyfully witness: "He has taken me to the banquet hall, and his banner over me is love" (2:4).

The Rose of Sharon commonly adorned the countryside with its delicate beauty and perfumed the air with its sweet fragrance. As a term associated with our Lord, it speaks to us of the beauty and fragrance he brings to those who know and love him.

In a valley of Romania, roses are grown for the Vienna market in great profusion and with much distillation of fragrance. It is said that if you were to visit that valley at the time of the rose crop, wherever you would go the rest of the day, the fragrance you would carry with you would betray where you had been.

If we company with the One who is the Rose of Sharon and the Lily of the Valley, something of the fragrance of his life will pass into ours. Then, infused with his presence, we will be a freshening influence to the world around us.

Catch for us the foxes, the little foxes that ruin the vineyards.

(Song of Songs 2:15)

A landmark of truth meets us on our journey through this love lyric. Our relationship of love with our Lord is a tender one, requiring the utmost vigilance against those things that would hurt and destroy.

There are many "little foxes" that would spoil the vine. It can happen ever so slyly, subtly, and swiftly — if we are not on guard. The little foxes will come into our spiritual vineyard through carelessness or neglect.

The text warns us to beware of the "little" things. For example, little things often make a difference in a relationship of love — a little remembrance, or a little forgetfulness, a little word of tenderness, or a little word of carelessness. A little compromise with the world, little neglects of duty — and the beauty and fruitfulness of the vine are sacrificed.

It is often not the big things in life that cause us the most trouble. They call forth our resources and the support of others and we get through them. The little things that make up our everyday determine our conduct and character and destiny. Let us beware of the "little foxes" that can spoil the tender vines of our lives.

"Come now, let us reason together," says the LORD. *"Though your sins are like scarlet, they shall be as white as snow; though they are red as crimson, they shall be like wool."* (Isaiah 1:18)

Isaiah stands foremost among the celebrated prophets of the Old Testament. The thunder of God's judgment can be heard rumbling through his pages as well as the resonating of his gracious call to salvation. In the midst of a dark picture of rebellion, God through his spokesman calls his children to repentance: "Wash and make yourselves clean. Take your evil deeds out of my sight! Stop doing wrong, learn to do right!" (1:16-17).

Then, through Isaiah is sounded in our selected text one of the most compelling invitations of the Bible. It declares the astonishing fact that God, the Creator of the cosmos, loves us and calls us back to himself even when we have forgotten and forsaken him.

God does not call us to a blind faith but graciously invites us to "reason" with him. The gift of reason, when exercised, will lead us to discover his love for us.

The royalty of Isaiah's day wore robes dyed deep scarlet and crimson. God promises his rebellious children of all ages that, though our sin be like scarlet or crimson, he will make our hearts as white as snow or wool.

Though Isaiah saw "through a glass darkly" that which would later be revealed on Calvary, he proclaims the message of God as a sorrowing yet loving Father who calls his rebellious children to return to him. It is a message all too relevant to our day of turbulence, political chaos, and moral breakdown.

They will beat their swords into plowshares and their spears into pruning hooks. Nation will not take up sword against nation, nor will they train for war anymore.   (Isaiah 2:4)

Religious sections of the secular bookstores are crammed with books today on "the new age," a sophisticated movement that espouses an eclectic type of religion. Isaiah here proclaims the true new age, God's glorious age of the future, when universal justice and peace shall reign.

The hope for a world without war has captured the imagination of peace and political movements throughout the world. The gift of a monument from none other than Russia to the United Nations has this classic text from Isaiah engraved on it. This noble text, also quoted by Micah (4:3), articulates man's deep and immemorial longing for peace. But true and lasting peace will only come in God's New Age.

Humankind has walked on the moon and developed amazing technologies. But we still have not learned how to live together in peace. War and violence dominate the headlines of our day. Isaiah's vision of the future offers the only and ultimate hope for humanity. God has a New Age coming. It will be an age of justice and peace, with a true "United Nations," people bonded together not by a paper treaty but by faith and love. And wonder of wonders we, through the grace of Christ, can be there!

Then I heard the voice of the LORD *saying, "Whom shall I send? And who will go for us?" And I said, "Here am I. Send me!"*
(Isaiah 6:8)

This chapter describes Isaiah's soul-shaking encounter with the glory and holiness of God and the commissioning of this prince of the prophets.

Crisis was at hand. The great King Uzziah was dead and Judah was in the path of Assyria's ominous war machine moving toward conquest of the entire Fertile Crescent.

God comes with a deeper clarity and closeness in the crises of life. Fulton Sheen records in his autobiography: "The greatest gift of all may have been His summons to the cross, where I found His continuing self-disclosure." The turning point in the life of Martin Luther came when his friend Alexis was struck by lightning and fell dead at his feet.

Isaiah comes to the temple to find guidance for difficult days ahead. Suddenly the temple is transformed into the very throne room of God. In his moving spiritual autobiography, Isaiah exultantly exclaims, "I saw the Lord seated on a throne, high and exalted" (6:1).

"Woe is me" is the heart cry of Isaiah as he stands before the thrice-holy God, overwhelmed with a sense of his unworthiness. God's response to Isaiah is immediate and remedial, bringing to Isaiah both pardon and purity, prerequisites for service for God.

The call of God is always wedded to a need and a task. In response to God's challenge, Isaiah responds, "Here am I. Send me!" God then commissions him, "Go and tell." What a glorious message it would be, resonating through the centuries!

Amid the crises of our world, God still calls, "Who will go for us?" May we respond, "Here am I. Send me!"

And he will be called Wonderful Counselor.   (Isaiah 9:6)

Isaiah has given us in this magnificent verse a constellation of titles. Its lofty appellations declare the superlative qualities of the Messiah to come.

Life is often perplexing, bewildering, complex, problematic, disconcerting. We have an inescapable need for guidance by the Divine Counselor.

A counselor is involved in the intimacies of life, directing it through its difficult times and crises. The inspired chronicler wrote: "He knew what was in a man" (John 2:25). This specialist of the human heart knows us better than we know ourselves.

This Wonderful Counselor is compassionate, loving, concerned for us. To him we are not a case, but a child; not a problem person, but a person with a problem and potential.

As our Wonderful Counselor he has all the resources of power and help to put at our disposal. He is wisdom incarnate, and will always guide our steps aright.

A counselor needs ability to communicate. We communicate with Christ in prayer, through the gentle stirrings of his Spirit, and by the manual of his Word for the human heart. He is always available, as close as the whisper of a prayer.

We may with confidence bring to him our hurts, failures, and deep needs and aspirations. Christ is the Counselor par excellence, the Wonderful Counselor.

Mighty God

And he will be called . . . Mighty God. (Isaiah 9:6)

Each new Advent season inspires us afresh with the immortal cadences of this lofty lyric in the enduring strains of Handel's *Messiah*. For some of us no Advent season would be complete without hearing the stirring refrain:

> For to us a child is born, to us a son is given,
> and the government will be on his shoulders.
> And he will be called Wonderful Counselor,
> Mighty God, Everlasting Father, Prince of Peace.
> Of the increase of his government and peace there will be no end.
> (9:6-7)

The four exalted titles in this refrain speak of four divine attributes of our Lord. *Wonderful Counselor* declares his omniscience, *Mighty God* his omnipotence, *Everlasting Father* his eternity, and *Prince of Peace* his omnificence — unlimited bounty on our behalf.

The title *Mighty God* attests to the divinity of Christ. He was the Mighty God in his preincarnate glory and splendor. He was the Mighty God in his ministry and miracles. He was the Mighty God in his death as our Savior from sin, and in his resurrection as he broke the bonds of death. He will be mighty when he comes again in his glory.

We may not only know of these attributes, but we can experience them in measure as Christ lives and works through us.

And he will be called . . . Everlasting Father.   (Isaiah 9:6)

We usually associate the name "Father" with the first Person of the Godhead, but here the title belongs to Christ. However, the original text does not denote "father" in the usual association we have with that word. It means in this verse "author" or "possessor." A more exact rendering of this verse would be "the Father of Eternity" as rendered by the Amplified Old Testament. It declares that Christ is eternal; he had no beginning and he holds eternity in his possession.

One of the most intriguing exercises for the imagination is to consider the eternity of Jesus. It staggers the mind to ponder that Jesus always was; he had no beginning. He is the unbeginning One.

The apostle Paul, centuries after Isaiah, writing of the eternal existence of Christ, states: "He is before all things" (Colossians 1:17). In that same passage he tells us Christ was an agent in the creation of all things (1:16). We reckon our time in terms of B.C. and A.D. — before or after Christ. But Paul is here speaking of P.W. time — "pre-world" time. Jesus himself referred to his pre-world splendor in his prayer in the Upper Room when he petitioned his heavenly Father: "glorify me in your presence with the glory I had with you before the world began" (John 17:5).

Because he is the Eternal One, Christ holds the future in his hands. We may not know what the future holds, but we know who holds the future, and when we are in the hands of the Eternal One, the future is as bright as his eternal love and grace to us.

Prince of Peace

And he will be called . . . Prince of Peace. (Isaiah 9:6)

P eace may well be the most sought for and at the same time the most elusive of treasures. History mocks the effort of world leaders and diplomats on behalf of peace. A French historian once computed that there had been 3,130 years of war in contrast to 227 years of peace from the fifteenth century B.C. to his own day. The world had seen thirteen years of war for every year of peace. Our own generation has never been without war and turmoil raging somewhere in the world.

Every new generation is today born under the ominous cloud that threatens to unleash a nuclear holocaust. We live not only in the age of the split atom but of the split personality as well. We are beset by neuroses and psychoses that undermine our peace from within. Human fears are so many and varied that psychologists have charted them all the way from *a* to *z*: from acrophobia, fear of heights, to zoophobia, fear of animals.

The heart of the problem is the problem of the heart. Jesus, the Prince of Peace, enables us to have peace with God by his work of reconciliation. He resolves the inner conflicts and tensions that rob us of peace of mind. When we are at peace with God and ourselves, then we will be at peace with others.

To Isaiah was given the prophecy of these magnificent titles of our Lord. But to us has been given the Person who fulfilled them. To Isaiah was given the expectation, but to us is given the experience of Christ and the radiant meaning of these titles in our lives.

You will keep in perfect peace him whose mind is steadfast, because
he trusts in you. (Isaiah 26:3)

Here in the midst of one of the darkest passages of this book shines
one of the most radiant gems of the prophet: "You will keep in
perfect peace him whose mind is steadfast, because he trusts in you."
The words "perfect peace" are translated from the Hebrew word *sha-*
lom, twice repeated in the original text. It is the beautiful Hebrew word,
often used as a farewell parting, meaning well-being and abiding
peace.

We ask: perfect peace, in the midst of the world's tragedies and sorrows? Perfect peace, in a world haunted by fear of nuclear holocaust?
Perfect peace, in a world beset with terrorism, strife, wars, turmoil?
Perfect peace, with the problems and trials we may personally confront? Perfect peace when it seems our world may come tumbling
down?

Christian experience through the centuries witnesses that when
darkness and turbulence rage about us, we can hear the Master of the
storm, saying, "Peace, be still."

The prophet lets us in on the secret of this perfect peace — our
steadfast trust in God. With John Greenleaf Whittier we affirm:

I know not where his islands lift
Their fronded palms in air;
I only know I cannot drift
Beyond his love and care.

The Way of Holiness

And a highway will be there; it will be called the Way of Holiness.
(Isaiah 35:8)

God calls us to holiness, to power and purity, for his marred image to be restored in us. We need not only to be adopted, but also to be adapted into the family of God. We stand in need, not only for atonement, but also for attunement. God provides not only for our salvation but also for our sanctification. Besides being "born of the Spirit," there is being "filled with the Spirit."

Holiness is not "having arrived." The prophet reminds us that holiness is not a place, but a path on which we continue to journey, not a state, but a lifetime walk.

Some years ago, with friends I took on the challenge of hiking up one of the 14,000-foot mountains in the Colorado Rockies. The day arrived, and as we made our ascent, we came to the timberline beyond which were only forbidding rocks and the heights beyond. Ahead of us loomed a high summit etched against an azure sky. But when we finally reached that point, we found yet another summit beyond, and to our surprise still higher peaks beyond each visible summit, opening more vast and beautiful vistas below.

That mountain experience became a parable of my own spiritual journey. Of course its final summit will not be reached in this life, but as we continue to make our ascent to the heights to which God calls us, we are enabled to go from "strength to strength," from "peak to peak," from "height to height." Isaiah described it long ago in his memorable metaphor: "And a highway will be there; it will be called the Way of Holiness."

Let's be excited about the further summits and exhilarating vistas God has in store for us as we make our pilgrimage on the Highway of Holiness.

"Put your house in order, because you are going to die."

(Isaiah 38:1)

"**P**ut your house in order, because you are going to die" was the disconcerting message Isaiah gave to King Hezekiah. The king pleaded to God to spare him from death in return for a vow. God granted his petition with a reprieve and an added fifteen years of life.

Life indeed is frail, fragile, and finite. We will not have such a summons as came to Hezekiah, but we will always be but a heartbeat away from death. The invincible reaper knocks ultimately, and often unexpectedly, at every door. We need always to have our "house set in order," for we know not what moment our fragile life may be ushered into eternity.

Following his recovery, Hezekiah reevaluated life's essentials, and he states that "by such things men live" (38:16), referring to the promises and gracious acts of God. We are led to ask ourselves, "What are the things by which I live? Do I live by life's true essentials? Or do I get caught up with the peripheral rather than the central, the material rather than the spiritual, the trivialities rather than the treasures, the ephemeral rather than the eternal?"

When one comes face to face with death and the finality of life, it often brings a new perspective on what really matters, to perceive life's true values and meaning, and to order life accordingly. Someday, some moment in time, and in some way, we will die. It is imperative that we "set our house in order," that we prepare for the ultimate summons of life, that of meeting our Maker.

But those who hope in the LORD will renew their strength. They
will soar on wings like eagles.   (Isaiah 40:31)

I saiah eulogizes the glory of God who "stretches out the heavens like
a canopy . . . who brings out the starry host one by one, and calls
them each by name" (40:22, 26). The prophet calls us to a theology of
the awesome transcendence of God.

This magnificent chapter culminates with one of the most inspiring passages and promises of the Bible. God's poet-prophet compares
the believer who trusts in God to an eagle that soars with unwearying
grace and strength. The eagle's noble inheritance is the heights of the
heavens, where it plays with the wind and builds its nest in lofty crags
beyond the reach of man.

The eagle soars to great heights, not by the power of its wings, but
by surrendering itself to the currents and power of the wind. So it is
with the believer. We soar and reach the heights of the spiritual life not
by our own finite power, but by surrendering to the mighty power of
the Holy Spirit, who renews our strength. This inner renewal is essential to the Christian life.

Joni Eareckson Tada has a beautiful recording with the title song,
"Spirit Wings." Her testimony in song can be the reality for each of us:

Spirit wings, you lift me over all the earthbound things.
And like a bird my heart is flying free.
I'm soaring on the song of Spirit Wings.
O Lord of all, you let me see a vision of your majesty.
You lift me up, you carry me, on your Spirit Wings.

God has destined us to soar on Spirit Wings. Let us rise up to our
noble inheritance.

"See, I have engraved you on the palms of my hands."

(Isaiah 49:16)

God's love and care for his children is expressed in a question by the Lord on the most tender of human relationships: "Can a mother forget the baby at her breast and have no compassion on the child she has borne?" (49:15a). We know all too well the sad answer to that question, of children throughout the world found abandoned or abused by a mother. The Lord responds to the question with a stunning affirmation of his love for us: "Though she may forget, I will not forget you! See, I have engraved you on the palms of my hands" (49:15-16).

This poignant metaphor presents one of the most beautiful portraits of God's love to be found in the Bible. The most eloquent expression of his love for us is the nail prints in the hands of our Lord. In this astonishing portrayal of our Lord, we see God's infinite love for us. Calvary has established an eternal memorial with God for every believer.

The story is told of a Russian citizen during the years of the Nazi occupation who had watched his young wife brutalized and killed after her newborn child had been snatched from her arms and given to a youthful officer whose wife was barren. Fearful of the days ahead and what cruelties might take from him his fragile mental powers, the prisoner did a startling thing. With his own knife he carved the name of the child in his right hand. Never would he allow himself to forget the object of his love.

The simple chorus penned by Albert Orsborn reminds us of this sacred truth:

He cannot forget me, though trials beset me;
Forever His promise shall stand.
He cannot forget me, though trials beset me;
My name's on the palm of His hand.

He was despised and rejected by men, a man of sorrows, and famil-
iar with suffering.   (Isaiah 53:3)

This title and portrait of the Master stands out as one of the cardinal titles of Christ. Some notable men are men of wealth, some men of fame, and some men of pleasure. Christ was a Man of Sorrows.

The last week of Christ's earthly life, with its record of deep sorrow, looms most prominently in the Gospels. One-third of Matthew, one-third of Mark, one-fourth of Luke, and one-half of John's Gospel are devoted to the last week of the life of Jesus. This is in striking contrast to the few pages of biography covering the death of other men of history. A biography of Abraham Lincoln, for example, has only twenty-five of its five thousand pages relating the dramatic account of his assassination and death. The amount of space in the Gospels devoted to Christ's suffering and death is so disproportionate as to underscore the paramount sacredness of that period in his life.

That incarnate Deity should be so predominantly characterized by sorrow makes us aware that this title ushers us into the holy of holies in the sanctuary of Christ's life. It evokes one of the most sacred truths of eternity, too deep to plumb its mystery and majesty.

The sorrows and anguish of Jesus defy description or definition. His love was wounded by the betrayal of those in his most intimate circle. His soul suffered imputed condemnation for man's transgressions. His body felt the torture of the cross. He had to endure ignominy, dereliction, and the death of the cross.

To what fathomless depths God descended to rescue a dying world! Such love transcends our understanding but wins our hearts.

He was wounded for our transgressions. (Isaiah 53:5 NKJV)

S ome years ago, during our family devotions, one of our little girls was struck by the fact that Jesus suffered so much on Calvary. Quite unaware of the theological profundity of her question, she asked in deep sincerity, "But if Jesus was God, why did he have to die?" As we contemplate the unexampled sorrows and sufferings of Christ, we cannot help but ask, "Why? Why?" Isaiah answers this question for us in immortal words:

> Surely He has borne our griefs and carried our sorrows;
> yet we esteemed Him stricken, smitten by God and afflicted.
> But He was wounded for our transgressions,
> He was bruised for our iniquities;
> the chastisement for our peace was upon Him,
> and by His stripes we are healed. (53:4-5 NKJV)

"He was wounded for our transgressions." The nails that tore through his sacred hands and feet were our sins. The thorns that pierced his brow and marred his visage were our sins. The scourge that lacerated the flesh of his back to ribbons was our sins. The wagging heads that mocked him and the tongues that vilified him were our sins. He took on himself our burden and penalty of sin. He suffered our condemnation. He died our death. Our Lord's suffering and death was a voluntary offering, a vicarious offering, and a victorious offering on our behalf.

Isaac Watts, in his enduring hymn, reminds us, "Love so amazing, so divine, demands my soul, my life, my all."

Seek the LORD while he may be found; call on him while he is near.

(Isaiah 55:6)

It is not surprising to find one of the most gracious invitations in the Bible shortly following Isaiah's peerless passage on the vicarious sacrifice of God's Servant. "Come, all you who are thirsty, come to the waters; and you who have no money, come, buy and eat!" (55:1). God's grace and gift of salvation is free to whomsoever. It satisfies the deepest thirst and hunger of our souls.

But such a priceless gift is conditional. The urgent call of the prophet reminds us that the day of grace will not last forever: "Seek the LORD while he may be found; call on him while he is near." Some people plan to be saved at the eleventh hour, but die at ten-thirty! Continued rejection of the Lord hardens the heart so that the soul may no longer be sensitive to God's call and grace.

We must not only seek God, but must also repent of our sins to receive God's gift of salvation and life eternal: "Let the wicked forsake his way and the evil man his thoughts. Let him turn to the LORD, and he will have mercy on him, and to our God, for he will freely pardon" (55:7).

The eternal God has provided for our pardon and made us heirs of the eternal promises. He has recorded the wonder and wooing of his love in his sacred Word. There comes a time in every life when God's day of grace has gone forever. Let us be sure to seek and find him "while he may be found, . . . while he is near."

Is there no balm in Gilead? (Jeremiah 8:22)

J eremiah became one of the dominant figures of the Old Testament, outlasting the pomp and power of the kings and conquerors of his time. His book, mainly poetic, is the longest book in the Bible, containing more words than any other.

Jeremiah, in masterful elegy, laments his people's lost condition: "The harvest is past, the summer is ended, and we are not yet saved" (8:20). The striking metaphor conveys a note of terrible finality. For each soul there may come that awful day when opportunity for salvation is gone and a person who has refused to turn to God becomes forever lost as the great reaper relentlessly wields his scythe of death.

In remorseless grief for his people's suffering, Jeremiah cries out:

Is there no balm in Gilead? Is there no physician there?
Why then is there no healing for the wound of my people? (8:22)

Gilead had long been known for its balm, made from the resin of the mastic tree and used by physicians of the Eastern world. But there was "no balm in Gilead" that could cure the Israelites' soul sickness that was a sickness unto death. In light of the New Testament and Calvary, the piercing pathos of the prophet's question has been answered in the traditional spiritual:

There is a balm in Gilead to make the wounded whole;
There is a balm in Gilead to heal the sin-sick soul.

Christ came as the Great Physician. He alone can cure the soul of its deadly infection of sin and give health and life to the one who trusts in him.

The Potter and the Clay

"Like clay in the hand of the potter, so are you in my hand."
(Jeremiah 18:6)

G od chose a common scene from Jeremiah's day for a classic para- ble. He told him, "Go down to the potter's house, and there I will give you my message" (18:2). Jeremiah did as the Lord commanded. He watched the skillful hands of the potter knead the clay and form it into a beautiful vessel. But, before the prophet's eyes, the potter suddenly broke it. He had a design in mind and something went wrong. The de- sign miscarried. Perhaps a foreign substance got into the clay.

Jeremiah observed that the potter did not discard the clay, but once more took the shapeless mass and kneaded and pummeled and shaped it on his wheel until he had fashioned it into an exquisite vessel. Then the Lord gives his message to the prophet: "O house of Israel, can I not do with you as this potter does? Like clay in the hand of the potter, so are you in my hand" (18:6).

Something had gone wrong with the clay of humanity. An impu- rity had entered into us by the Fall of our first parents. God had des- tined humankind for holy living, but sin marred the design. What an eloquent parable of the indomitable patience of the Divine Potter who has not cast us aside.

God is the potter. We are the clay, the vessel in the making. Clay has no intrinsic worth; it is not valued for itself but for its potential. In the hands of this potter we can become a vessel of eternal worth and value. Calvary provided a second chance for humankind to be made over again. Praise God, who recreates the marred vessel! He removes the imperfections and makes us into exquisitely beautiful and useful ves- sels for his service.

Great is your faithfulness. (Lamentations 3:23)

The book of Lamentations, with its mournful cry of anguish over the sufferings of Judah and Jerusalem, is an appendage to the book of Jeremiah. Jerusalem, destroyed and desolate, is personified as a lonely widow (1:1). Her crown of sorrows is remembering happier days (1:6, 7). Her plaintive cry longs for sympathy: "Is it nothing to you, all you who pass by? Look around and see. Is any suffering like my suffering?" (1:12).

In the midst of this incomparable dirge, with its tears and terrors, comes one of the brightest jewels of the Bible: "For his compassions never fail. They are new every morning; great is your faithfulness" (3:22-23). In the midst of our failures and sorrows, God's compassion and faithfulness endure. This textual jewel inspired Thomas Chisholm to write the song that has blessed an innumerable company with the truth of this golden text:

> Great is thy faithfulness, O God my Father,
> There is no shadow of turning with thee;
> Thou changest not, thy compassions they fail not;
> As thou has been thou forever wilt be.
>
> Great is thy faithfulness! Great is thy faithfulness!
> Morning by morning new mercies I see;
> All I have needed thy hand hath provided;
> Great is thy faithfulness, Lord, unto me!

Bridging the Gap

"I looked for a man among them who would build up the wall and stand before me in the gap." (Ezekiel 22:30)

Our society and world today are imperiled by great cleavages and gaps. The holocaust of abortion, the scourge of pornography and AIDS, the disintegration of marriage and family, the perversions of our day, the atrocities of terrorism and violence — all signal that the moral structures of our society and nation are in need of serious repair.

God calls for men and women who today will stand in the gap, to help rebuild the foundations of life, of family, of community, of nation. As someone has asked: "If not you, who? If not now, when?"

Christ calls his followers to be the salt that will keep the world from pollution, to be the light that will overcome the darkness. He calls to servanthood, to a vulnerable involvement amid the moral breakdowns of our world.

Billy Graham has described his first meeting with Mother Teresa, the saint of the gutters in Calcutta. When he was introduced to her, she was ministering to a dying person, holding him in her arms. He waited while she helped the man face death. When he expired, she prayed quietly, gently lowered him to his bed and turned to greet Graham. He records: "Mother Teresa looks past the physical features of every needy man, woman or child and sees the face of Jesus staring up at her through them. In every starving child she feeds, she sees Jesus. By every lonely, dying man she cradles in her arms, is Jesus. When she ministers to anyone she is ministering to her Savior and Lord." Mother Teresa provided a living and loving example of what it means to stand in the gap for God.

"I will give you a new heart and put a new spirit in you."
(Ezekiel 36:26)

The heart of the problem for rebellious Israel, as well as for all those who are outside of the will of God, is the problem of the heart. In a high peak of Ezekiel's prophecy, God promises to give a spiritual heart transplant. He takes away the heart of stone (v. 26), the heart that has been hardened against his call, and puts in its place an obedient heart.

This promise is for nothing less than the radical transformation of our inner life. The biblical word for "heart" has volitional overtones, not merely emotional ones as in the English. To be a Christian, then, is to become a new person in Christ. Old desires and ways of life give way to a whole new orientation and value system.

Sin is a fatal disease of the heart. God alone has the cure. It was provided for all on Calvary. Praise God, the Divine Cardiologist gives us a new heart. He puts a new spirit within us. He performs the radical surgery that we need to become, in the words of the apostle Paul, "a new creation in Christ."

God also declares, "And I will put my Spirit in you" (36:27). This is the secret of the spiritual heart transplant, of the transformation of life in Christ. The Holy Spirit does his creative work within us, of both re-generation and sanctification.

Valley of Dry Bones

He . . . set me in the middle of a valley; it was full of bones.
                                                              (Ezekiel 37:1)

The prophet is transported by the Spirit to a valley of dry bones scattered over its desert floor. Looking at the vast number of bones, God asks Ezekiel, "Can these bones live?" He knows dry bones can't live, but he answers carefully, "O Sovereign LORD, you alone know."

Then the Lord said to him, "Prophesy to these bones." Of all the bizarre things God had told him to do, this was the most preposterous! "What was that again, Lord?" we can hear him say. "I said, 'Prophesy to these bones.'" Perhaps he felt he had been preaching to the dead before, but never as dead as these bleached bones! In spite of his incredulity, Ezekiel starts to preach to the dry bones, that God would restore them to life.

Imagine his spine-tingling surprise as he is preaching, and hears a clanking and a rattling as the bones click into place and become whole skeletons. Then before his awe-struck gaze, the skeletons become clothed with flesh and sinew and wrapped in skin.

God then tells the prophet to call for the wind to come into the lifeless bodies. As he did so, "breath entered them; they came to life and stood up on their feet — a vast army" (37:10). Ezekiel witnessed the transformation of a bone yard into a battalion.

God tells Ezekiel that the dry, bleached bones lying lifeless on the valley floor are the scattered Israelites whom the Lord will ultimately restore to the land of their covenant. For the exiles whose existence was a living death, this was a message of great hope. The miraculous fulfillment of this promise in our time is one of the great phenomena of history.

The prophet's vision becomes the proclamation of the gospel — that though dead in trespasses and sin, the Lord has an abundant and eternal life for those born of the Spirit.

"If we are thrown into the blazing furnace, the God we serve is able to save us from it." (Daniel 3:17)

The edict of King Nebuchadnezzar proclaimed that all must prostrate themselves and do homage before the image of gold he had set up. His decree warned: "Whoever does not fall down and worship will immediately be thrown into a blazing furnace." As the orchestra struck the note, all the people fell down and worshiped the image. All, that is, except the three devout friends of Daniel — Shadrach, Meshach, and Abednego.

Their defiance reported, the monarch gave them one more chance to repent and worship his god. With courage, the faithful three answered: "If we are thrown into the blazing furnace, the God we serve is able to save us from it."

The fire, stoked seven times hotter, scorched to death the executioners who had bound the Hebrews and thrown them into the furnace. The king and his officials looked on in astonishment as they saw "that the fire had not harmed their bodies, nor was a hair of their head singed; their robes were not scorched, and there was no smell of fire on them" (3:27). The king acknowledged the God of the faithful three, decreed his protection, and promoted them in the kingdom.

History gives witness to those who kept the faith when tried by fire — Stephen praying as his battered body became covered with a mound of stones, Polycarp keeping the faith amid the flames at the stake, Bonhoeffer believing as he went to the gallows.

The distance from Nebuchadnezzar's furnace is not that great. Even now, Christians in certain countries are suffering for their faith, some facing death. There have been more martyrs for the faith in our time than in all previous history.

Circumstances may take hold of us and put us through a fiery test and trial. If it does, may we, as the three faithful servants of old, say, "Our God is able!"

The Banquet of Death

"You have been weighed on the scales and found wanting."
                                                    (Daniel 5:27)

The scene is a royal banquet at the king's palace, with a thousand nobles and their wives and concubines. One may imagine a glitter of jewels and a rustle of silk mingled with drunken laughter and song. King Belshazzar is at the peak of his power. Significantly, the king and his most honored guests are imbibing out of gold goblets plundered from Jerusalem's temple.

But suddenly, what is that on the plastering of the wall? What did they put in that wine? Fingers of a hand writing on the wall! My God, what is it? There is a spreading gasp of horror! The king is shaken. Never has a drunken man sobered so quickly.

He shouts frantically for his experts to explain this mystery. They cannot. The Queen Mother comes to the rescue, telling the king of Daniel, who has "ability to interpret dreams, explain riddles and solve difficult problems" (5:12).

Daniel is brought into the banquet hall, brushes aside the king's offered baubles, and goes straight to the crisis facing the drunken king and his empire. He tells the king that he has set himself up "against the Lord of heaven." Daniel then gives the interpretation. God has numbered the days of his reign and brought it to an end; Belshazzar has been weighed on the scales and found wanting; his kingdom is to be divided among the Medes and Persians.

Belshazzar had felt secure, his city of Babylon impregnable. But death burst in upon that banquet scene, turning his glee into gloom and his desecration into destruction. Human blood became the wine and dying groans the music, amid the murdered guests and the battered corpse of a dead king.

Sin has spread a great banquet in the earth today. It invites all to come and feast at its table. But sooner or later death breaks in upon sin's banquet, with every soul weighed in the judgment scales of God. Let us be sure in that day that we will not be found wanting.

"Those who are wise will shine like the brightness of the heavens, and those who lead many to righteousness, like the stars for ever and ever."   (Daniel 12:3)

"There will be a time of distress such as has not happened from the beginning," prophesies Daniel (12:1a). If "coming events cast their shadows before them" are we not seeing such foreboding shadows on our landscape today? The imminent threat of nuclear holocaust, continual strife and wars, devastating famines and environmental concern, may make us wonder if we are foreseeing Daniel's forecast of the word "finis" on the canvas of history.

But the great book of Daniel does not end on the doleful note of trouble, but on the ringing note of triumph. It modulates from minor to major key in these final verses. It is like going from Tchaikovsky's *1812 Overture* to his *Swan Lake*.

There will be deliverance, a conditional deliverance — for "everyone whose name is found written in the book" (12:1b). Daniel gives a great prophecy: "Multitudes who sleep in the dust of the earth will awake: some to everlasting life, others to shame and everlasting contempt" (12:2). Here the doctrine of resurrection breaks through into the faith of man as a sea beating at the dikes of human aspiration, which at last forces a breach and floods the human soul. The great truth dawns in this moment: God has made us for eternity.

With this prophecy of resurrection is one of the most radiant promises of the Bible: "Those who are wise will shine like the brightness of the heavens, and those who lead many to righteousness, like the stars for ever and ever" (12:3). Those who are wise in the things of God and those who are soul winners are God's stars, reflecting his glory and bringing his illumination to a darkened world. Wonder of wonders, this can include you and me!

"Many shall run to and fro, and knowledge shall increase."
(Daniel 12:4 NKJV)

D aniel, in his final chapter, gives two intriguing prophecies and hallmarks of the end time. First, "many shall run to and fro." The fastest mode of transport in Daniel's time was a horse-drawn chariot. Today, with the ubiquity of freeways and air travel, and with spacecraft that circle the earth at 17,000 mph, Daniel's prophecy of speed and mobility seems to have been fulfilled.

The second hallmark Daniel gives of the end time is that "knowledge shall increase." We live in "the information age." The computer, which burst upon the scene around 1950 with its mind-staggering capabilities, has become a major force behind the knowledge explosion of our age. The silicon chip, "an educated grain of sand," has spawned astonishing knowledge, from the cells of the human body to the rings of Saturn. Orbiting telescopes probe the heavens and yield dramatic revelations about the universe. Daniel's prophecy of a knowledge increase finds ample resonance in our day.

Our generation has had its collision course with the future. Just think: many of us were alive before television, air conditioners, frozen foods, microwave ovens, dishwashers, credit cards, ballpoint pens, before split atoms, and before men walked on the moon.

This magnificent book of the Bible ends with Daniel confirmed as an heir to the resurrection, a ringing note of victory for the aged prophet: "You will rest, and then at the end of the days you will rise to receive your allotted inheritance" (12:13). Praise God, we too may share in that glorious promise!

They sow the wind and reap the whirlwind.   (Hosea 8:7)

"They sow the wind and reap the whirlwind" (8:7) is the universal judgment upon sin. There is a correspondence between what we choose to do and the results or consequences. Some expositors interpret wind as "the way of passion and of disloyalty" and whirlwind as "the tornado of destruction."

The succeeding chapters of Hosea present a poignant profile of prostitute Israel's reaping the "whirlwind" as a painful penalty for its faithlessness. A history of anguish is summed up in the words, " . . . because they have not obeyed him; they will be wanderers among the nations" (9:17), a prophecy pathetically fulfilled through the centuries.

The consequences of sin always outweigh the initial act and intention. What we sow we will reap many times over. As someone has said, "Deed is seed, which is multiplied in harvest." Israel had sown the seed of infidelity and reaped the harvest of destruction. Our lives, too, will bear the fruit of what we sow, be it good or ill.

Many live by the code, "Sin now, pay later." Indeed, sin will ultimately exact its wages. God's Word reminds us, "the wages of sin is death" (Romans 6:23). To pay a lifelong and eternal regret for an hour's pleasure is a fool's bargain.

May we so live that the thoughts, words, and deeds we sow each day will reap character and an eternal destiny in Christ.

"I will heal their waywardness and love them freely."

(Hosea 14:4)

Hosea is eminently the prophet of God's grace, the St. John of the Old Testament. The burden of his message is God's undying love and compassion for wayward Israel.

Israel's folly and faithlessness were poignantly depicted in Hosea's tragic personal story of his marriage to a harlot. The story dramatizes the costliness of love and proclaims the love of God, as do few other books. Israel might forget and forsake God, but he does not forsake or forget them. God is, in the great phrase of Francis Thompson, "The Hound of Heaven," ever pursuing us to return to him.

Hosea's love story is our love story. Gomer, the unfaithful and fallen wife who represents humankind, was restored. The story portrays the redeeming love fully poured out in the life and death of Christ. By the grace of Christ we claim and experience this gracious promise of God: "I will heal their waywardness and love them freely."

Salvationist poet John Gowans beautifully expressed the truth of our text:

> Don't assume that God dismissed you from his mind,
> Don't assume that God's forgotten to be kind;
> For no matter what you do, his love still follows you;
> Don't think that you have left him far behind.
> For his love remains the same, He knows you by your name,
> Don't think because you failed him he despairs;
> For he gives to those who ask, his grace for every task,
> God plans for you in love for he still cares.

"I will pour out my Spirit on all people." (Joel 2:28)

The promise of the Holy Spirit is the high-water mark of the book of Joel. This promise became the text for Peter's sermon on the day of Pentecost (Acts 2:16-21). When others saw the startling results of Pentecost they thought the disciples were intoxicated. Peter defended their experience by interpreting the event as the fulfillment of Joel's prophecy: "This is what was spoken by the prophet Joel."

As this passage declares, the promise of the Holy Spirit is for all believers. The bestowal of this gift is universal. It breaks down barriers of age, sex, and class — it is for the young and old, for men and women; there is no distinction between slaves and free. The Holy Spirit is God's gift to his children.

After a rain, we often see "diamonds" coruscating on every limb of the spruce in our backyard. What takes place is that the remote, enormous incandescence of the sun suffuses and transforms these small, pale, cold droplets of rain. The permanent illumines the transient. Power caresses fragility. The interplay of the far and near takes place before our eyes. As we behold the translucent beauty of these multifaceted diamonds, they speak to us metaphorically of the work of the Holy Spirit in our lives. The all-encompassing flame of God reaches down from heaven to humankind, to transform our common lives into a radiant reflection of our Lord himself.

God has poured his Spirit "on all people." And that includes us!

Plucked from the Burning

"You were like a burning stick snatched from the fire."
(Amos 4:11)

He was a boy of five on the winter night when his family's house was swept away in flames. A nurse carried his five-month-old brother Charles to safety. But he was by an upstairs window surrounded by flames. Many onlookers felt that there was no way he could be rescued; his father, thinking him lost, commended his soul to God. But a man stood beneath the window and another climbed up on his shoulders and was able to take the boy in his arms and lower him to safety. At that very moment the roof fell in and the flames consumed the spot where he had been standing only seconds before.

The boy never forgot that night. Throughout his life John Wesley referred to himself as "a brand snatched out of the burning."

Amos says to the people of Israel: "You were like a burning stick snatched from the fire." On the brink of destruction, each of us is saved by the grace of God. Christ, at the tremendous cost of his own life, came into the midst of the destructive power of sin, stretched out his loving arms to us, and plucked us from destruction.

"Prepare to meet your God."   (Amos 4:12)

The thunderclap of Amos's message sounds forth: "Prepare to meet your God." The moment of ultimate accountability for Israel has come.

Meeting God on the Day of Judgment is inevitable for each of us. Sooner or later we must each meet our God. But the judgment of God need not be retributive. For those who have been faithful in love and obedience to him, it will be remunerative. God has joy and rewards that transcend anything we have known on earth.

An old song, written by "Anon," still speaks its solemn message:

Your garments must be white as snow,
Prepare to meet your God:
For to His throne you'll have to go;
Prepare to meet your God.

People will make elaborate preparations for meeting an important person. They will pay great attention to their appearance, preparation of thought, precision of schedule, observance of protocol, etc. But many never think of their preparation to meet the Creator of the universe and the Savior of the world.

May you and I, dear reader, be prepared to meet our God. If we are not prepared at this moment, let us put aside everything else and make this the top priority of our lives.

"The pride of your heart has deceived you."   (Obadiah 3)

O badiah is the shortest book in the Old Testament and the only book with just one chapter. But it packs a powerful message.

The Edomites literally lived "in the clefts of the rocks" (v. 3). They considered their position impregnable, secure in their impenetrable strongholds high up in the rocky gorges. Obadiah punctures their inflated pride of security with the Lord's prophecy of their doom. In poetic hyperbole he describes their high position, like that of the eagle soaring and safely secluded in its high aeries; but even so they will be brought down. In 578 B.C. Edom was left desolate by the Babylonians, later to disappear from history, fulfilling this prophecy.

Have we not known something of pride in national security? Of a sense of impregnability? Do we not know something of deceptions that infiltrate and threaten to destroy? And have we not with pride based our national security on our nation's position and military prowess? Surely the message and metaphors of the prophet resonate in our day.

Any sense of our invulnerability was shattered on 9/11/01. The ominous threat of instant apocalypse through weapons of mass destruction in the hands of terrorists has awakened us to the fragility of our security. Our national security is no longer taken for granted, and is considered by many to be gravely imperiled.

The message of Obadiah should remind us that the most impregnable defenses always prove to be insecure in the end. This Old Testament book is a wake-up call to us today: God and his righteousness alone are the security of the believer and the nation.

But the LORD provided a great fish to swallow Jonah, and Jonah was inside the fish three days and three nights.   (Jonah 1:17)

The word of the Lord had come to Jonah to go and preach to Nineveh, but Jonah sought to run away from the Lord, and booked passage on a ship at Joppa. The path away from God is a slippery slope that leads down to a maelstrom of destruction. The sea may look calm and inviting at first, and the boat appealing; but anyone who tries to run away from God is headed for a storm.

Our text tells us that Jonah was inside the great fish for three days and nights. The *Princeton Theological Review* in 1927 reported that the structure of the sperm whale and its habits make it perfectly possible for a man to be swallowed alive and after an interval vomited up again, also for him to remain alive for two or three days within the whale.

Man's extremity is God's opportunity! Entombed in the fish and in the depths of the sea, Jonah prayed: "In my distress I called to the LORD, and he answered me." At the end of his prayer he affirmed, "Salvation comes from the LORD" (2:9). Jonah then turns up in Nineveh by way of the first amphibious landing in history!

If we feel we have been "swallowed alive" by circumstances, if we are discouraged, disheartened, or defeated, let us remember that God is still the God of miracles. If the story of Jonah's failure finds an echo in your heart, remember that our God is the God of the second chance, and the second hundredth chance. May we be obedient to the word of the Lord and be his faithful witnesses wherever he may lead us.

And what does the LORD require of you? To act justly and to love mercy and to walk humbly with your God. (Micah 6:8)

Micah was a son of the soil, a plowman who became God's penman. His book is termed "minor," but his message is mighty. His fiery sermons thundered against business, government, and religious leaders for their corruption and oppression of the poor. His preachment culminates with some of the most extraordinary and best-known texts in the Bible.

He poses the pivotal question for our lives: "What does the LORD require of you?" Our destiny for this life and the next hangs in the balance in our answer to that question.

Micah tells the Israelites that it is not their burnt offerings or their rituals that God desires from them (6:6-7). God's plowman turned prophet cuts a deeper furrow to let his hearers know the meaning of true religion. In a text that has become one of the towering mountain peaks of the Bible, God defines true religion in a single terse statement: "To act justly and to love mercy and to walk humbly with your God" (6:8).

"To act justly" speaks of honesty and integrity. Our world of duplicity and corruption cries out for justice, for truth in action. "To love mercy" speaks of kindness, compassion, love, tenderness. People around us desperately need to see these qualities in us.

In God's trilogy of requirements he takes us from the horizontal to the vertical relationship and calls us "to walk humbly with [our] God." It declares the essence of what our faith is all about. Our faith is not a ritual; it is a relationship. To walk with God — what a priceless privilege! To walk with God — what a sacred responsibility!

The LORD is good, a refuge in times of trouble. He cares for those who trust in him.   (Nahum 1:7)

The winds of war blow through the book of Nahum and it can only be understood in the context of Nahum's world and Nineveh, the object of God's wrath and destruction.

The one radiant promise of this book declares: "The LORD is good, a refuge in times of trouble. He cares for those who trust in him" (1:7). True, he will punish the unrepentant sinner, but he will be the security and comfort of the believer.

"Nothing can heal your wound; your injury is fatal" (3:19) — this is the divine diagnosis on Nineveh. Nineveh's heinous sins put them beyond hope. Little could the powerful kings of Assyria know that their vassal Jerusalem would flourish long after the glory and grandeur of Nineveh had become a heap of ruins, buried in the sands of time.

Rudyard Kipling wrote a poem of celebration for the diamond jubilee of Queen Victoria in 1897, when the British Empire was at its apex of power. His "Recessional" baffled and angered many of his countrymen, as they read its stern warning:

> Lo, all our pomp of yesterday
> Is one with Nineveh and Tyre!
> Judge of the Nations, spare us yet,
> Lest we forget — lest we forget!

Let us hear and heed the message of Nahum, that God holds accountable both individuals and nations. Let us not forget, but remember the God of history and of grace.

"Write down the revelation and make it plain."   (Habakkuk 2:2)

As we brush the dust off the Old Testament book of Habakkuk, this illuminating text leaps out at us. First, it gives to the prophet the divine imperative, "Write the revelation." To some, that divine summons still sounds forth. The call to write may come as an inner urging, a haunting drive, a constant impulse, an inescapable constraint, a specific call.

The Lord not only gives to the prophet the divine imperative, he also gives the divine instruction: "Make it plain . . . that he may run who reads it" (2:2 NKJV). God's communicators today must be clear, lucid, and understandable.

"That he may run who reads it" suggests the urgency of the message. We are commissioned to address a world that is running fast and wild, at a dizzying pace. It will not be easy to capture its attention and response. We will fail if we are obscure, complex, or writing with a stained-glass vocabulary. Never has there been a greater urgency for the message our Lord calls us to bear.

For those who will write the vision the Lord also provides the inspiration. The prophet will "look to see what he will say to me" (2:1). For those so called, we need to listen to hear the clear accents of his Spirit to decipher meaning in life's struggles, to see the eternal above the temporal. God himself will inspire and give the message. From our communion with God will come our communication to others. Through the Holy Spirit we may hear those immortal cadences that will anoint and use our writing for the glory of God.

"The righteous will live by his faith."   (Habakkuk 2:4)

Habakkuk, though one of the briefest, is one of the mightiest and most memorable books of the Old Testament. Its towering truth became a landmark of New Testament theology and altered the course of spiritual and church history.

Some years ago we entered the church of St. John's Lateran in Rome. In it is a marble staircase said to be the one Jesus ascended in Pilate's judgment hall. We witnessed pilgrims mounting it on their knees, a step at a time, saying prayers as they ascended.

Centuries earlier a monk was performing this rite as he sought his salvation through works and rites of the church. What happened to Martin Luther on those stairs was recorded by his son: "As he repeated his prayers on the Lateran staircase, the words of the prophet Habakkuk came suddenly to his mind: 'The just shall live by faith.' Thereupon he ceased his prayers, returned to Wittenberg, and took this as the chief foundation of all his doctrine."

In that moment, as the mighty truth of this text given to the prophet Habakkuk gripped Luther's mind and soul, the Reformation was born that would sweep across Europe and spread throughout the world. Luther himself testified: "When by the Spirit of God, I understood those words, 'The just shall live by faith!' I felt born again like a new man." This text from Habakkuk became the battle cry of the Reformation.

God would remind us once again through this timeless text that it is only on the merit of the grace of our Lord and our faith in him that we are justified. It is not what we do for God that will get us into heaven, but what God has done for us, on Calvary.

> *"The LORD your God is with you, he is mighty to save."*
>
> (Zephaniah 3:17)

The prophet Zephaniah wastes no words but gets right down to the burden of his message, the divine judgment upon Judah's sin that will bring total devastation. He flings out his mighty message, "The great day of the LORD is near" (1:14). "The day of the LORD" or its equivalent is repeated no fewer than twenty times in this brief book. The horrors of the judgment of that day tumble from his lips as an avalanche of woes upon the nation (1:15-16).

But the message of doom is not the final word. There is good news for those who "may call on the name of the LORD" (3:9). God's penman concludes with one of the most beautiful assurances in the prophetic tradition: "The LORD your God is with you, he is mighty to save. He will take great delight in you, he will quiet you with his love" (3:17).

From this little-known book of the Old Testament comes an enduring message to all generations. First, God is sovereign. History and events are working toward his ultimate design. Second, God will bring a day of universal judgment upon sin. Third, the justice and plan of God will ultimately triumph over evil. Fourth, a remnant will be saved. To the prodigal nation comes the divine promise, "I will bring you home" (3:20).

The great day of the Lord will ultimately come for every person. Let us in continued obedience to God be prepared for this grandest event of all.

"Give careful thought to your ways." (Haggai 1:5)

N o fewer than four times do we find the statement "give careful thought" in this thirty-eight-verse, two-chapter book (1:5, 7; 2:15, 18). God sends Haggai to call the people to their long-neglected job of rebuilding their place of worship, summoning them from apathy to action.

"Give careful thought" is ever a contemporary message from God. What place does God have in the everyday matters of our life — in our home, our business, our devotional life, our physical life, our relationships? Does God have first place in all these areas?

"The time has not yet come for the LORD's house to be built" (1:2) was the excuse of the people. Procrastination can rob us of doing God's will and work when it should be done. The road of "maybe someday" leads to the land of "never ever."

With a touch of irony, God asks, "Is it a time for you yourselves to be living in your paneled houses, while this house remains a ruin?" (1:4). Do we not tend to find time for what is most important to us personally? The problem is not time, but priority. Properly ordered priorities will rescue us from living under the tyranny of the urgent.

The frantic and feverish activity of our day is echoed in Haggai's description of his hearers: "You have planted much, but have harvested little. You eat, but never have enough" (1:6). The ancient text of Haggai is not all that remote from where we live.

Giving careful thought to what God has for us to do, we can claim the encouraging promise: "Be strong . . . and work. For I am with you, declares the LORD Almighty" (2:4).

"Not by might nor by power, but by my Spirit," says the LORD Almighty. (Zechariah 4:6)

W hat is the key, the secret for excellence and effectiveness in our spiritual life? I once heard Billy Graham give a needed word of caution to a group of Christian leaders, "Sometimes I think we depend more on computers than on the Holy Spirit."

God's Word declares that the secret of spiritual success is, "Not by might nor by power, but by my Spirit." Only by the Holy Spirit can we truly be God's people, and do God's work.

Charles Haddon Spurgeon was considered the greatest preacher in the late nineteenth century, with overflow crowds of six thousand persons every Sunday for thirty years at his Metropolitan Tabernacle in London. People throughout the world read printed versions of his sermons each week. His preachment of the gospel reached a larger audience than anyone of his day. Spurgeon's integrity, vigorous thought, eloquent language, grasp of gospel truth, and force of presentation made him without peer among preachers, earning for him the name, "Prince of the Pulpit."

What was the secret of his greatness, his effectiveness for God? Spurgeon himself answered: "Without the Spirit of God I feel I am utterly unable to speak to you." Each Sunday as he mounted the fifteen steps of his pulpit, he said to himself on each one, "I believe in the Holy Ghost. I believe in the Holy Ghost." After fifteen repetitions of this creedal affirmation, when he entered the pulpit he relied on the Holy Spirit's enabling presence and power.

That, I believe, was the secret of this Prince of the Pulpit, and that I believe is the secret of spiritual excellence and greatness in any person of God.

"I have loved you," says the LORD. (Malachi 1:2)

"**I** have loved you," says the Lord in the opening message of this last book of the Old Testament. God does not allow the oracles of the prophets to close without once more affirming his unchangeable love for his people.

God declares, "I the LORD do not change" (3:6). God is the same today as he was a billion years ago. He will always be just. He will always be holy. He will always be omnipotent and omniscient. He will always be loving. Though we may fail and falter, God's love for us is unchanging. One of God's most assuring attributes is his immutability.

With a touch of impudence, Israel asks of Yahweh, "How have you loved us?" In other words, "If you really loved us, you would not let these things happen to us." They looked for worldly prosperity as proof of his love.

This key word, "how," or its equivalent, recurs seven times in the debating style of this short book. Malachi's message does not come from a cloistered study, but was hammered out in the verbal conflicts and debates of the marketplace, where assertions had to be defended against cynical objections. Seven times his hearers throw this rebuttal, "How?," at the prophet, denying his statements of God's love and their corruption.

Love is ever in danger of being taken for granted. A husband can take for granted the faithful love of a wife; a grown child the sacrificial love of a parent. The people of Israel became blind to the love of God and turned to moral laxity.

God's word to us in this final book of the Old Testament is that he loves us. Let our hearts return that love in devotion and glad obedience.

THE NEW TESTAMENT

"You are to give him the name Jesus, because he will save his people from their sins." (Matthew 1:21)

G od sent his own messenger from the heavenly courts to announce that his name should be Jesus. It is his earthly name, and the name by which we know him best. In the Gospels he is called by this name over five hundred times, with the name occurring 909 times in the New Testament.

Of all the names and titles of Christ this one has been most endearing to his followers. The contents of a hymnbook add eloquent testimony of that fact: John Newton gave us "How sweet the name of Jesus sounds"; Edward Perronet exalts this name with "All hail the power of Jesus' name!" Bernard of Clairvaux exclaims, "Jesus! The very thought of Thee."

It is the name that denotes the great purpose of his life: "He shall save his people from their sins." Above all else he came to be our Savior. Imagine knowing Tennyson, but not as a poet; Socrates, but not as a philosopher! Unless we know Jesus as Savior, we miss the preeminent message and mission of his life. The Scriptures declare: "Salvation is found in no one else, for there is no other name under heaven given to men by which we must be saved" (Acts 4:12).

With Will J. Brand, we would exultantly sing:

There is beauty in the name of Jesus,
    Passing time can ne'er extol;
All the splendour of its clear unfolding
    Will eternal years enrol.

"The virgin will be with child and will give birth to a son."
(Matthew 1:23)

Gabriel, God's heavenly messenger, delivered a stunning announcement in the small village of Nazareth where he appeared to Mary, who was pledged to be married to Joseph. Gabriel announced that she would give birth to a son who "will be great and will be called the Son of the Most High. His kingdom will never end" (Luke 1:26-33).

"How will this be," Mary asked, "since I am a virgin?" Gabriel answered, "The Holy Spirit will come upon you. For nothing is impossible with God." Mary replied, "I am the Lord's servant. May it be to me as you have said" (Luke 1:34-38). Luke the physician records, with no ambivalence, that Mary was impregnated by the Holy Spirit (Luke 1:35).

If any law of science is established as immutable, it is that human reproduction is not possible without the contribution of both genders. The virgin birth of Jesus violates this inviolable, mutates this immutable. Biologically, a virgin birth is an impossibility. But so was the raising of Lazarus from the dead. So was the resurrection of Christ.

God, who created the world *ex nihilo* — without preexistent matter, certainly can produce the birth of a baby by supernaturally fertilizing an egg in a woman's womb. It defies logic to grant the greater but deny the lesser.

Joseph did not have to be an obstetrician to know that babies do not come from storks when his betrothed came to him with her crushing revelation. He was the first hard-core skeptic of the Virgin Birth until an angel visited him and made him a believer.

"Nothing is impossible with God" (Luke 1:37). The presence of mystery in the Gospel narrative is the footprint of the divine, the God of miracles.

"They will call him Immanuel" — which means, "God with us."
(Matthew 1:23)

G od had this name written three times in his Word: Isaiah 7:14; 8:8; and here in Matthew. Christ alone was great enough to be called Immanuel. No one else could fill its glowing meaning — *God with us.*

John presents a graphic portrait of Christ when he wrote that he "became flesh (human, incarnate), and tabernacled — fixed his tent of flesh, lived awhile — among us; and we [actually] saw his glory" (John 1:14, ANT). The statement staggers the imagination. Yet that is precisely what happened with the Incarnation.

The miracle and the marvel of *Immanuel* — God with us — defy description. The hands of God that had scattered galaxies into space became the small chubby hands of an infant. Jesus was the heart of God wrapped in human flesh. He was God in the garb of humanity. He was God walking the earth in sandals.

From that feeding trough in the cattle shed of lowly Bethlehem, the cry from that infant's throat broke through the silence of centuries. For the first time on Earth, there was heard the voice of God from human vocal chords. *Immanuel* speaks to us of the unfathomable act of God becoming human and dwelling among us.

A young child looked at a picture of her absent father and longingly said, "I wish Father would step out of that picture." For centuries, men had a yearning for God to step out of the picture — to become more tangible, to make himself known, to be communed with. At Bethlehem, Jesus became God's authentic self-disclosure.

What a reassuring thought, that he is still *Immanuel* to his followers — God with us.

The Wise Men

Wise men from the East came, saying, "We have seen his star in the East and have come to worship him." (Matthew 2:11 NJKV)

Devout astrologers who gazed for long hours at the heavens one night observed the appearance of a spectacular new star. They saw it as signaling the birth of a great king, and journeyed far over difficult and dangerous routes to where the star led them.

The Wise Men made a long and hazardous journey to find Christ. We too must make a journey to find him — a journey from afar, from the land of self and sin — and make our spiritual pilgrimage to the Son of God.

The Magi brought their best treasures to Christ. They came with perfumes from Edom, myrrh from the forests, and gold from the mines. Christ deserves nothing less than our best, our utmost for his highest.

Warned by God in a dream of the murderous plot of King Herod, the Wise Men returned by a different way. When we find Christ, life can never be the same again; we can no longer travel the same path. Christ changes our destination and our destiny.

The star observed by the Wise Men reminds us that God leaves no one without a sign of himself. There are many signs from God along life's road — his Word, the church, wonders of nature, godly parents and loved ones, an experience of joy or sorrow, the leading of the Holy Spirit. Let us follow the signs that would lead us to God.

The Wise Men foresaw, they forsook, they followed, and they found the Christ. The wise seek and find him still.

"Blessed are the poor in spirit, for theirs is the kingdom of heaven."
(Matthew 5:3)

For many, happiness becomes the supreme quest of life. Men spend their wealth, energy, and their lifetime seeking it. Some seek it in possessions, position, power, wealth, and fame. Others seek it in sex, drugs, and selfish pursuits, all of which turn out to be dead ends. Christ teaches that if you want to be truly happy, the Beatitudes are the way.

The Sermon on the Mount (Matthew 5, 6, 7) represents the core and essence of the teaching of Christ. He had just called his disciples. Now he tells them what true discipleship means, and the secret of happiness.

The setting for the Beatitudes is a mountain, symbolic of the loftiness of the teaching and the heights to be scaled. Each Beatitude begins with the word "blessed." The Greek word, *makarios,* denotes the highest stage of happiness and well-being, a joy independent of the chances and changes of life. Happiness is not something we find outside of ourselves but within, a byproduct of the virtues commended in the Beatitudes.

Our Lord presents a revolutionary teaching — a transvaluation of the world's values. He challenges selfishness. We say blessed are the achievers, the powerful. He says blessed are the poor in spirit. This Beatitude does not speak of material poverty. Nor is it a suppression of personality. But the Lord speaks of the poverty of spirit, a complete absence of pride.

Pride is the root of sin; poverty of spirit is the root of virtue. Pride is the dethronement of God from his rightful sovereignty in the human heart. Poverty of spirit is the dethronement of pride and the enthronement of God.

"Blessed are those who mourn, for they will be comforted."

(Matthew 5:4)

The world shuns mourning. Its philosophy is, forget your troubles. Its motto is, "Enjoy! Eat, drink, and be merry!" But in our text Christ says, "Mourn to be blessed."

Believers mourn for their sins. They mourn for the suffering and tragedies of others in the world. Such sorrow finds comfort and meaning in life. An anonymous poet writes:

I walked a mile with Pleasure,
She chattered all the way,
But left me none the wiser
For all she had to say.
I walked a mile with Sorrow,
And ne'er a word said she,
But, oh, the things I learned from her
When sorrow walked with me!

Someone has said that Negro spirituals are "pain set to music." When our trust is in God, trials work for us, not against us. They build a spiritual maturing and character into our lives. As the Japanese evangelist Toyohiko Kagawa once wrote, "The sanctification of suffering is the ultimate art of God."

No words can express the debt the world owes to sorrow. Most of the Psalms were born in times of trial. Most of the epistles were written in prison. Great hymn writers and poets often "learned in suffering what they taught in song." The sorrows, which threaten to blight our joy, become our source of comfort and blessing when our trust is in the Lord.

"Blessed are the meek, for they will inherit the earth."

(Matthew 5:5)

M eekness is often confused with weakness, a self-effacing humility. But meekness is not weakness. True meekness is great strength.

The Greek work for "meek," *praus,* means far more than our English word *meek.* It has no English equivalent. The word *praus* was used for an animal that has been tamed and trained. Thus it denotes the God-controlled person. Meekness is submission to the will of God. Others assert their rights, but the meek are concerned about their duties. Others advertise themselves; the meek walk in quiet godliness.

This Beatitude ran counter to the ethos of Jesus' day. The Jews asserted their pride of race, the Romans their pride of power, the Greeks their pride of knowledge. But Christ teaches a sharp denial of the world's standards. He calls his followers away from pride to humility, away from assertiveness to meekness.

The astonishing reward of the meek is that they inherit the earth. Possession of the earth is given to the meek — of all people! This is surely one of the startling paradoxes of the Christian faith.

Jesus himself gave the supreme example of meekness, stating, "I am meek and lowly in heart." We see it in his whole life and ministry. He humbled himself, became a servant, and suffered rejection and death for our salvation.

For the Christian, meekness is a virtue produced by the Holy Spirit. In Galatians 5:23 the word is translated "gentleness" — one of the fruits of the Spirit, planted and nurtured and blossoming forth in the life of the Christian.

The Deeper Hunger

"Blessed are those who hunger and thirst for righteousness, for they will be filled."   (Matthew 5:6)

All the trouble in the world today is due to the fact that human beings are not right with God. Because we are not right with God we have gone wrong everywhere else.

Righteousness is being right with God. Jesus calls us to an intense desire for rightness. The psalmist summed it up in the words, "My soul thirsts for God, for the living God" (Psalm 42:2).

Everything seems designed for happiness. The pervasive and seductive advertising of our day relate to people's hunger and thirst for happiness. But in the end it eludes them, for if we want to be truly happy and blessed we must hunger and thirst after righteousness.

A desire for righteousness is a desire to be right with God, a desire to be rid of sin, because sin is that which comes between us and God, and dulls our spiritual appetite. The person who truly examines himself not only discovers that he is in the bondage of sin; still more serious is the fact that he likes it — that even after he has seen it is wrong he still wants it. But the person who hungers and thirsts after righteousness is someone who wants to get rid of that desire for sin. It is nothing less than the longing to be holy, to exemplify the Beatitudes in his daily life.

The result of such longing and seeking is "they shall be filled." God satisfies the deep longing of our heart for a right relationship with him and for living a holy life.

"Blessed are the merciful, for they will be shown mercy."

(Matthew 5:7)

M atthew is the teaching Gospel, presenting Jesus as the Teacher. The Beatitudes Jesus gave in this mountaintop seminar to his disciples are the "be-attitudes" for Christians. They depict what should be our attitude, our psyche — our philosophical outlook and our action in the world at large.

The follower of Christ, having obtained mercy through the grace of our Lord, in turn becomes a channel of mercy to others. Mercy lays claim upon us wherever there is suffering. The word in the original text denotes not mere sympathy, but empathy, an identification in the suffering of others, entering into another's problem with understanding and support. Mercy is one of the great acts of God toward us, what he did for us in Christ; identifying with us and suffering on our behalf.

To be merciful is to receive mercy. Let us be among the "twice blest" as described by Shakespeare in the memorable lines of *The Merchant of Venice:*

The quality of mercy is not strain'd,
It droppeth as the gentle rain from heaven
upon the place beneath; It is twice blest;
It blesseth him that gives and him that takes:
'Tis mightiest in the mightiest:
It becomes
the throned monarch better than his crown.

The Pure in Heart

"Blessed are the pure in heart, for they will see God."

(Matthew 5:8)

J esus makes an astonishing statement in saying that the pure in heart shall see God. A parallel verse in the Epistle to the Hebrews summons us "to be holy; without holiness, no one will see the Lord" (12:14). That is true in this life as well as hereafter. Sin blurs our vision and distorts our perception. There is a vision known alone to the eye of faith and purity. We can only realize God as a presence when our hearts are pure.

What an amazing blessing is promised to the pure in heart! They shall see God! Imagine, you and I may someday see God! We can have an audience with the King of the universe. No earthly thrill can begin to compare with that most momentous event ever. Let us then heed the advice of the apostle John when he wrote: "We shall see him as he is. Everyone who has this hope in him purifies himself" (1 John 3:2-3).

Tennyson willed that at the end of any collection of his poetry there be his "Crossing the Bar." The words of that immortal poem affirm the Christian hope:

> Sunset and evening star,
> And one clear call for me!
> And may there be no moaning of the bar,
> When I put out to sea,
> . . . .
> For though from out our bourne
> of Time and Place
> The flood may bear me far,
> I hope to see my Pilot face to face
> When I have cross'd the bar.

"Blessed are the peacemakers, for they will be called sons of God."
(Matthew 5:9)

We are called not only to have the peace of God within our hearts but to be peacemakers, to help bring peace to others and to our world. God's peacemakers do not bring strife but serenity, not conflict but concord, not hostility but harmony, not enmity but amity, not ill will but good will, not contention but cooperation.

The Greek word *eirene,* and its Hebrew equivalent, *shalom,* means not only freedom from trouble, but everything that makes for man's highest good. That is what God wants us to contribute to the lives of others and to our world.

In Greek mythology, a young man named Damocles used flattery to endear himself to Dionysius, tyrant ruler of ancient Syracuse. To instruct and warn the ambitious youth, Dionysius invited the flatterer to a banquet and seated him under a sword suspended over his head by a single hair. This graphic story was designed to illustrate the perilous nature of one's happiness and peace.

Many today consider that the whole human race sits under a sword of Damocles, a sword of mass destruction that any day may be unleashed by terrorists in the world. Some fear that humankind may self-destruct by pushing a button that will destroy much of the planet. Never in history has there been such a need for peacemakers. Let us, as children of God, help create and spread peace in our respective circles of relationships and influence.

The Persecuted

"Blessed are those who are persecuted because of righteousness, for theirs is the kingdom of heaven." (Matthew 5:10)

J esus, in this last Beatitude, makes an amazing statement. He tells us what to expect when we truly embrace his teachings. This description of the Christian is integral to the whole teaching of the New Testament.

Not every persecution is pronounced blessed. Some persecution may be for foolishness' sake, for fanaticism, or because of self-righteousness, which we call down on our own heads. The motive must be "for righteousness' sake . . . for my sake."

When the church is true to its Lord it will be the conscience to the society and nation. If our expression of faith becomes tepid, the world then may simply ignore it.

Today, more than ever, Christians are paying the ultimate cost of discipleship. Some fundamentalist Muslim countries both suppress and oppress Christian witness, and all too often in our day Christians in these countries and cultures suffer severe persecution.

The character traits of the Beatitudes are not natural to our disposition but are produced by the Holy Spirit who makes them hallmarks of our discipleship. Dietrich Bonhoeffer, in *The Cost of Discipleship*, warns against "a cheap grace" and in contrast writes of a "costly grace." He himself paid the high cost of discipleship when he was martyred at the age of 39 because he dared to stand against the heresy and atrocities of Nazism.

May God give to us needed wisdom and courage, so that if our faith must some day go through a fiery trial, we may have the assurance of this Beatitude.

"You are the salt of the earth."   (Matthew 5:13)

The Christian does not live in isolation from the world. Christ does not call us to monasticism but to mission. In this respect, our Lord describes the Christian with two great metaphors — they are to be the salt and the light of the earth (Matthew 5:13-16).

The principal function of salt is to preserve and to act as an antiseptic. Before refrigeration salt was the main means of preserving food. In the ancient world it was the most common preservative. Those listening to Christ had no doubt seen fish, heavily salted, transported on the back of donkeys from the shores of the Galilean Sea.

If Christians need to be the salt of the earth, then by implication our world tends toward corruption. Our society today suffers with decay from materialism, lust, pride, family breakup, war, violence, environmental pollution. Our world is infected by the microbes of sin and evil, which unchecked bring disease and death.

Another function of salt is to provide flavor to food, to prevent it from being insipid. Life without Christ lacks that which enables it to reach its full potential. What we are and do has an effect on others around us. By a godly life and character we become the salt of the earth of which Christ speaks.

Today when we wish to compliment a person of worth and usefulness, we use the proverbial expression, "He is the salt of the earth." May we be among those that are "the salt of the earth," bringing the enrichment of Christ and helping to preserve our world from moral pollution.

"You are the light of the world." (Matthew 5:14)

J esus makes this most astounding statement to the simple people gathered before him, "You are the light of the world." The "you" of this statement refers not only to those to whom these words were first spoken, but to ourselves. It is a summons to every believer.

By implication, Christ describes the world as in a state of moral darkness. The darkness of the world has never been more evident than in our day. News headlines scream to us each day of its bleak condition. Christ alone can save it from the dark night of sin.

Our planet Earth has no light of its own. Our earthly light comes from the sun. Our spiritual light is as a borrowed ray from the Sun of Righteousness. How wonderful that we can catch his radiance and reflect Christ to a darkened world!

Although not of the world, we are called to live in it. The mandate of the Master to his followers is, "Let your light shine before men, that they may see your good deeds and praise your Father in heaven" (Matthew 5:16). Our purpose is not to call attention to ourselves but to glorify God.

Jesus declared, "I am the light of the world" (John 8:12). Because Christ dwells within us, his light becomes a part of us and we become reflectors of that divine light. A. W. Tozer said that he believed in communion with God to the point of incandescence. Praise God instead of cursing the darkness around us, for we are called to be spiritually incandescent as bearers of the eternal light.

*"This is how you should pray: 'Our Father in heaven, hallowed be
your name.'"*   (Matthew 6:9)

Jesus, knowing that his disciples would be totally dependent on the
resource of prayer, gives them a lesson on how they should pray.
Even prayer, he taught, can be wrongly practiced, with hypocrisy, os-
tentation, or vain repetitions (Matthew 6:5-8).

The result of our Lord's mountain seminar on prayer is that Christians in the ages since have been the beneficiaries of "the Lord's Prayer,"
which could more appropriately be termed "the Disciples' Prayer," for
it is the prayer that he taught his followers to pray.

The first word, "our," rescues prayer from egocentricity, a selfish
mindset. It is a key word that if left out makes the prayer read, "Give
me, forgive me, lead me, deliver me."

None of the saints before Christ ever ventured to address God as
"Our Father." This invocation evokes the wonderful revelation by Jesus
that God is our heavenly Father.

"Hallowed be your name" is the first of the three petitions directed
for God's glory. The name of God stood for his very nature and his
attributes. "Hallowed" means "revered, kept holy." "Your kingdom
come" prays for the reign of God here in the hearts of believers. The
third petition, "Your will be done," represents the ultimate in human
achievement.

The last three petitions, directed to our needs, are all-encompassing.
Our daily bread relates to our need for physical sustenance, forgiveness
of sins to our need for salvation, and deliverance from evil to our need
for sanctification.

Some late manuscripts of the Bible add the postscript to the Lord's
Prayer: "For yours is the kingdom and the power and the glory forever."
To this model prayer, it offers an appropriate praise and doxology in its
ascription of glory to God forever.

Treasure in Heaven

"Store up for yourselves treasures in heaven, where moth and rust do not destroy, and where thieves do not break in and steal."
(Matthew 6:20)

J esus warns of a common folly: "Do not store up for yourselves treasures on earth, where moth and rust destroy, and where thieves break in and steal" (Matthew 6:19). There is an element of decay in all earthly things, all of which will inevitably perish.

The most beautiful flower begins to die the moment we pluck it. The most comely countenance will someday succumb to the aging process. The strongest physique will eventually become weak. Our trophies tarnish; the plaudits of the crowd die away. Jesus reminds us that worldly treasures have upon them the kiss of death.

"Thieves break in and steal." We may think that we are safe only to find that our dearest treasures are ransacked by accident, disaster, illness, economic loss, aging, and finally, death. Time, the greatest thief of all, ultimately will claim all that we may possess.

In our text, the Lord goes from the negative to the positive side: "But store up for yourselves treasures in heaven, where moth and rust do not destroy, and where thieves do not break in and steal" (6:20). No thief can rob us of our spiritual treasures, for God himself is the guardian who keeps our treasures in heaven incorruptible and invulnerable, forever untouched by earth's decay and death.

Christ enunciates a central principle that governs life, "For where your treasure is, there will your heart be also" (6:21). What we treasure motivates and governs our life. He addresses the quintessential question, "What is it that really matters?" He calls us to view the things of this world with a holy detachment, and to seek the eternal treasures of heaven.

"Therefore, I tell you, do not worry about your life."

(Matthew 6:25)

"Do not worry" is a cardinal teaching of Christ, repeated four times in this passage (Matthew 6:25, 28, 31, 34). It does not veto wise preparation, but warns against borrowing trouble from the future.

"Do not worry about tomorrow" (6:34) is hard counsel. Concerns and anxieties for people and things of importance impinge upon us. We become concerned about our work, loved ones, security, health, world issues. Worry can be a constant and nagging companion.

There are two days in the week about which we should never worry — two carefree days kept free from anxiety. One of these days is yesterday, with its pains and mistakes, forever beyond our recall. The other is tomorrow, with all its possible burdens and dangers. Jesus reminds his hearers, "Each day has enough trouble of its own" (6:34). He calls us to live one day at a time. God promises, "Your strength will equal your days" (Deuteronomy 33:25).

Jesus, referring to God's care for the flowers and birds, teaches that worry is a contradiction of our status as children of an all-loving and caring God (6:26-30). But let us remember that no one works harder than the sparrow to survive. Faith is always wedded to works. The antidote to worry is complete trust in God (6:33).

The following was "overheard in an orchard":

Said the robin to the sparrow, "I should like to really know
Why these anxious human beings rush about and worry so."
Said the sparrow to the robin, "Friend, I think that it must be
That they have no Heavenly Father such as cares for you and me."

Ask, Seek, Knock

"Ask and it will be given to you; seek and you will find; knock and the door will be opened to you." (Matthew 7:7)

This text is one of the most gracious promises of the Bible. To give it emphasis Jesus repeats it in an even stronger form: "For everyone who asks receives; he who seeks finds; and to him who knocks, the door will be opened" (Matthew 7:8).

Surely this text does not suggest that God is a cosmic Santa Claus who will give us anything for which we ask. That would be a contradiction of his character as well as not in our best interests.

Jesus had just presented the tremendously high standard of the Sermon on the Mount. The challenge that no doubt came to the disciples and comes to all of us is, "How can we ever live up to this lofty standard? Who is equal? Where can we find the grace and strength to measure up?" Jesus answers with this great promise that the resources of God are available to us.

The threefold invitation suggests a progression in our spiritual pilgrimage. First, there are times of helplessness when, as children, we must ask God for our needs. Then there comes a searching and pursuing of what God has for us. And sometimes it seems as though the door is tightly shut and we must knock, as in sickness or death.

Jesus uses the familiar method of arguing from the lesser to the greater with the analogy of the earthly father who, though sinful, gives good gifts to his children. Then he says, "how much more" (7:11) will an all-loving God be gracious and good to his children.

Just think, the boundless blessings of God await our asking, seeking, and knocking!

"Enter through the narrow gate. For wide is the gate and broad is the road that leads to destruction, and many enter through it."
(Matthew 7:13)

Jesus in this text gives a graphic description of the two ways of life, and warns that only a few find the "narrow road that leads to life."

Every worthy path of life has a narrow entrance. The accomplished musician must submit to endless hours of practice; the champion athlete must give himself to an arduous regimen; the surgeon must spend years in preparation.

The word Jesus uses for "enter," which in some translations is rendered "striving," is the Greek word from which we derive "agony." The road to greatness is always the fruit of toil, discipline, and renunciation, and requires leaving behind encumbrances of the world.

We all confront the ultimate choice between the two ways of life that our Lord describes. The person who starts out on a long journey and does not consider his destination will lose his way. Life is a journey toward an eternal destination. Jesus tells his hearers that the broad way leads to destruction but the narrow way leads to life. John Oxenham echoes the truth of our text:

> To every man there openeth a way and ways and a way;
> And the high soul treads the high way, and the low soul
>   gropes the low;
> And in between on the misty flats the rest drift to and fro;
> But to every man there openeth a high way and a low;
> And every man decideth the way his soul shall go.

"Peace, be still!" (Matthew 8:39 NKJV)

The Sea of Galilee is notorious for sudden and terrifying squalls. Nearly seven hundred feet below sea level, it is surrounded by high hills that act as huge funnels through which the winds spiral, creating a raging turbulence upon its surface.

Such was the tempest the disciples found themselves in while out on their boat. The storm is called a *seismos,* the Greek word for earthquake, emphasizing its violence. Even the seasoned fishermen on board had never encountered a storm quite like this one.

As the winds howled, the waves mounted, and the water filled the boat, Jesus slept, exhausted from his crowded days of teaching and healing. Terror-stricken, the disciples awakened him. In response to their plight, Jesus stretched his hand over the tempest-tossed sea and commanded, "Peace, be still!" The winds ceased. The seething water smoothed its face, changing into a sudden calm. In amazement the disciples fell before Jesus and cried out, "What manner of man is this that even the winds and sea obey him?"

Journeying with Jesus does not make us immune to the storms and tempests of life. But to voyage with Jesus is to be with the Master of the sea and storm who brings peace, even amid life's severest tempests. He will speak the word that brings calm amid chaos, peace amid panic.

"Come to me, all you who are weary and burdened, and I will give you rest." (Matthew 11:28)

I n one of the most gracious promises in the Bible, Jesus invites "all who are weary and burdened" to come to him and he will give them rest. This promise brings hope to the countless number in the world who carry heavy burdens.

"Come," the first word of the promise, is a simple word but full of meaning. "To come" is to leave one thing and advance to another. To begin with, we have all at one time carried the heavy burden of sin. It has been said that Atlas with the world upon his back had a light load compared with a sinner upon whom rests sin and God's judgment. Jesus invites us to come, to forsake our sin and let him lift its burden from us.

Strange that after having received this rest, we are asked, in the very next verse, to shoulder another burden: "Take my yoke upon you." Having just had our burden lifted, are we to have another one thrust upon us? But we note that it is Christ's yoke, and he tells us that his yoke is easy.

A yoke was tailor-made to fix the ox, with two oxen usually yoked together. The yoke would not work if one were to lie down and the other to stand up. But when they are both of one mind, to lie down or go forward, the yoke is easy. A Christian, yoked together with Christ, will find the shared yoke to be both bearable and blessed.

Joy Webb has expressed this truth in her beautiful devotional song:

Share my yoke and find that I am joined with you.
Your slightest movement I shall feel and be there too!
Share my yoke and come the way that I must go!
In our "togetherness" my peace you'll know;
The world beholding us will see it so!

The Pivotal Question

"But what about you?" he asked. "Who do you say I am?"
(Matthew 16:15)

O ur text brings us to one of the most dramatic and critical moments in the life of Jesus. The scene portrays this penniless Galilean carpenter, with twelve very ordinary men gathered around him,
standing amid the motley temples of pagan gods. Here in Caesarea
Philippi, the religious fortress of the pagan world, this itinerant teacher
asks men who they believe him to be, and expects them to respond,
"The Son of God!"

Against the background of man's opinions, he confronts them
personally: "But what about you? Who do *you* say I am?"

In response to Jesus' probing question, Peter takes a giant leap of
faith and answers on behalf of the disciples, "You are the Christ, the
Son of the living God." His confession acknowledges both the messi-
anic fulfillment and the divinity of Jesus.

The world offers many verdicts in its continuing "search for the
historical Jesus." Some say he was a myth, a fanatic, an idealist, merely
an inspiration for social causes or a great teacher, but obsolete in our
modern world.

This question, timeless and universal, is a personal one. Sooner or
later, each person must answer Christ's searching question. It demands
a verdict, whether openly or quietly within the soul. In answering, we
need to see the Christ of the Gospels, uncluttered by our cultural accre-
tions and ecclesiastical structures.

Just as Jesus confronted his disciples with this burning question, so
he comes to each of us and asks, "What about you? Who do you say
that I am?" Jesus' identity is not at stake. Ours is.

"If anyone would come after me, he must deny himself and take up his cross and follow me." (Matthew 16:24)

C aesarea Philippi marked a crossroads in the life of Jesus. Here his public ministry ended and his path turned toward the cross, a scant six months away. Peter's historic confession acknowledging Christ as the Messiah, and the Lord's dialogue with his disciples, was a watershed in his life and ministry. It was here he made the first announcement of his impending suffering, death, and resurrection.

Jesus concluded this seminar at the foot of Mount Hermon with one of his greatest declarations and dominant themes: "If anyone would come after me, he must deny himself and take up his cross and follow me." Luke adds to this command a telling word: "Let him take up his cross *daily*" (Luke 9:23). There can be no discipleship without self-denial and a full life commitment to the cross.

The geographical heart of London is named Charing Cross, known simply as "the cross." All distances in London are measured from it. The heart of the gospel is the cross of Christ, with all our spiritual bearings reckoned from Calvary.

Jessie Pounds has put in song our Lord's inescapable requisite for discipleship:

I must needs go home by the way of the cross,
There's no other way but this;
I shall ne'er get sight of the Gates of Light,
If the way of the cross I miss.
The way of the cross leads home.

"For whoever wants to save his life will lose it, but whoever loses his life for me will find it."   (Matthew 16:25)

Jesus here gives one of the great paradoxes of truth found in the Bible, recorded in all three synoptic Gospels. If we seek to save our life, we will lose it, but if we lose our life for Christ, we will find it.

The person preoccupied with saving his lower life will lose his higher life. To be consumed with pursuit of the passing things of this world is to lose the eternal riches of the world to come.

Jim Elliot, one of the missionaries martyred in the jungle of Ecuador when he sought to bring the gospel to the primitive Auca tribe, had said, "He is no fool who gives what he cannot keep to gain what he cannot lose." In his dedication he did lose his transient earthly life, but gained life eternal. The seeds of his sacrifice and ministry have reaped a bountiful harvest through the continued ministry of his wife Elisabeth, not only in that jungle setting, but in her inspiring books telling their story. This very summer of 2002, almost a half century later, our 17-year-old granddaughter is part of a Teen Missions International team that is rendering a practical ministry to children of the same Auca tribe.

Indeed, in the divine paradox of life, losing is finding, giving is gaining, and dying is living. Hymn writer George Matheson has expressed this truth in his song:

> Make me a captive, Lord,
> And then I shall be free;
> Force me to render up my sword,
> And I shall a conqueror be.

"For where two or three come together in my name, there am I with them."
                                                                (Matthew 18:20)

"Christians cannot reach the full blessing God is ready to bestow through his Spirit," writes Andrew Murray, "until they seek and receive it in fellowship with each other." It was to those praying in one accord, under the same roof, that the Spirit came in mighty power at Pentecost. It is still so: in the union and fellowship of believers the Holy Spirit manifests his presence and power.

"Come together" speaks of being in accord with each other. "In my name" speaks of purity of motive. "Two or three" reminds us that the church does not depend on numbers. "With them" assures believers that none other than Christ himself is present.

Corporate prayer is as a golden chain that binds and bonds us together in the fellowship and spirit of Christ. A powerful spiritual synergism takes place — a multiplying of results — when two or more come together to pray.

Eighteenth-century hymn writer William Cowper versified this truth for us:

Jesus, where'er thy people meet,
There they behold the mercy seat;
Where'er they seek thee thou art found,
And every place is hallowed ground.

"How many times shall I forgive?"   (Matthew 18:21)

Forgiveness may be the most difficult thing for a person to give. As Alexander Pope reminds us: "To err is human; to forgive is divine." Peter, thinking of what Jesus said about a brother who may sin against you, wanted to know how often he had to forgive his brother. Peter proposed magnanimity, going beyond the rabbinic rule of three times, extending it to seven.

But Jesus responded, "seventy times seven." Jesus, known to be fond of hyperbole, did not intend a precise mathematical 490 times for forgiveness and then quit. Rather, he clearly meant unlimited forgiveness. The spirit of the Lord's answer is not earthly calculation, but celestial arithmetic; it is a precept for conduct, not for mathematics.

Forgiveness is not only hard, it is costly. What of malicious slander that has deeply wounded? Or treachery where there should be friendship or love? True forgiveness means to forget as well as to forgive.

Jesus taught his followers to pray, "Forgive us our trespasses as we forgive those who trespass against us." God's forgiveness and our forgiveness are inseparably linked. To be forgiving is to be forgiven; to be unforgiving is to be unforgiven.

Luke records that when the disciples heard this requirement, they exclaimed, "Increase our faith!" Indeed, such teachings of Jesus have an unfathomable depth and seem almost more than we can bear. But he has given us the Holy Spirit to make us adequate. Let us take for our example the One who on the cross modeled his teaching by forgiving the very ones who crucified him.

"What good thing must I do to get eternal life?"

(Matthew 19:16)

I n one of the best-known stories in the Bible, recorded in all three synoptic Gospels, a young man comes to Jesus with a troubling question. Rich, personable, and respectable, what more could he want? This young aristocrat came to the penniless preacher on his way to becoming an outlaw with a death sentence, and asked him, "What good thing must I do to get eternal life?"

The young man said that he had always kept the commandments. "Go, sell your possessions and give to the poor," said Jesus, "and you will have treasure in heaven." He then added, "Come, follow me."

Jesus was not setting down a universal rule for discipleship, but a prescription for the particular need of this person. One thing he lacked — the self-forgetfulness that would enable him to surrender to Christ. It was not so much what this man possessed as what possessed him that kept him from Christ and eternal life.

Our last glimpse of the young ruler is with his head down, his back to Jesus, retreating into the idolatry of his riches. Little could he realize as he saw that small company of men disappear down the dusty road that they were walking into the greatest romance of history. He missed life's choicest friendship and the realization of his true potential. Who knows? He might even have written a fifth Gospel. He forfeited all of it for a few bags of gold and a few acres of land.

No earthly treasure is worth forfeiting Christ's eternal riches.

The God of Impossibilities

"But with God all things are possible."   (Matthew 19:26)

Following the sorrowful turning away of the rich young ruler who had just come to Jesus in his search for eternal life, our Lord employed his memorable hyperbole to illustrate a truth. "Again I tell you, it is easier for a camel to go through the eye of a needle than for a rich man to enter the kingdom of God" (v. 24). It is believed that he referred to the opening in the city gate, so narrow that it was known as a "needle's eye," and certainly not able to allow a camel to pass through. The disciples upon hearing this "were greatly astonished and asked, 'Who then can be saved?'" (v. 25). In response to their question Jesus declared, "With man this is impossible, but with God all things are possible."

Many things other than privilege and wealth can keep us from the kingdom of God. The "needle's eye" through which we cannot pass can be any number of obsessions as well as possessions that take hold of us and keep us from life's richest treasure. We may yield to the circumstances that crowd in upon us so that life's priorities get lost in the shuffle. It has been said that if a letter were sent to that most influential person called "circumstances," most of us could end it by saying, "I am, sir, your most obedient servant."

But what we cannot do for ourselves, God can do for us: when we turn to God he enables us to become what we ought to be and makes us an heir to eternal life. The songwriter Oscar Eliason put it this way:

> Got any rivers you think are uncrossable?
> Got any mountains you can't tunnel through?
> God specializes in things thought impossible.
> He can do what no other power can do!

"For I was hungry and you gave me something to eat, I was thirsty and you gave me something to drink, I was a stranger and you invited me in."   (Matthew 25:35)

This notable text is taken from the passage vividly depicting the Last Judgment (Matthew 25:31-46). It follows the *Parousia* parables dealing with the Lord's announcement that he will return in glory and judge all nations gathered before him, to be separated, symbolically, as sheep (the good people) and as goats (the wicked people).

Jesus said that to have shown compassion to those in need was as showing it to him, and to have withheld it was as withholding it from him. A deed of love "for one of the least of these" is a deed of love for Christ (v. 40). Mother Teresa beautifully exemplified this text when she said that in the face of every dying person she attended on the streets of Calcutta she saw Christ.

William Booth, founder of the Salvation Army, declared in his last public speech:

While women weep as they do now, I'll fight!
While little children go hungry as they do now, I'll fight!
While men go to prison, in and out, I'll fight!
While there is a drunkard left,
While there is a poor girl left upon the streets,
While there remains one dark soul without the light of God,
    I'll fight!
I'll fight to the very end!

These words became the Army's battle cry and its century-old dictum, "Heart to God, Hand to man," remains an enduring principle of this infantry of the Christian church. God cares and holds us responsible for others whose need lays claim upon our caring and compassion.

"Watch and pray so that you will not fall into temptation. The spirit is willing, but the body is weak." (Matthew 26:41)

There is no scene like this in all history. Amid the shadows and agonies of Gethsemane, Jesus fought a battle, the like of which there had never been. The salvation of the world hung in the balance as the tempter sought to deflect him from the cross. Here with the forces of good and evil locked in deadly combat, Christ took on his armor of prayer. In his supreme hour of trial, he poured out his soul in prayer.

To his sleeping disciples, he pleads, "Watch and pray, lest you enter into temptation. The spirit indeed is willing, but the flesh is weak" (KJV). This word of our Lord in Gethsemane becomes the watchword for each of us.

In the city of Krakow, Poland, a bugle sounds from the steeple of St. Mary's church, but always with the last note muted as though some disaster has overtaken the bugler. This ritual commemorates a heroic trumpeter who from the same tower seven centuries ago summoned the people to defend themselves as Mongol hordes stormed the city. As he was sounding the last note on his trumpet, an arrow from one of the Tartars struck and killed him. Thus the muffled note at the end.

In the garden of Gethsemane, Jesus sounded the bugle to pray. Surrounded by enemies ready to put him to death, he warned his closest followers to watch and pray. For each of us, the lesson of Gethsemane is the lesson of prayer.

"My God, my God, why have you forsaken me?"
(Matthew 27:46)

Words of the world's great men and women are chronicled in the books and libraries of the world. Many are engraved upon marble monuments. But the most sacred words of all are the words of Jesus, engraved upon the hearts of his followers. Among his immortal statements, the seven sayings from the cross are held in deepest reverence and devotion. They are as seven windows to the Savior's mind and soul in those moments when he took upon himself the world's burden of sin.

From the cross came an astonishing cry too deep for our understanding: "My God, my God, why have you forsaken me?" This fourth word from the cross is a cry of abandonment, quoted from the psalm of the cross (22:1), identifying with its prophecy. In this moment Jesus felt the utter loneliness and desolation of the cross as a result of the world's sin he bore.

This word of Christ from the cross is a mystery too sacred and profound for human comprehension. But we know it was our sin that caused that awful moment of aloneness. He loved us with such infinite love that he was willing to endure that abandonment. His heavenly Father had to turn his back on Calvary and enshroud it in darkness, as his beloved Son became the sin-bearer of humankind.

The cry itself, though an utterance of despair, yet takes hold of the eternal: "My God, my God!" In this final hour of supreme trial, he placed himself in the arms of God.

Because Christ uttered this word of desolation, we need never utter them.

The Great Commission

"Therefore go and make disciples of all nations, baptizing them in
the name of the Father and of the Son and of the Holy Spirit."
(Matthew 28:19)

Jesus here met with his eleven disciples on a mountain for this final event recorded in the Gospel of Matthew. There he declares his ultimate victory and preeminence: "All authority in heaven and on earth has been given to me" (v. 18).

In what has become known as the "Great Commission" Jesus sends forth his followers to make disciples, and in doing so institutes the "threefold formula" of what has become known as the Trinity. God's complete work is thus represented — God the Father as our Creator, God the Son as our Savior, and God the Holy Spirit as our Sanctifier.

It was this universal commission that prompted many early missionaries to go, at great sacrifice, throughout the world and bring the gospel where it had not yet been heard.

God's penman concludes and climaxes his manuscript with one of the most remarkable promises of Jesus: "And surely I am with you always, to the very end of the age."

When David Livingstone was asked what had sustained him in all the perils of his missionary work in Africa, he answered by quoting this verse. When his wife died in Africa, he helped prepare her body for burial; he helped make the coffin and lower it into the grave. Then he opened his New Testament, read this text, and said to his African comrades, "These are the words of a gentleman of the strictest and most sacred honor and He will keep His word. Let us now get on with our task."

The risen Christ still commissions his followers to go forth to our troubled and tortured world to witness of his saving grace and power. And surely, he will be with us!

"Come, follow me," Jesus said, "and I will make you fishers of men."
(Mark 1:17)

The moment had come for Jesus to pick his team. On their shoulders would rest the tremendous responsibility of building the kingdom of God.

Christ did not go to the Temple or to the halls of learning or power to find his men. He went along the shore of the Sea of Galilee. There he saw two brothers fishing, Peter and Andrew, and called to them, "Come, follow me, and I will make you fishers of men." The record states, "At once they left their nets and followed him." A short distance farther he called two other fishermen, James and John. Something magnetic and authoritative about Christ drew these two brothers to also leave their nets and follow Christ.

These ordinary men made up the inner circle of Christ. They were disciples in clay, the raw material with which Christ would build his kingdom. Peter was impulsive, Andrew outgoing, James and John had short fuses, earning them the nickname "sons of thunder." But our Lord saw in them the sturdy qualities of fishermen needed as disciples. He likened the catching of men to the skills and art of fishing. Without the right effort the nets would come up empty.

Little could these four men have realized that, as they left their nets and boats and fishing business, they were walking into the greatest adventure of history.

Christ today invites us. "Follow me," he calls, "and I will make you fishers of men." We will never have a better offer than that. Cecil Alexander has lyricized this calling of Christ to us:

Jesus calls us! O'er the tumult
Of our life's wild, restless sea,
Day by day His sweet voice soundeth,
Saying: Christian, follow me.

As of old apostles heard it
By the Galilean lake,
Turned from home and toil and kindred,
Leaving all for His dear sake.

"What good is it for a man to gain the whole world, yet forfeit his soul? Or what can a man give in exchange for his soul?"

(Mark 8:36-37)

This penetrating and rhetorical question of our Lord resonates across the centuries. Many prefer to gain even a small part of the world and forego the dubious gain of some future life. They choose the tangible over the intangible, the ephemeral over the eternal.

We are each a sum of our choices. Our decisions determine our destiny. Each life is confronted with the decision to choose Christ or the world, the material or the spiritual, the temporal or the eternal, the earthbound or the heavenly.

The beloved baritone voice of George Beverly Shea has blessed millions around the world in his solos just before Billy Graham's preaching. In his early manhood Shea was offered a lucrative contract to use his rich voice in another direction. He chose to use it for the Lord, and now for over half a century he has been part of the Billy Graham evangelistic team, blessing more people than any other Christian singer in history. A song he composed and has sung at countless crusades gives witness to his far-reaching choice:

> I'd rather have Jesus than silver or gold,
>   I'd rather be His than have riches untold;
> I'd rather have Jesus than houses or lands,
>   I'd rather be led by His nail-pierced hand.
>
> I'd rather have Jesus than men's applause,
>   I'd rather be faithful to His dear cause;
> I'd rather have Jesus than worldwide fame,
>   I'd rather be true to His holy name.

The Precious Children

"Let the little children come to me, and do not hinder them, for the kingdom of God belongs to such as these." (Mark 10:14)

According to the custom of the time, mothers would bring their children to be touched and blessed by a distinguished rabbi. Mothers with squirming and squealing babies pushing for a place in line to Jesus did not fit in with the disciples' priority for teaching by the Lord.

At the strong remonstrance of the disciples, Jesus flashed indignation. He not only comes to the defense of the children, but also commends their simple, uncomplicated childlikeness and guilelessness as keys to the kingdom.

Our Lord's strongest condemnation was pronounced against any who would hurt innocent, helpless children. He sternly warned, "It would be better for him if a millstone were hung around his neck, and he were drowned in the depths of the sea" (Matthew 18:6; Mark 9:42; Luke 17:2). This referred to the large millstone turned round and round by a donkey to grind grain. The nineteenth-century hymn by William Hutchings captures the story of our text:

When mothers of Salem
    Their children brought to Jesus,
The stern disciples drove them back,
    And bade them depart;
But Jesus saw them ere they fled,
    And sweetly smiled and kindly said:
Suffer the little children to come unto me.

"Love the Lord your God with all your heart and with all your soul and with all your mind and with all your strength."

(Mark 12:30)

A lawyer, in an attempt to trap Jesus, posed a probing and subtle question. There were no fewer than 613 commandments, 365 negative and 248 positive. How could one be chosen as supreme in that great body of religious law without slighting the rest?

But Christ, the master dialectician, distilled that entire body of 613 commandments to one central simplicity — love for God. Later, Augustine added his postscript, "Love God and do as you please!" For if we love God we would not violate those commandments that relate to our reverence and responsibility toward him.

Our Lord was quoting the text in Deuteronomy 6:5. However, Jesus added one dimension to the Deuteronomic text, that of loving God with "all our mind." With that addition he annexed the whole world of science and knowledge and intellectual discipline. In other words we are to love God with every faculty and the totality of our being: with all our heart — our affectional nature, with all our strength — our physical nature, with all our soul — our spiritual nature, and with all our mind — our intellectual nature.

Jesus then added the second greatest commandment: "Love your neighbor as yourself." It is obvious that if we love our neighbors we would not think of harming or doing any injustice toward them, but would work for their well-being.

"All the Law and the Prophets," added Jesus, "hang on these two commandments" (Matthew 22:40). On that day, morality took a quantum leap, from prohibition to love. May our lives ever be a living postscript to these two greatest commandments.

"He has risen! He is not here." (Mark 16:6)

"**H**e has risen" was the glorious announcement of the heavenly messenger to the women who came to the tomb to anoint the body of Jesus on that first Easter morning. Supposing we had seen someone die, and then two days later heard that he was alive. "He has risen!" — startling, stunning, incredible words, indeed.

No three words in history have ever counted for more than these words. Without doubt, they altered human destiny and turned the world upside down. Now, almost two millennia since first spoken, they still remain supremely significant, and no message is more needed today than just to know that Christ has risen and gives us hope.

Those three words passed like wildfire from lip to lip and heart to heart. They transformed the disciples, stunned the chief priests, and startled and amazed all who heard them.

Women were the first to hear this most amazing announcement. They ran back to tell the disciples, "He is risen!" Peter and John rushed to the tomb to see for themselves and within the hour were telling James, Philip, Nathaniel, and the rest, "He is risen!" All that day the words went winging from friend to friend and follower to follower. Women put aside household tasks and went next door to break the news to a neighbor. Children carried hastily scrawled notes to a friend or relative. The whisper of it grew until it became a triumphant chorus, a song of tumultuous joy — "He is risen!"

All other events of history pale before the awesome moment of this text. Let us, as the followers of old, ever live under the spell of them, and go forth to spread the news to our world around us.

I myself have carefully investigated everything from the beginning.
(Luke 1:3)

J esus Christ is the foundation upon which our faith is built. We must face the unassailable fact that virtually all we know about Jesus is what is recorded in the Gospels. Our Christian faith stands or falls on the credibility of the Gospels.

How reassuring then to come upon this preface in the Gospel of Luke in which he validates its authenticity. He does not base his life of Christ upon secondary sources but cites "eyewitnesses" for his account. The earliest biography of Alexander the Great was written by Plutarch more than four hundred years after Alexander's death, yet historians consider it trustworthy. In contrast, Luke's biography of Christ was written some forty years after his death, within the lifetimes of eyewitnesses of his life.

Luke asserts that he "carefully investigated everything from the beginning." The words "carefully" and "investigated" invest his writing with authority in his research. Luke also has given to us the history book of the New Testament, his Acts of the Apostles, these two books comprising one-fourth of the New Testament. Having confidence that this first-century journalist gives us an accurate record assures us that our faith is valid.

Astronaut John Glenn said of the compass that is used to guide airplanes in their flight: "Although we can't see, hear, or touch the force that runs the compass, we see it pointing a certain direction. All of us who fly have staked our lives thousands of times on the fact that this compass will give us the proper reading and will guide us where we should go."

We of the Christian faith can confidently stake our lives upon the Word of God, given to us by the inspiration of the Holy Spirit, and unerringly pointing us in the right direction.

Miracle in the Manger

She wrapped him in cloths and placed him in a manger.

(Luke 2:7)

Each Advent season brings to us once again the familiar story of the decree by Caesar Augustus that required Joseph and Mary to travel the eighty miles from Nazareth to Bethlehem, where the event of the ages took place: "While they were there, the time came for the baby to be born, and she gave birth to her firstborn, a son. She wrapped him in cloths and placed him in a manger, because there was no room for them in the inn."

What took place in that lowly manger in the cattle shed of Bethlehem those two millennia ago was the miracle and marvel of the ages. The Son of God stepped across the stars to become the Babe in Bethlehem's manger.

Imagine, God in a cradle! God in the lap of a virgin mother. The strangest event of history — God becoming clothed in human flesh — took place in a stable. No tongue of man or brain of scholar can explain this marvel, this mighty transition that wrapped Deity in the dust and burden of human flesh.

In our visit to the Holy Land we made the pilgrimage to the Church of the Nativity in Bethlehem, built by the emperor Constantine. Beneath the high altar of that church is the cave believed to have been the one in which the Christ child was born. In order to descend into the cave we had to stoop or kneel to enter. On the floor of the cave is a star and a Latin inscription, "Here Jesus Christ was born of the Virgin Mary." A beautiful truth is symbolized by the fact that the pilgrim must kneel to enter the birthplace of our Lord.

To ponder the mighty miracle in this simple text fills us with reverence and awe at the infinite love of God, unveiled in that manger. We are "lost in wonder, love and praise!"

There was no room for them in the inn. (Luke 2:7)

"No room at the inn." These words have become a familiar refrain of the Christmas story. The birth of Jesus took place in a cattle shed because the inn, where Mary and Joseph had stopped at the hour Mary was due to deliver, was full.

The innkeeper has been portrayed as the Mr. Scrooge of Bethlehem. There was no room for the Christ, who could have blessed his hostel with the marvel of the ages.

An anonymous poet has captured something of this saga of the innkeeper:

What could be done? The inn was full of folks
As Bethlehem had never seen before.
Of course, if I had known them, who they were,
And who was He that should be born that night
I would have turned the whole inn upside down,
And sent all the rest to stables.
And if He comes again, tell him,
That all my inn is His to make amends.
Alas, alas! To miss a chance like that!
This inn might be chief among them all —
The birthplace of the Messiah — Had I but known!

Today Christ comes and seeks admission, to make our hearts his abiding place. Let not our hearts be as the crowded inn with no time or room for the One who would bring his rich bounty of blessing. We cannot afford "to miss a chance like that!"

A Model for Growth

Jesus grew in wisdom and stature, and in favor with God and men.

(Luke 2:52)

D r. Luke, in the chronology of the life of Christ, gives us one of the intriguing and illuminating episodes in the Gospels. He ushers us into what is known as the "Silent Years" — that long interval between our Lord's birth and flight to Egypt until the beginning of his ministry at 30 years of age, giving us the only window into that unknown period.

When Jesus was 12 years old his parents made their annual pilgrimage to Jerusalem for the Feast of the Passover. On the return home, they discovered Jesus was missing. "When they did not find him, they went back to Jerusalem to look for him."

After three days they found him in the temple sitting among the teachers, listening to them and asking them questions. "Amazed" is the word used of the learned men with whom he discoursed. "Astonished" were his parents at this evidence of his precocity.

This illuminating episode culminates with the statement: "And Jesus grew in wisdom and stature, and in favor with God and men" (v. 52). Jesus grew in wisdom — intellectual growth; in stature — physical development; in favor with God — spiritual maturation; and in favor with men — social development.

God did not create us to be static. Each part of our being has great potential for development that we might reach our potential, and render our highest service. This portrait of the young manhood of Jesus is a model for the development of every person. Oliver Cromwell's inscription in his Bible can well serve as a motto for us all: "He who ceases to be better ceases to be good."

"Do to others as you would have them do to you."   (Luke 6:31)

The Golden Rule is one of the best known and most quoted of the teachings of Jesus. William Barclay in calling it "The Everest of Ethics" says, "With this commandment the Sermon on the Mount reaches its summit and its peak."

If this rule were practiced there would be no unkindness, violence, or wars in the world. Yet, though admired and praised, it is too seldom practiced. Why is it that we do not treat others in accordance with this rule? Why are there disputes, unkindness, and troubles between persons, families, and nations?

It is because we cannot practice the Golden Rule without the foundation of a commitment to Christ's total teaching and standards of his Sermon on the Mount. In order to practice this rule our own moral condition and standards need to be governed by Christ-centeredness and love, rather than self-centeredness and concern primarily for our own well-being. The Sermon on the Mount provides the foundation in the heart of the "be-attitudes" of love and consideration for others, needed to live out the Golden Rule.

We should all be grateful that God does not treat us as we deserve. We are unworthy of his love, yet he has showered his numberless blessings upon us. The Golden Rule was not meant to be praised, but to be practiced. Let us then treat others, not always as they may deserve, but as we would have them do to us.

"The harvest is plentiful but the workers are few."   (Luke 10:2)

T he Gospel records of Jesus that, "when he saw the crowds, he had compassion on them. . . . Then he said to his disciples, 'The harvest is plentiful but the workers are few'" (Matthew 9:36-37).

There is an urgency implied in the analogy of the harvest. It must be gathered in before the winter or it will be lost. The Lord's message is that there was no time to waste; days were hurrying by and God's work in the heart must take place before the harvest.

Workers were urgently needed, those willing to take on the hard and urgent task. God uses human instrumentality to get his work done. He wants laborers, not loiterers, workers not wishers, those who will go out into the field and help reap the harvest.

William Gladstone, the renowned Prime Minister of Great Britain, was one morning preparing an important speech to be delivered that day to Parliament. Early that morning, he heard a timid knock on his door at No. 10 Downing Street in London. He opened the door to a boy whose confidence and friendship he had earlier won. The boy said, "Mr. Gladstone, my brother is dying. Will you please come and show him the way to heaven?"

Leaving his important political work for the most important work any Christian can do, Gladstone soon arrived at the bedside of the dying boy and led him to the Savior.

Returning to his office, Gladstone wrote at the bottom of the speech he was preparing, "I am today the happiest man in England!"

For every Christian, there is no more important or rewarding work in the world than sharing our faith. Let us be among God's harvesters for the greatest work in the world.

"Go and do likewise."   (Luke 10:37)

The Parable of the Good Samaritan had its setting on the Jericho Road. Every thief in Palestine had heard of that seventeen-mile mountainous stretch known as the "bloody pass." This desolate terrain, and the number of travelers on it, made it a haven and happy hunting ground for bandits.

Jesus describes a man on the Jericho Road who is ambushed, robbed, beaten in true gangland style, and left by the side of the road. There he lay — bruised, broken, bleeding.

He's in luck, for here comes a priest! But Jesus says, "When the priest saw him he passed by on the other side." Theological propriety may have kept him from acting with compassion.

Next comes a Levite. How lucky can a victim get! Surely this man, whose life was the church, will stop and help. Jesus keeps his parable moving and says, "The Levite looked on him, and passed by on the other side." His motto may have been "safety first" or he may have been in a hurry to make a Jericho Improvement meeting!

But here comes a Samaritan! A "Samaritan"! The very term was a reproach to Jews. Quick glances were exchanged among listeners. Samaritans were the bitterest enemies of the Jews. "Surely," thought some, "the Samaritan might just finish him off." The wounded traveler could have no claim on him. The Samaritan could excuse himself from the bother of stopping much more easily than the priest or Levite.

But instead, the Samaritan demonstrated a concept of brotherhood that transcended prejudices of race, differences in creed, and enmities rooted in history. He tended the wounded man, took him to an inn, paid the bill, and offered to cover any further needs.

The Jericho Road stretches around the world. It is near at hand to each of us, calling for our caring and compassion, for a Christianity with its sleeves rolled up, binding the wounds of broken humanity. "Go and do likewise" was the final word of Jesus to his hearers, and to us. Jesus calls us to a vulnerable involvement amid the agonies of our world.

"Father, forgive them, for they do not know what they are doing."
(Luke 23:34)

J esus' first word from the cross was, "Father." His first utterance was a prayer: "Father, forgive them, for they do not know what they are doing."

When righteousness seemed trampled underfoot and wrong triumphant, when his body quivered with the pain of the flogging and the spikes of the cross, when his soul felt the even sharper sword of desertion and betrayal, when every breath was a pain and every heartbeat an agony, Jesus still was able to say, "Father."

This utterance to heaven from Golgotha is the highest reach of faith known to man. When it seemed God's hand was withdrawn from the rudder of the universe, Jesus called out to his Father. It was an acknowledgment of the authority of God in spite of the misrule of men. It evoked the presence of God in life's most desolate moment. It testified to the love of God triumphant over the violence of man. It demonstrated the care of God amid life's cruelty and callousness.

This first word of the cross reminds us that when life comes tumbling down, we too may know the unfailing presence of God our Father. It assures us we need never bear life's crosses alone. It also teaches us the lesson of forgiveness. Tradition has it that these words were spoken as soldiers were driving the spikes through our Lord's hands and feet. The teachings and the example of Jesus beautifully intersected at Calvary, and serve as a model for our faith and striving toward holiness.

"I tell you the truth, today you will be with me in paradise."
(Luke 23:43)

Two thieves were crucified with Jesus, one on each side of him. Any beautiful dreams they may ever have had now turned into a horrible nightmare. There was nothing behind them but error, nothing before them but terror, nothing behind them but the ashes of a misspent life, nothing before them but the eternal fires of Hell.

The first thief joined in the taunts and sneers, "If you are the Messiah save yourself and us!" Then the other says, "Don't you fear God? We are getting what our deeds deserve. But this man has done nothing wrong." Turning to the One impaled next to him, he pleaded, "Jesus, remember me when you come into your kingdom." The final plea of a life with its hands quite empty laid hold on the grace of our Lord Jesus Christ.

Here was a man with one foot in eternity. Life was ebbing from him. A dying man does not look to another dying man for salvation, but this man did! He saw in Christ the Victor over death, the gateway to life eternal. He asked only to be remembered, knowing that if Christ remembered him, he need have no fear for eternity.

Christ replied: "Today you will be with me in paradise." What a day it turned out to be for the dying thief! When he awakened that Friday morning, A.D. 33, he was a thief and condemned criminal. But by midday he was converted; by nightfall in paradise. Every soul finds its true destiny when it meets Jesus Christ. May we affirm with the hymn writer William Cowper:

> The dying thief rejoiced to see
> that fountain in his day,
> And there may I, though vile as he,
> wash all my sins away.

The Word of Victory

"Father, into your hands I commit my spirit."   (Luke 23:46)

Luke records that this word from the cross was spoken "with a loud voice." It was not as though in a final weak effort he managed to mumble these words. Jesus was the Master of death. He was not death's victim, but its Victor.

This word of victory by Christ makes it possible for us to share in his triumph over death. The apostle Paul exulted in this glorious truth: "Where, O death, is your victory? But thanks be to God! He gives us the victory through our Lord Jesus Christ" (1 Corinthians 15:55, 57).

This final word from the cross was a quote of Psalm 31:5. Jesus had so saturated his heart and mind with Scripture that it came naturally to him in the hour of death. For us too, the promises of God can be our anchor amid the storms of life and in our final "putting out to sea."

Jesus had left heaven for thirty-three long years. Now he was going to be reunited with his Father and all the host of heaven. We too can look forward to that grand reunion with those of the family of God, those, in the words of Tennyson, "whom we have loved and long since lost awhile."

The surest thing about life is death. May God grant us grace so that when our life has run its course we may be able to pray, "Father, into your hands I commit my spirit."

"Were not our hearts burning within us while he talked with us on the road and opened the Scriptures to us?" (Luke 24:32)

For the two crestfallen disciples on the dusty road to Emmaus, their sun had set when Jesus had been taken down from the cross and placed in a tomb. Their bright promise of tomorrow had been shattered by the tragic frustration of yesterday.

As they talked about these things Jesus himself drew near, but they did not recognize him. Cleopas and his unnamed companion shared the reason for their obvious sadness, following which "beginning with Moses and all the prophets, he explained to them what was said in all the Scriptures concerning himself" (v. 27). What an exposition that must have been, the Light of the World illuminating the word!

At the end of their journey they invited Jesus to linger with them. As he broke bread they recognized him, and then he disappeared from their sight. In that moment of awareness they jubilantly exclaimed, "Were not our hearts burning within us while he talked with us on the road and opened the Scriptures to us?" Christ had walked and talked with them until those seven miles of country road seemed as a golden path.

We too may be called upon to walk a road of shattered dreams, dashed hopes, disappointment, and sorrow. But we also may find that the Christ of the human road draws near to commune with us and open the luminous meaning of Scripture for our need. The old song has expressed it beautifully:

He's the Christ of the human road,
And He offers to carry our load,
In all times of need He's a true friend indeed,
This Christ of the human road.

The Promise

"I am going to send you what my Father has promised; but stay in the city until you have been clothed with power from on high."

(Luke 24:49)

This text records the final words of our Lord, spoken just before his ascension. He tells his disciples that he will soon send to them the promise of his Father for them. To what promise was Jesus referring? And why, in his final moment on earth, does he single this out as the special promise among all the promises of God?

It was what God had promised through the prophet Joel in the eighth century B.C.: "I will pour out my Spirit on all people" (2:28). It was the same promise repeated a century later by Isaiah: "I will pour out my Spirit on your offspring" (44:3). The promise was renewed a century later by Ezekiel: "I will put my Spirit in you" (36:27).

Of all the promises, this was preeminent, because all others are of God's gifts to us. But in this promise God offers the greatest gift that can ever be given — the gift of the Giver. It is no less than a promise of the gift of God himself to the believer, the Third Person of the Trinity to empower and dwell within the life of the Christian.

It is an unparalleled promise, the heritage of every child of God. The Holy Spirit is God's most precious gift to us, the very gift of his coming to dwell within us. Without the Holy Spirit there can be no regeneration, no cleansing, no empowering, no anointing for service, no divine comfort, no fruit of the Spirit. The Holy Spirit, singled out and promised in the last words of our Lord to his followers, is the Christian's indispensable gift.

Let us each day claim this heritage from God.

In the beginning was the Word, and the Word was with God, and the Word was God. (John 1:1)

This verse has been described by one Bible commentator as the most breathtaking opening in any piece of literature. John, who had the most intimate contact with Christ, launches his mighty manuscript with three transcendent truths about Christ, the Word.

First, he makes the staggering claim of the eternity of Christ — he was "in the beginning." Our finite mind cannot grasp this attribute of the Lord; we can but stand in awe at its mystery and majesty. We are but a child of the hour in which we were born, a brief momentary episode in eternity. But Christ is the Timeless One. He always was. He is the Unbeginning One as well as the Unending One.

Second, Christ was part of the divine fellowship — "the Word was with God." John climaxes his opening statement with the most unambiguous assertion about the divinity of Christ to be found in the Bible — "and the Word was God." John had seen his mighty miracles, had seen the risen Lord, and had witnessed his ascension. He knew beyond the shadow of a doubt that Christ was divine. His own great purpose was to tell the good news to all the world, and he did so by this incomparable record of the life and lordship of Christ.

The Greek word *logos*, translated "Word," is one of the titles of Christ, combining the idea of expression and wisdom. Jesus was God expressed in a new and living language. He was God's supreme articulation.

The Grand Miracle

The Word became flesh and lived for a while among us.

(John 1:14)

"The Word became flesh and blood, and moved into the neighborhood. We saw the glory with our own eyes, the one-of-a-kind glory, like Father, like Son" — Eugene Peterson's paraphrase in *The Message* — clothes this timeless truth in our idiom. Malcolm Muggeridge opens his book *Jesus* with the seminal statement: "The coming of Jesus into the world is the most stupendous event of human history." C. S. Lewis calls the Incarnation, God becoming man, "the grand miracle."

G. K. Chesterton, in *The Everlasting Man*, has expressed it memorably: "Right in the middle of all these things stands up an enormous exception. It is quite unlike anything else. It is news that seems too good to be true. It is nothing less than the loud assertion that this mysterious maker of the world has visited his world in person." Indeed, God in Christ, "moving into the neighborhood," is the "enormous exception" of all history.

Astronaut James Irwin had the extraterrestrial thrill of driving a vehicle on another world, discovering the Genesis rock, and seeing the planet Earth suspended in space as an iridescent jewel. The commander of *Apollo 15*, who knew the spine-tingling experience of walking on the moon, put the Incarnation in perspective for us. He testified upon his return, "God walking on the earth in Christ is far more important than man walking on the moon."

Wonder of wonders, this grand miracle of the ages was all on our behalf!

"Look, the Lamb of God, who takes away the sin of the world!"

(John 1:29)

J ohn the Baptist heralds the Lord's coming and mission with the stunning announcement: "Look, the Lamb of God, who takes away the sin of the world!" Peter later records that we were redeemed "with the precious blood of Christ, a lamb without blemish or defect" (1 Peter 1:19). From Adam, all humankind has inherited original sin. From Christ comes the universal remedy.

But someone asks, "How can the sacrifice of One avail for all?" The answer is in the worth of the One who made the sacrifice. When Christ sacrificed himself as the Lamb of God, it was not an ordinary man who died. It was God himself. Thus his sacrifice has infinite merit.

In Revelation, John the seer portrays Christ as the Lamb no fewer than twenty-nine times. But it is not the familiar figure found in the fourth Gospel. A different word is used for "lamb," and Christ is portrayed as the exalted Lamb of God at the celestial throne who has accomplished the redemption of God's people.

May we one day gather with that innumerable host around the throne of God and raise our voices in the great doxology: "Worthy is the Lamb, who was slain, to receive power and wealth and wisdom and strength and honor and glory and praise!" (Revelation 5:12).

"You must be born again." (John 3:7)

How intriguing that Nicodemus, as "a member of the ruling council," a leader and lay theologian of the Jews, sought out an itinerant teacher to enquire about the kingdom of God. At the start of his midnight interview with Jesus he made the astonishing acknowledgment: "Rabbi, we know you are a teacher who has come from God. For no one could perform the miraculous signs you are doing if God were not with him."

Jesus came directly to the heart of the matter, replying, "I tell you the truth, unless a man is born again he cannot see the kingdom of God" (3:3). This mystical statement was not quite what Nicodemus expected. He was compelled to ask, "How can a man be born when he is old? . . .Surely he cannot enter a second time into his mother's womb to be born!" (v. 4).

It is a new life generated by the Spirit, explained Jesus, a supernatural act of God within the human heart. To be born again is to undergo such a radical change that it is like a new birth, as being born all over again. It is as powerful and mysterious as the wind. It is a change of our very nature; we become "a new creation" in Christ (2 Corinthians 5:17). There can be no salvation without regeneration, no life eternal without the transforming experience in Christ of the new birth.

The word "you" in the Greek is plural, for which we have no English equivalent. These words to Nicodemus announced the invariable requisite for all humankind.

Let us be sure that we are among the twice born; for to be born once is to die twice, but to be born twice is to die once!

"For God so loved the world that he gave his one and only Son."
                                                    (John 3:16)

This golden text is one of the most beloved in the Bible, a towering peak of eternal truth in the Word of God. John 3:16 has been called "the gospel in a nutshell."

It speaks to us of the divine Person, God the Father — "For God." Its truth deals with the Infinite, the Ultimate Reality, our Creator and heavenly Father.

It speaks to us of the divine passion — "so loved." It would have been incredible enough for God to love us. But this verse speaks to us of the intensity and the passion of his love for us.

It speaks to us of the divine provision — "He gave his one and only Son" signifies the incalculable divine sacrifice. The NIV rendition, "his one and only Son," denotes the unique and special relationship between the Father and the Son.

We often contemplate the sacrifice of the Son, but this verse would remind us of the sacrifice of God the Father. For thirty-three years the Godhead was impoverished as our Lord left his Father's home and took on himself our finiteness and infirmities. It was his only Son whom he saw endure the shame, the mockery, the cruelty, the violence of men. Some have suggested that the darkness that veiled Calvary at the crucifixion was because God could not bear to look on that scene of the unspeakable suffering of his Son.

For whom was this sacrifice on the part of God the Father? Our text speaks to us of the person — "whoever believes." If you are a Christian believer, this was all for you! God loves you, made the supreme sacrifice for you, and as the remainder of the verse declares, he will give you eternal life!

The Bread of Life

"I am the bread of life." (John 6:35)

The multitude had witnessed the miracle of the feeding of the five thousand with the five loaves and two fishes. To escape the press of the crowd, Jesus crossed over the lake, but the people followed him. Their enquiries revealed that they were still looking for his miraculous loaves. However, Jesus pointed to the Giver and said, "I am the bread of life."

Christ discerned that the seeking of the crowd was for the material rather than for the spiritual. He said, "You are looking for me, not because you saw miraculous signs but because you ate the loaves and had your fill" (v. 26).

Have we not at times sought, even in religion, the temporal instead of the eternal, the shadowy instead of the substantial? The transient pleasures, the phantom charms, the evanescent fame and success are as bubbles. They sparkle, and like children we reach out to them only to find that when we grasp them their charm vanishes.

Jesus in this text refers to the deeper hunger of life, a hunger that no earthly bread can satisfy. Only Christ, who is the bread of life, can satisfy the deepest hunger and yearning of our soul.

We need to take Christ into our inmost being, to assimilate the truths and the reality of his presence into our daily lives. He will sustain us and replenish our spent strength.

"I am the light of the world."   (John 8:12)

Wbat light is to the earth, Jesus is to humankind. Light is indispensable to life. It is a great mystery, yet it is one of man's greatest friends. In many ways physical light is analogous to the One who is the light of the world.

The world needs light. It cannot exist or survive without it. Darkness and barrenness would prevail without light. Nothing could grow; nothing could live.

Light is the great revealer. The beautiful flowers, the majestic mountains, are obscured in inky blackness until they are rescued from the night and bathed in the sunlight. Christ releases the hidden splendor within us and clothes life with beauty.

Light guides. In the dark we may easily stumble and fall. Light makes possible a sense of direction and destiny. Christ guides us each step of our pilgrim way.

Light permeates. It travels at its phantom speed of 186,000 miles a second, unhindered by space and time. Christ transcends the barriers of time and space.

Light is pure. Water may start out as a pure spring but becomes impure when it comes close to man's habitations. Wind and air become contaminated with man's toxic chemicals. But light may shine through the foulest medium and yet remain pure. Christ mingled amid earth's moral pollution and yet remained spotlessly pure.

May the devotional verse of George Matheson be our prayer:

O Light that followest all my way,
I yield my flickering torch to thee;
My heart restores its borrowed ray,
That in thy sunshine's blaze its day
    May brighter, fairer be.

"I am the good shepherd." (John 10:11)

The portrait of the good shepherd is delineated in the beloved 23rd Psalm and other shepherd passages. The shepherd of the East had a much more intimate relationship with his sheep than the shepherd of the West, knowing each by name (John 10:3).

"He goes on ahead of them" (10:4). The shepherd did not drive his sheep; he led them. Christ has journeyed before us through life's thorn-grown wilderness. The good shepherd led his sheep safely from a rushing current that might sweep the flock to destruction, or from an approaching predator. Our Good Shepherd protects us from the deadly enemies of our soul.

The context of this verse also portrays the heart of the good shepherd. "When he saw the crowds, he had compassion on them, because they were harassed and helpless, like sheep without a shepherd" (Matthew 9:36). We, like sheep, are often foolish and prone to wander. His is an urgent, active love on our behalf.

In Luke 15:4-6, Jesus likens himself to the shepherd who had a hundred sheep. Ninety-nine were safe in the fold and one was lost. The shepherd went into the wilderness, sought and found the lost sheep. He brought it back on his shoulders and called his neighbors to celebrate with him: "Rejoice with me; I have found my lost sheep." We were each the lost sheep that he sought and found.

Jesus said, "The good shepherd lays down his life for the sheep" (John 10:11). His love for us was so great that he laid down his life to save us. It is a blessed assurance to be sheep in the safe keeping of his green pasture.

"I am the resurrection and the life. He who believes in me will live,
even though he dies."   (John 11:25)

T hese words were spoken in the midst of a drama of human death
and gloom. It is an agony well known to the human race, as the
tender ties of affection are severed. The little home of Bethany that had
so often been a retreat and a haven of rest for the Master had now become a morgue of gloom and dismay. Lazarus had died.

In this darkest of settings Jesus performs his greatest miracle, raising Lazarus from the dead, and gives us one of his most radiant titles.
Many consider this the climax of his "I am" statements, a supreme expression of his authority over life and death.

In the history of humankind, there was another momentous day
that seemed ominous with defeat. When the decisive battle of Water-
loo was fought, the people of London anxiously awaited the outcome.
From the top of Winchester Cathedral came the message by sema-
phore code, "Wellington defeated" and then a blanket of fog veiled the
signalers. London was in deep despair; all seemed lost. But later that
day the fog lifted and again the message was signaled. Again they read,
"Wellington defeated" — but this time there was more to the message.
It read, "Wellington defeated the enemy." Gloom changed to glory, despair to delight. Tragedy had become triumph.

So too when the fog had lifted following Calvary, the glorious message passed like wildfire, "He is risen!" Defeat was changed into victory. Christ became the great Victor over death instead of its victim.
Christ the Mighty Conqueror came and cut the Gordian knot of death
by the decisive thrust of his resurrection. May we ever be kept under
the spell of his mighty resurrection and promise of immortality.

"Do not let your hearts be troubled. Trust in God; trust also in me."

(John 14:1)

This golden text is taken from the longest and most sacred discourse of Christ — his farewell message to his disciples in the Upper Room (John 13–17). They usher us into the Holy of Holies in the life of our Lord. His words float as soft music through the night air, with eternity in every word.

To the disciples, Jesus had been their dearest friend, their leader, and the One upon whom all their hopes had been cast. Now he announces that he will be leaving them and they will not be able to follow where he is going. On this eve of his departure, to his bewildered and grief-stricken disciples, he imparts his words of comfort that have resonated across the centuries: "Do not let your hearts be troubled. Trust in God; trust also in me. In my Father's house are many rooms; if it were not so, I would have told you. I am going there to prepare a place for you. And if I go and prepare a place for you, I will come back and take you to be with me that you also may be where I am" (14:1-3).

We too will face days of trouble, even of danger and, as the disciples of old, the dread of separation and death. Jesus gives the antidote to trouble — trust in God. Faith will give the victory that will enable us to overcome whatever difficulties may come our way.

The assuring word of Jesus to his disciples and followers of all ages is: "I will not leave you as orphans; I will come to you" (14:18). He announces to his inner circle in that Upper Room that he will send another, the divine Paraclete — the Holy Spirit, who will abide with his followers (John 16:7). Our Lord's bequest to each of us is the Holy Spirit, who dwells within us, empowers us and makes us adequate.

"I am the way."   (John 14:6)

J esus had just said some astonishing things to his disciples. Here, in his farewell discourse in the Upper Room, he had spoken of his Father's house and mansions and going away where the disciples would not be able to follow. These mystical statements were too much for Thomas with his practical bent of mind. He was constrained to ask, "How can we know the way?"

Thomas's question, "How can we know the way?," comes echoing down the centuries. It is the pivotal question that every life must ask. We are glad Thomas asked it, for in response we have one of the radiant textual jewels of the Bible. In reply, Jesus declared, "I am the way and the truth and the life. No one comes to the Father except through me."

Other religions and cults claim they are the way. Science and technology offer their panacea for the world's ills. Many succumb to the spurious claims of drugs, sex, hedonism, materialism. In our world of sharply conflicting claims and ideologies, how can we know the way?

Above the clamor of all other voices, we hear from our text the authoritative voice of Christ, declaring: "I am the way!" He did not say he is a way among many other ways. He stated, "I am THE way." He is the only way. All other ways are dead ends.

"I am . . . the truth." (John 14:6)

"I am the truth" is the second of this great trilogy of titles Jesus gives in response to the bewildered question of Thomas in the Upper Room. God's truth was incarnate in Jesus. He was without dissimulation, his life and words totally authentic. Jesus is not only the way we must follow, he is the infallible and sovereign truth we must believe. In Christ we find the truth that makes us free.

There has never been a greater need to know the truth than in our day of deceit and duplicity. For many, deception has become a way of life; for nations, it is often a policy. What sage or Solomon of today can discern the truth between the conflicting claims that make the headlines of every day's news?

Dr. M. Scott Peck, integrating the insights of psychology and religion in his book *People of the Lie,* makes the statement, "Wherever there is evil, there's a lie around. Evil always has something to do with lies." This best-selling author has no illusion about the source of lies: "I know no more accurate epithet for Satan than the Father of Lies."

How easy to lie, even for religious people. Lying takes many subtle forms — exaggerations to make impressions, shading the truth on an income tax return or a compensation form, lack of complete truth in appealing for funds, twisting a meaning to gain a point, offering a false excuse to cover a failure or protect our image.

In this day when it may seem, as James Russell Lowell expressed it, "Truth forever on the scaffold," Christ, the Truth, calls each of us to the high standard of truth, to be authentic in all our communications and relationships.

"I am . . . the life."   (John 14:6)

"I am the life" is the final title of this sublime trilogy given by Christ in the Upper Room. It is an astonishing statement. Any other person would have to say, "I am a life." But Christ declared, "I am *the* life." Once again the definite article makes our Lord's statement resonate as a seminal truth.

The life in our cosmos is derived from the provision and providence of the Trinity. The air we breathe, the water we drink, the food we eat, our very being — all comes to us by divine providence.

Dag Hammarskjöld, in diary selections published under the title *Markings,* records an incisive comment on the tragedy of missing out on life: "He was a member of the crew of Columbus' caravel. He kept wondering whether he would get back to his home village in time to succeed the old shoemaker before anyone else could grab his job." We smile — but what trivialities do we permit to dominate our lives? What petty ambitions or obsessions keep us from life's richest discoveries, its immortal quests?

Christ helps us become the best that we can be. In him we become creative, productive, our potential most fully actualized. The Lord is also our Source of eternal life.

In response to this text, let our prayer be:

Christ the Way, lead me, for without You there is no going.
Christ the Truth, illumine me, for without You there is
    no knowing.
Christ the Life, live in me, for without You there is no growing.

"I have told you this so that my joy may be in you and that your joy may be complete."   (John 15:11)

"Joy is the gigantic secret of the Christian," writes G. K. Chesterton. William Barclay reminds us that "joy is one of the commonest New Testament words." The Christian life is not a drag but a delight, not a bother but a beatitude, not an endurance but an enjoyment.

"The mark of a saint is the ability to laugh," is the observation of Thomas Merton. There is nothing frivolous about the fun of a Christian. He takes seriously his delight of life. In Paul's listing of the fruit of the Spirit, joy is the runner-up virtue, right after love.

This fullness of joy is a recurring theme in John's writing. Earlier in his Gospel he quotes our Lord's words that speak of the abundant life: "I have come that they may have life, and that they may have it more abundantly" (John 10:10 NKJV). In my series of treasured devotional books by E. Stanley Jones, long out of print, he writes in his preface to *Abundant Living*, "The business of life is to live and to live well and adequately and abundantly. But this age knows almost everything about life except how to live it. We are long on analysis and short on synthesis."

Jesus calls us to Life with a capital L. He gives us "the gigantic secret" for joy. He calls us to the abundant life, life that is full, life that is fruitful, and life that is felicitous.

"As my Father hath sent me, even so send I you."

(John 20:21 KJV)

A s the disciples met in fear behind locked doors, the risen Christ appeared and encouraged them with his words, "Peace be with you." Peace was just what they needed, as they mourned the loss of Christ and feared for their own safety from his enemies.

But now the mission that Christ had started must go on. To these men, and to followers who could come after, would be entrusted the proclamation of the gospel's redeeming message. Before his departure from them, Christ commissioned them, "As the Father hath sent me, even so send I you."

But the mission to which Christ called was beyond them. They would need a superhuman resource and power. For the mission before them, that is exactly what Christ gave to them: "He breathed on them and said, 'Receive the Holy Spirit'" (v. 22). To all who would be his disciples, Christ speaks the same words of commission and enablement. E. Margaret Clarkson has incorporated our text in her familiar hymn:

So send I you — to take to souls in bondage
The word of truth that sets the captive free,
To break the bonds of sin, to loose death's fetters —
So send I you, to bring the lost to me.

So send I you — My strength to know in weakness,
My joy in grief, My perfect peace in pain,
To prove the power, My grace, My promised presence —
So send I you, eternal fruit to gain.

"But you will receive power when the Holy Spirit comes on you."
(Acts 1:8)

W hat were the very last words of our Lord while here on earth? With angels hovering near, and harps of glory sounding in his ears, to his disciples — weak, persecuted, faced with a formidable task, he assured them: "But you will receive power when the Holy Spirit comes on you." This is the key verse in the book of Acts, and the key to victory for the follower of Christ. It announces the priority and the power of the Christian faith.

"You will be my witnesses," declared Jesus. Evangelism, the proclamation of the gospel, became the priority for the Christian church. A Christian leader had a motto on his wall to remind him of what his work was to be about: "The main thing is to keep the main thing the main thing." This golden text identifies the priority for the Christian church and the Christian. We are to be witnesses for Christ. We must beware of the danger of becoming "keepers of the aquarium instead of 'fishers of men.'"

"You will receive power when the Holy Spirit comes on you." The Holy Spirit is the dynamic that enables us to meet the demands of the Christian life. He is the explosive and expulsive power that makes us more than conquerors in Christ.

An "old-time" chorus offers a prayer needed by each follower of Christ:

The old-time power, Lord I am seeking today.
The old-time power will help me to watch and to pray.
Life's too short to trifle; I need thee every hour.
Come, Lord, and give us again, the old-time power.

"And everyone who calls on the name of the Lord will be saved."

(Acts 2:21)

This golden text comes to us from the first Christian sermon ever preached, that by Peter on the day of Pentecost. It set a preaching standard — biblically based, Holy Spirit anointed, and Christ-centered. Peter put in perspective God's plan of redemption with the fulfillment of prophecy in the incarnate life, atoning death, and triumphant resurrection and exaltation of Christ, and the coming of the Holy Spirit, all in 569 words!

In the heart of Peter's sermon was the proclamation of God's gracious offer of salvation: "And everyone who calls on the name of the Lord will be saved." Good preacher that he was, Peter "drew the net," calling his hearers to repentance and to receive forgiveness of sins and the gift of the Holy Spirit. "About three thousand were added to their number that day," which brought to 3,120 the initial membership in the church born on that day.

Salvation came to those who called "on the name of the Lord." Peter later declared, "There is no other name under heaven given to men by which we must be saved" (Acts 4:12). An anonymous poet reminds us of the wonder-working power in the name of Jesus:

I know a soul that is steeped in sin,
That no man's art can cure;
But I know a Name, a Name, a Name,
That can make that soul all pure.

"It is more blessed to give than to receive." (Acts 20:35)

This verse is set in the context of Paul's moving farewell speech as he met with the elders of the church in Ephesus before going on to Jerusalem where danger awaited. He said that none of them "will ever see [him] again." He enjoined them to keep watch over themselves and "Be shepherds of the church of God, which he bought with his own blood" (20:28).

The apostle gave an account of his faithful stewardship, and before they knelt by the seashore, prayed, and tearfully embraced, he gave to them his final benediction: "Now I commit you to God and to the word of his grace, which can build you up and give you an inheritance among all those who are sanctified" (20:32).

Paul reminded his hearers that he had supplied his own needs and the needs of his companions. He stated that the Christian life is expressed in the servant role — that of "hard work" and to "help the weak." Then he quoted the highest source for his now familiar dictum, "the words the Lord Jesus himself said: 'It is more blessed to give than to receive.'"

These words reverse the world's order of values, which believes that it is more blessed to receive. But the Christian's model is Christ, who made the ultimate sacrifice of himself so that we might know the eternal riches of the kingdom.

Years ago we found among the papers of my saintly mother-in-law the handwritten lines: "What I spent — I had; what I kept — I lost; what I gave — I have." The love and grace that emanated from her life remain an enduring legacy. In the grand paradox of Christian living, it is only what we give in life that remains.

I am not ashamed of the gospel, because it is the power of God for the salvation of everyone who believes.   (Romans 1:16)

O f Paul's thirteen epistles, Romans holds the preeminence, as both the longest and the weightiest. John R. W. Stott writes: "The Epistle to the Romans is the fullest and most coherent manifesto of the Christian gospel." Romans is the quintessence of the mind and theology of the apostle Paul, where he unfolds the whole plan of salvation and the implications of the gospel.

In this first chapter, Paul strikes the keynote of the entire letter: "I am not ashamed of the gospel, because it is the power of God for the salvation of everyone who believes." The heart of Paul's theology is the doctrine of salvation.

Paul himself had experienced its amazing power that transformed him from "the chief of sinners" to a devoted follower of Christ, from the persecutor into the peerless professor of the faith. He had also witnessed its transforming power in the lives of the many who believed its message.

Its power avails for "everyone who believes." There is no aristocracy of privilege; the power of the gospel is available to all. The ground is level at the foot of the cross.

The apostle was not ashamed of the gospel; rather it became the irrepressible theme of his life and preachment. Its good news was utterly new on the scene of history, declaring God's love and intervention on man's behalf through Christ. There had never been, nor will there ever be, a greater and more powerful message than that. May we know and ever unashamedly proclaim its life-changing power.

A Liberating Text

"The righteous will live by faith." (Romans 1:17)

This verse proclaims the central theme of Paul's epistle to the Romans, as he flings out the great truth that became pivotal in the history of Christendom, quoted from Habakkuk 2:4, and also recorded in Galatians 3:11.

In 1515 Martin Luther, Augustinian monk and doctor of theology, as he was preparing his lectures from the book of Romans, came to the trenchant truth of our text, "The just shall live by faith." A lightning bolt of truth flashed upon his soul. The brilliant light of that text lit the great fires of the Reformation that spread as a conflagration around the world. Luther's soul became liberated from the legalism that had mastered him, and this Romans text became the battle cry of the Reformation that changed the course of history.

On May 24, 1838, a spark from that fire fell upon the soul of John Wesley, who upon reading Luther's preface to Romans recorded in his journal, "I felt my heart strangely warmed." The fire that warmed Wesley's heart in that moment spread to light the fires of the evangelical revival.

The God who spoke through this text to Luther and Wesley, and to succeeding generations, also calls each of us to the liberating reality of living by faith.

For all have sinned and fall short of the glory of God.

(Romans 3:23)

W e were born with a genetic endowment from which no one is immune. David put it memorably in his prayer of penitence: "Surely I was sinful at birth, sinful from the time my mother conceived me" (Psalm 51:5). At the Fall, the venom of sin entered the bloodstream of humanity, and we are by nature prone to disobedience to God's will. Sin is a rebellion against God with devastating consequences.

Sin is in our DNA, a spiritual condition we inherit from our first parents, Adam and Eve, in their rebellion against God. Sin is also a conduct, our own acts of disobedience to the will of God for our lives. In these two ways, by condition and conduct, we are all sinners.

In our culture the very concept of sin is an endangered species, under threat of extinction. It is common to view sins as nothing more than mistakes, rather like minor traffic offenses. Such a superficial attitude to sin reflects a failure to realize the immensity of man's moral plight before God.

The New Testament Greek word for "sin" is *hamartia*. It means to miss the mark. It is a shooting word. Sin is missing the target of life God has for us, missing the high goal of what we ought to be. Sin is failure to realize life's potential as ordained by God.

"All have sinned." Sin is a universal malady, a spiritual cancer of the soul, fatal unless treated with the only cure provided for it. For this universal malady God has provided a universal remedy, the salvation of Christ, procured at Calvary for whomsoever.

*The wages of sin is death, but the gift of God is eternal life in Christ
Jesus our Lord.* (Romans 6:23)

The apostle Paul here uses a double metaphor to teach a twofold
truth. Wages are earned. We have earned death. But God has given
us the free gift of eternal life.

Sin leads to tragic separation from God and servitude to sin, which
in the end earns God's decree of death. It is not so much that God sends
judgment upon man as the fact that the sinner brings judgment upon
himself, for evil is ultimately self-destructive.

This is powerfully illustrated in the story connected with Leo-
nardo da Vinci's masterpiece, "The Last Supper." Long and in vain the
artist sought for a model for his Christ. At length he found a young
man who sat in the choir of a church in Rome, named Pietro
Bandinelli. He was not only a young man of beautiful countenance, but
of a pure and beautiful life. "At last I have found the face I wanted," exclaimed da Vinci.

Years passed on, and still the great painting was not finished. The
eleven faithful apostles had all been sketched on the canvas, and the
artist was hunting for a model for his Judas. Long and far he searched
until one day in the streets of Rome he came upon a beggar in rags,
with a face of such villainous stamp that even the artist was repulsed.
But he knew that at last he had found his Judas to sit as his model.
Upon completion of the painting da Vinci said, "I have not yet asked
your name, but I will now." "Pietro Bandinelli," replied the man. He,
whose fair face had been the inspiration for the face of Christ, had now
become so disfigured by the sins of his life that no trace was left of the
beauty that had been the admiration of men.

The wages of sin is death. However, our text ends with the exultant
truth, followed by that all-important word "but" — "the gift of God is
eternal life in Christ Jesus our Lord."

For what I want to do I do not do, but what I hate I do.

(Romans 7:15)

In the seventh chapter of Romans the apostle Paul lays bare his heart and soul. In this moving spiritual autobiography Paul reveals the duality he found in his nature — a civil war within his soul — his struggle between the carnal and spiritual natures.

Paul's use of the word "war" in the context is apt, as we find two selves at war within us. The Phillips translation renders verse 15: "My own behavior baffles me. For I find myself not doing what I really want to do but doing what I really loathe."

The story of Dr. Jekyll and Mr. Hyde is the story of every person. There lives within each of us these two selves described by Paul — the carnal and the spiritual. His melancholy frustration and failure is two-pronged — sins of omission and of commission.

Have not each of us struggled with this spiritual warfare of the divided self? Have we not also found that often when we would do good, evil is present within us and we have done what we really loathe? Try hard as we may to do right, we have come to frustration and miserable failure. Our hearts have echoed the apostle's anguished cry, "What a wretched man I am! Who will rescue me from this body of death?" (Romans 7:24).

God does not leave us there, struggling with the desires and depravity of our fallen nature, with an irreconcilable conflict between the flesh and the spirit, with an unfulfilled longing of deliverance from indwelling sin. We too can claim the apostle's assuring testimony in response to his desperate cry for rescue: "Thanks be to God — through Jesus Christ our Lord!" (7:25). Praise God, we can have victory in this civil war within.

Through Christ Jesus the law of the Spirit of life set me free from the law of sin and death. (Romans 8:2)

In chapter 7 of Romans we saw where Paul was incapable of overthrowing the tyranny of his carnal nature, with its vulnerability to sin and temptation. Life was spiritually frustrated, dominated by the dictates of the flesh.

Chapter 8 brings us into a new and radical relationship of life in Christ. God has done for us what we could never do for ourselves. A new era is ushered in for the believer, an era of liberty through life in the Spirit, releasing us from the captivity of the carnal nature. Paul states that we no longer "live according to the sinful nature but according to the Spirit" (8:4).

The Holy Spirit produces in us a new mindset of holy desires (8:5-8). Life becomes redirected toward God. "The Spirit of God lives in you" (8:9a). The word Paul uses for "lives" means to dwell as in a home. The Christian's life becomes the dwelling place for the Spirit of God, one of the great marvels of the Christian faith.

"And if anyone does not have the Spirit of Christ," warns Paul, "he does not belong to Christ" (8:9b). The Holy Spirit's indwelling is not a luxury, or a provision for the spiritually elite, but is the privilege and requisite for every believer.

E. Stanley Jones calls the life in the Spirit "the undiscovered country of Christianity, the land where our spiritual resources lie." He declares, "The Holy Spirit is the secret to power and poise." May we discover — and live by — that sublime secret.

We do not know what we ought to pray for, but the Spirit himself in-
tercedes for us with groans that words cannot express.

(Romans 8:26)

P rayer is at the same time the noblest and most difficult exercise of
the soul. We are burdened with our mortality, wearied with our
busyness, beset with our preoccupations, and hindered by our lack of
discipline.

From birth we learn the rules of self-reliance. Prayer becomes an
assault on our human autonomy, alien to our proud nature. We confess our inertia and aversion to meeting with God.

But the apostle Paul in our text tells us that our inarticulate longings are made known to God by the intercession of the Spirit. The Holy
Spirit interprets our heart's longing for both that which is unspoken as
well as that for which there is no human language.

The following verse states that "the Spirit intercedes for the saints."
Imagine, the Third Person of the Trinity, interceding for us at the
throne of God! Such a marvel is too deep for our understanding, over-
whelming us with God's amazing grace on our behalf.

James Montgomery eloquently describes the grace of unspoken
prayer in his hymn:

> Prayer is the soul's sincere desire,
> Unuttered or expressed,
> The motion of a hidden fire
> That trembles in the breast.
>
> Prayer is the burden of a sigh,
> The falling of a tear,
> The upward glancing of an eye
> When none but God is near.

And we know that in all things God works for the good of those who love him, who have been called according to his purpose.

(Romans 8:28)

Paul has learned the truth of this text from his own many trials. "We know" is his confident statement. This is not a promise for a sunfilled life without its clouds and storms. It does not say that all things are good, as any who have known life's hardships and evils can attest. Rather, Paul says that God brings good even out of the trials and traumas of life.

In 1967 at age 17, Joni Eareckson dived into Chesapeake Bay and broke her neck; since then she has been confined to life in a wheelchair as a quadriplegic. Joni testifies to the truth of our text, saying, "I praise God not in spite of my paralysis, but because of it, for it has drawn me nearer to God. His grace enables me to rejoice because of my disability. God has a way of reaching down and wrenching good out of it. He has gotten so much more glory through my paralysis than through my health!" Her worldwide ministry to those with physical handicaps, and the difference she is making, is eloquent testimony to the powerful truth of our text.

We should note that this promise is for those who love God and have answered his call and purpose for their life. To such, God brings forth a golden harvest from the furrows that pain has cut. He turns their sorrows into servants, their difficulties into dividends, their obstacles into opportunities, their brokenness into blessing, their stresses into strengths, their tragedies into triumphs, and their stumbling blocks into stepping-stones.

Let us be among the company who love and follow the Lord, so that the troubles that come to us along the way will become the treasures of God's grace to us.

*In all these things we are more than conquerors through him who
loved us.* (Romans 8:37)

I n lyrical lines the apostle Paul catalogs the most potent forces that
can assault us: "Who shall separate us from the love of Christ? Shall
trouble or hardship or persecution or famine or nakedness or danger
or sword?" (8:35). He resoundingly answers, "No, in all these things we
are more than conquerors through him who loved us." We not only
overcome life's hardships but through God's grace we snatch a blessing
from their onslaught.

Paul goes on to present an all-inclusive list of life's challenges: "For
I am convinced that neither death, nor life, neither angels nor demons,
neither the present nor the future, nor any powers, neither height nor
depth, nor anything else in all creation, will be able to separate us from
the love of God that is in Christ Jesus our Lord" (8:38-39).

Nothing can thwart the eternal purpose of God in the Spirit-
indwelt life. No earthly affliction can separate us from the love of God.
The mighty forces of the world, the flesh, and the devil are powerless to
separate us from the impregnable love of God. As Paul confidently asserts, "If God is for us, who can be against us?" (8:31).

One with God is always a majority. Let us then live the victorious
life in the Spirit that God has destined for us.

Total Commitment

Offer your bodies as living sacrifices, holy and pleasing to God.
(Romans 12:1)

Paul's letter to the Romans up to this point has been dealing with the fundamentals of faith. As he comes to the close of his great epistle, he moves from the fundamentals of faith to its practice in daily life. For Paul there was no divorce between theology and daily life. Belief is sterile if it does not issue in a new quality of life. Paul made no distinction between principle and practice, belief and behavior, creed and conduct, doctrine and deed.

His word "therefore" at the opening of the twelfth chapter is the link between the doctrine that has gone before and the ethical section that follows. This ethical section is not a mere appendix but an integral part of this gospel according to Paul. "In view of God's mercies" (12:1) indicates that God's infinite love expressed through Christ is the basis of Paul's appeal for Christ-like conduct.

A tone of urgency resonates from Paul's letter: "Therefore, I urge you, brothers, in view of God's mercy, to offer your bodies as living sacrifices, holy and pleasing to God — which is your spiritual worship." The Christian faith is not an otherworldly concept, but very practical, affecting us in the totality of our being and everyday living. No part of us is exempt from the claims of the gospel. A complete surrender of all we are and have — our body, mind, and spirit — is the secret of the Christian life.

Such a commitment is "reasonable," is the rendering by the Authorized Version, because of who God is and what he has done for us. The only proper response to the boundless grace of God is the consecration of our total being — our body, mind, and spirit.

Do not conform any longer to the pattern of this world, but be transformed by the renewing of your mind. (Romans 12:2)

There is a pull of the environment and world around us that would disarm our spiritual alertness and conform us to its secularism and selfishness. Our Lord described this tension between the Christian and the world when he said that we are "in the world but not of the world."

We are not to be conformed to the world. J. B. Phillips translates this verse graphically: "Don't let the world around you squeeze you into its own mold, but let God remold your minds from within." The word Paul uses for "transformed" is the root word for "metamorphosis" — the term used for the amazing change from a caterpillar to a butterfly. Christianity involves a radical and revolutionary change, making us a new person in Christ.

One of the greatest thieves of the mind today is television, with the exorbitant amount of time many allow for it to infiltrate their mind, and consequently their thoughts and heart. God's Word calls us to daily renewal of our mind, which will have a transforming impact upon our character and conduct.

Fanny Crosby, in one of her hymns, ushers us into a secret chamber for renewal:

I am praying, blessed Savior,
To be more and more like thee;
I am praying that thy Spirit
Like a dove may rest on me.

Thou who knowest all my weakness,
Thou who knowest all my care,
While I plead each precious promise,
Hear, O hear, and answer prayer!

For none of us lives to himself alone and none of us dies to himself
alone.   (Romans 14:7)

T ucked away in Paul's letter to the church at Rome is the statement
of fundamental truth: "For none of us lives to himself alone and
none of us dies to himself alone" (14:7).

The temptation to make islands of our lives is a powerful one. Islands are places of escape, idyllic settings where we can indulge our
fantasies and take refuge from the hectic pace that drives our lives. But
the philosopher poet John Donne reminds us:

No man is an island, entire of itself;
every man is a piece of the Continent,
a part of the main . . .
Any man's death diminishes me,
because I am involved in mankind.

The death of any person impacts upon others. When we lose
someone dear to us, something in us dies as well. That person was a vital part of our life that is gone. We do not live or die solely unto ourselves.

The greater truth Paul states is that, "If we live, we live to the Lord;
and if we die, we die to the Lord. So, whether we live or die, we belong
to the Lord" (Romans 14:8). Paul's affirmation in another of his letters
amplifies this great truth: "For to me, to live is Christ and to die is gain"
(Philippians 1:21). These verses provide our compass both for living and
for dying.

No eye has seen, no ear has heard, no mind has conceived what God has prepared for those who love him. (1 Corinthians 2:9)

The deep things of God cannot be discovered by unaided reason. "No eye has seen" — they cannot be discerned by earthly vision. "No ear has heard" — they are not unveiled in the schools of philosophy. "No mind has conceived" — intellectual insight and intuition cannot uncover them.

The story is told of a woman who had been diagnosed with a terminal illness and had been given three months to live. As she was getting her things in order, she asked her pastor to come to her house to discuss her final wishes. She told him which songs she wanted sung at the funeral service, what Scriptures she would like read, and what outfit she wanted to be buried in. The woman also requested to be buried with her favorite Bible.

As the pastor was preparing to leave, the woman suddenly remembered something else. "There's one more thing," she said excitedly. "What's that?" asked the pastor. "This is very important," the woman continued; "I want to be buried with a fork in my right hand." The pastor stood looking at the woman, not knowing quite what to say.

"That surprises you, doesn't it?" the woman asked. "Well, yes, to be honest, I'm puzzled by the request," said the pastor.

The woman explained. "In all my years of attending church socials and potluck dinners, I always remember that when the dishes of the main course were being cleared, someone would inevitably lean over and say, 'Keep your fork.' It was my favorite part because I knew that something better was coming. Something wonderful.

"So I just want people to see me there in that casket with a fork in my hand and to wonder 'What's with the fork?' Then I want you to tell them: 'Keep your fork, for the best is yet to come.'"

As people at the funeral were walking by the woman's casket, they saw the pretty dress she was wearing and her favorite Bible, and the fork placed in her right hand. Over and over the pastor heard the question: "What's with the fork?" And over and over he smiled. During his message, the pastor told the people of the conversation he had with the woman shortly before she died. He also told them about the fork and what it symbolized to her, "the best is yet to come."

Indeed, the best is yet to come for those who love the Lord. And I don't want to miss it! How about you?

God is faithful; he will not let you be tempted beyond what you can bear. (1 Corinthians 10:13)

Paul in his letter to the church at Corinth makes an astonishing statement about himself. He confesses his need for the discipline of his body, "lest, when I have preached to others, I myself should become disqualified" (1 Corinthians 9:27 NKJV). It seems inconceivable that the great apostle Paul could become a "castaway" as one translation puts it. Yet he maintains that he had to persevere in the Christian life.

In an interview I was privileged to conduct with Billy Graham, he said, "The thing I fear more than anything else is that I may make a mistake and bring disrepute upon the Gospel. If ever I should be tempted to fail, I pray the Lord will take me immediately." If these two giants of the faith, the apostle Paul and Billy Graham, had such a concern, how much more we of far less stature need to be constantly vigilant and disciplined.

The full statement of Paul with this text provides both a warning and assuring words for the believer in his confronting temptation: "So, if you think you are standing firm, be careful that you don't fall! No temptation has seized you except what is common to man. And God is faithful; he will not let you be tempted beyond what you can bear. But when you are tempted, he will also provide a way out so that you can stand up under it" (1 Corinthians 10:12-13).

So if you feel helpless against some fierce temptation that besets you, take heart. The temptation you face is common to many. The world, the flesh, and the devil will all be against us, but God is for us. His promise is that there is help for the helpless and power to turn our temptation into triumph.

There are different kinds of gifts, but the same Spirit.

(1 Corinthians 12:4)

Paul cites a representative list of nine gifts to illustrate the variety of gifts bestowed (12:8-10) and later appends a further list (12:28-30). The purpose of the gifts is not for self-glory or gratification, but "for the common good" (12:7) and to "build up the church" (14:12). Those who would qualify as saints must validate their credentials as servants.

A poet delightfully reminds us:

> Isn't it strange that princes and kings
> And clowns that caper in sawdust rings,
> And common people like you and me
> Are builders for eternity?
> Each is given a bag of tools,
> A shapeless mass, a book of rules;
> And each must make ere life is flown,
> A stumbling block or a stepping-stone.

"Each is given a bag of tools." Every believer is gifted by the Holy Spirit and has a unique contribution that will enrich the church fellowship and ministry.

"Do not neglect your gift" (1 Timothy 4:14) is the admonition of Paul to Timothy and to all Christians. What a waste and loss to allow God's gift to lie dormant and unused for God. Antonio Stradivarius said, "If my hand slacked, I should rob God."

Our Lord needs the gift each of us has to bring. He needed Peter's unpolished frankness, Matthew's penmanship and gift of detail, Paul's schoolroom learning. Let us as faithful stewards of his gifts be a "stepping-stone" for others on their pilgrimage of life.

And now these three remain: faith, hope and love. But the greatest
of these is love. (1 Corinthians 13:13)

Paul introduces his celebrated Hymn of Love by urging his readers
to "eagerly desire the greater gifts" (12:30) and adds, "Now I will
show you the most excellent way" (12:31). The lyrical lines of chapter 13
present some of the grandest prose and loftiest teaching of the Bible.

The apostle inserted a new word into the Christian vocabulary,
agape, denoting a vulnerable love bestowed on others. It is the same
word John used when he wrote his immortal text: "God so loved the
world" (John 3:16), and when he was inspired to declare: "God is love"
(1 John 4:8).

The ancient world of Paul's day was divided into three great cultures — the Greeks with their emphasis on eloquence, the Hebrews
with their emphasis on prophetic powers, and the Romans with their
emphasis on action. Paul stepped onto that stage of history and said, "If
I speak (Greeks), know (Hebrews), and do (Romans), but have not love,
then I speak nothing; I know nothing; I do nothing; I am nothing." He
declared that the absence of love negates all other gifts.

Paul presents in fifteen succinct phrases this superlative gift of love
in its practical aspects. This is love where it counts, love in action, love
expressed in relational theology.

Indeed, "Love makes the world go 'round." It is the highest good
and crowns every human relationship. When all else that seems permanent is gone, love will endure, for love is eternal. Paul's final word to
us on this subject is, "Follow the way of love" (14:1).

Reality of the Resurrection

But Christ has indeed been raised from the dead.

(1 Corinthians 15:20)

1 Corinthians 15 is one of the most supremely important chapters of the entire Bible. A faith can be no stronger than its foundation, and the foundation of the Christian faith is the resurrection of Jesus Christ. This chapter gives the earliest and fullest record of the resurrection of Christ, written in A.D. 54, within twenty-one years of the event, and preceding the earliest Gospels by almost fifteen years. Many, influenced by the pagan philosophy of Paul's day, had difficulty accepting the doctrine of the resurrection of the body. Thus Paul found it necessary to state the proofs and philosophy for this doctrine.

First, there was the testimony of the Scriptures on the resurrection of Christ (v. 4). The risen Christ himself expounded to the disconsolate travelers on the Emmaus Road how his death and resurrection fulfilled the Old Testament prophecies. Today we have the inspired and confirming witness of the New Testament.

Second, there was the impressive number of personal witnesses to the resurrection. There was Peter (v. 5), the Twelve (v. 5), James the brother of the Lord, and "more than five hundred of the brothers at the same time, most of whom are still living" (v. 6). There was no doubt in Paul's mind about the authenticity of the resurrection, and if his readers cared to do so they could verify his statements by checking them out with the impressive number of witnesses still alive.

The lives of witnesses to the resurrection were radically transformed. Peter changed from cowardice to courage, Thomas from skeptic to believer, the disciples from meeting in fear behind closed doors to boldly proclaiming the gospel and being willing to suffer and even be martyred for their belief in the risen Christ. Through two thousand years this miracle of changed lives has continued, with millions affirming the power of the risen Christ.

Let us also affirm, "I know he lives, because he lives within my heart!"

"Death has been swallowed up in victory." (1 Corinthians 15:54)

The apostle climaxes his magnificent resurrection chapter with one of the most graphic and spine-tingling descriptions of the Second Coming of Christ found in the Bible: "We will all be changed — in a flash, in the twinkling of an eye, at the last trumpet. For the trumpet will sound, the dead will be raised imperishable, and we will be changed.... Then the saying that is written will come true: 'Death has been swallowed up in victory. Where, O death, is your victory? Where, O death, is your sting?'... But thanks be to God! He gives us the victory through our Lord Jesus Christ" (vv. 51-57).

The word "victory" appears only three times in all of Paul's writings. He reserved these few lines for all of them, in which he celebrated the glorious victory of the risen Christ over the twin evils of sin and death.

Malcolm Muggeridge, a latecomer to the faith, became one of its most brilliant apologists. He wrote of the prospect of death, affirming: "So, like a prisoner awaiting his release, like a schoolboy when the end of a term is near, like a migrant bird ready to fly south . . . I long to be gone. Extricating myself from the flesh I have too long inhabited, hearing the key turn in the lock of Time so that the great doors of Eternity swing open. . . . Such is the prospect of death."

Our Gospel ends not with a corpse, but with a Conqueror, not with a tomb, but with a triumph, not with a victim of death, but with a Victor over it! Because of that radiant truth, the great apostle exhorts us all: "Therefore, my dear brothers, stand firm. Let nothing move you. Always give yourselves fully to the work of the Lord, because you know that your labor in the Lord is not in vain" (v. 58).

For we must all appear before the judgment seat of Christ.
(2 Corinthians 5:10)

Paul, in his epistles, writes as a citizen of two worlds, with one foot in time and the other in eternity. His binocular vision takes in the inexorable event for each of us in the afterlife: "For we must all appear before the judgment seat of Christ, that each one may receive what is due him for the things done while in the body, whether good or bad" (5:10). This life becomes the testing ground for eternity and the verdict of God. There will be for each person an accounting and reward or punishment according to the life we have lived.

For believers the judgment will be a time, not of fear, but of eternal felicity as they hear, "Come, inherit the kingdom prepared for you from the foundation of the world." For sinners the judgment will be a time of dread as they hear the verdict, "Depart from me" (Matthew 25:34, 41).

The judgment of God equates with justice. If there were no judgment there would be no justice. Good would be unrewarded and evil unpunished. The judgment of God also equates with the holiness of God. A holy God cannot tolerate sin and evil and a holy God rewards righteousness.

God's Word declares, "Now is the day of salvation" (2 Corinthians 6:2). Now, while there is opportunity; now, while the Holy Spirit moves upon us. Let the words of Amos, which have echoed across the centuries, be our watchword, "Prepare to meet your God" (Amos 4:12).

*Though outwardly we are wasting away, yet inwardly we are being
renewed day by day.*   (2 Corinthians 4:16)

From the obstacles Paul encountered comes one of his radiant jewels of promise: "Therefore we do not lose heart. Though outwardly we are wasting away, yet inwardly we are being renewed day by day. For our light and momentary troubles are achieving for us an eternal glory that far outweighs them all" (4:16-17).

This promise becomes more precious with the passing of years. Though we may experience outer decay, inner renewal comes day by day from the Lord's fresh spiritual resources. The years, which take away physical strength and beauty, can add loveliness and sinew to the soul. Among the promises of God, studded throughout his Word as bright stars in a dark sky, are these of his sustaining grace "day by day."

Annie Johnson Flint has penned this radiant truth in memorable verse:

> God hath not promised skies always blue,
> Flower-strewn pathways all our lives through;
> God hath not promised sun without rain,
> Joy without sorrow, peace without pain.
> But God hath promised strength for the day,
> Rest for the labor, light for the way,
> Grace for the trials, help from above,
> Unfailing sympathy, undying love.

And he died for all, that those who live should no longer live for
themselves but for him who died for them and was raised again.

(2 Corinthians 5:15)

I n the context of our verse, we find one of the profound theological
statements of the Bible: "God was reconciling the world to himself
in Christ" (5:19). This truth speaks of humankind's estrangement from
God, caused by rebellion, sin, and selfishness. But God, in his infinite
love, took the initiative on Calvary, there to restore human beings' relationship as children of God.

"He died for all." There are no exceptions. Race, nationality,
wealth, position, status, and gifts — all fade away in the light of Calvary. There we see ourselves as we really are — sinners in need of the
redeeming love of God, and with an eternal destiny.

Such infinite love compels us, exclaims the apostle, to a reversal of
the life-principle of living for self, to a life-principle of living for Christ,
who made the ultimate sacrifice for us on Calvary. The words of Isaac
Watts's classic hymn witness our response to this amazing love:

> When I survey the wondrous cross
> On which the Prince of Glory died,
> My richest gain I count but loss,
> And pour contempt on all my pride.
>
> Were the whole realm of nature mine,
> That were a present far too small;
> Love so amazing, so divine,
> Demands my soul, my life, my all.

*Therefore, if anyone is in Christ, he is a new creation; the old has
gone, the new has come!*   (2 Corinthians 5:17)

The transformed life is described by Paul in these unforgettable
words of our text. The apostle is not merely describing a cosmetic
treatment but an inner and total transformation, nothing less than "a
new creation," being remade in Christ.

Each of us who know the salvation of Christ readily identify with
this experience. When Christ came into our lives, we became a new
person, with a new purpose and power for living. The change went to
the very roots of our life. Old things passed away, new desires and motivations were born. We no longer lived for ourselves but for God's
high and holy purpose.

Paul himself was the classic example of the transformed life in
Christ. History witnesses to this powerful truth with such examples as
Augustine, John Newton, and in our day almost a modern counterpart
to Paul in the dramatic conversion of Watergate's Chuck Colson and
his far-reaching prison ministry. When President George W. Bush was
asked on a nationally televised interview, "Who has had the greatest influence on your life?" without hesitation he replied, "Jesus Christ." The
transforming power of Christ in human lives is still at work.

Over a century ago the hymn writer Rufus McDaniel sought to express this transformation in his song: "What a wonderful change in my
life has been wrought,/Since Jesus came into my heart!" Indeed, the
saving power of Christ imparts a metamorphosis to our soul, lifting us
from the chrysalis of our sin-bound life to the glorious beauty and liberty that enable us to soar to heights of unspeakable joy.

A Cameo of Christ

For you know the grace of our Lord Jesus Christ, that though he was rich, yet for your sakes he became poor, so that you through his poverty might become rich. (2 Corinthians 8:9)

This cameo of Christ speaks to us of the possessions of Jesus — "He was rich." Jesus, in his preincarnate existence, was fabulously rich. J. B. Phillips renders this statement, "He was rich beyond our telling." All creation, all the cosmos belonged to him.

The text speaks to us of the poverty he assumed at his Incarnation — "He became poor." Paul elsewhere writes, "He emptied himself." No theologian can fathom the mystery and majesty of that mighty transition when Deity wrapped himself in the dust and decay of human flesh, when he exchanged his ivory palaces for a cow barn, and when he who was the richest of all became the poorest of men.

This text also relates the purpose of Jesus' coming to earth — "for your sakes." Jesus went from riches to rags that spiritually we might go from rags to riches. He became bankrupt that we might have imperishable riches. He descended the steps of glory that we might ascend with him to worlds unknown. He became what we were that he might make us as he is.

This marvelous truth that transcends our understanding leads us with Charles Wesley to exclaim, "Master, I own thy lawful claim, Thine, wholly Thine, I long to be."

*And God is able to make all grace abound to you, so that in all
things at all times, having all that you need, you will abound in every
good work.* (2 Corinthians 9:8)

I confess that I turn to this promise each time I have a major preaching or teaching engagement, to again affirm that the Lord compensates for my unworthiness and weakness with his all-sufficient grace. We may not feel able to adequately cope with a task or a situation, but this promise reminds us that "God is able."

In our worship, the chorus by Rory Noland and Greg Ferguson resonates this truth:

He is able, more than able
To accomplish what concerns me today.
He is able, more than able
To handle anything that comes my way.
He is able, more than able
To do much more than I could ever dream.
He is able, more than able
To make me what He wants me to be.

Five times Paul employs the Greek word *pas,* meaning "all" or "every," to emphasize God's abundant provision for our need — "all grace," "in all things," "at all times," "having all that you need," "abound in every good work." And what is it that relates in all these areas of our life? Nothing less than the grace of God, provided for our every spiritual need. Holding firm to this promise, we can face with confidence whatever life may send us.

The Indescribable Gift

Thanks be to God for his indescribable gift!

(2 Corinthians 9:15)

The apostle Paul, writing to the church at Corinth on the subject of giving, climaxed his discourse with an exclamation of how extravagantly God has given to us, describing Christ as God's "indescribable gift" to us.

God's gift of Christ to the world is indeed an indescribable gift. No words can define or describe God's gift of his Son. It defies description, transcends superlatives, and exceeds our imaginative powers.

Charles Wesley exclaimed: "O for a thousand tongues to sing/My great Redeemer's praise,/The glories of my God and King,/The triumphs of His grace." But even then we would not find words to adequately describe the meaning and majesty of the gift of Christ to humankind. This gift of infinite love is beyond the finite grasp of our minds.

A young child was having trouble going to sleep and was heard crying in her bed. Her father brought her all the things that might solve the problem, including her favorite stuffed animals — but nothing helped. Finally he asked, "What is it that will make you stop crying?" The child answered, "If you will stay with me."

The greatest gift we can give another is the gift of ourselves. As the poet reminds us, "The gift without the giver is bare." The gift of Christ is no less than the gift of God himself to the world. It is the highest and costliest gift he could give to us. It is "his indescribable gift."

"My grace is sufficient for you, for my power is made perfect in weakness."   (2 Corinthians 12:9)

The apostle Paul, with obvious reticence, opens his heart to share a very personal experience. He modestly relates it in the third person, telling of an indescribable experience of rapturous revelation within the courts of heaven (1 Corinthians 12:1-6).

To keep Paul from perilous pride for such a surpassing experience, he was given a "thorn in the flesh." We do not know what it was, but the figure of speech stands for an irritating, bothersome bodily infirmity. Three times he pleaded for its removal. God answered his prayer, but not with "yes." The answer he received was: "My grace is sufficient for you, for my power is made perfect in weakness" (12:9). As George Meredith has discerningly written: "Who rises from prayer a better man, his prayer is answered."

Paul adds his triumphant testimony: "For when I am weak, then I am strong" (12:10). What a paradox! We live in a power-conscious, power-driven age. People today boast of megatons, megahertz, and megabytes, and worship at the shrine of power. Weakness is not in style. Yet Paul here says, "I delight in weaknesses" (12:10). Why?

It was because he discovered the great secret that his self-sufficiency, yielded to God's great sufficiency, allows God to turn our weakness into strength. Joni Eareckson Tada testifies confidently from her wheelchair: "The weaker we feel, the harder we lean. The harder we lean, the stronger we grow spiritually. God delights in using human weakness." May we, with Paul, experience this paradox of our faith — the yielding of our weakness to gain God's mighty strength.

The Threefold Benediction

May the grace of the Lord Jesus Christ, and the love of God, and the fellowship of the Holy Spirit be with you all.

                                                                    (2 Corinthians 13:14)

This verse has given the Christian church the familiar apostolic benediction, incorporated in its worship and often used as a closing benediction. Paul offers this benediction four times in his epistles.

It is theologically noteworthy that the apostle's inspired benediction links the Son and the Spirit with the Father as of equal status with him. It consummates all previous suggestion in Scripture, and sets the standard in all subsequent teaching.

"Grace" is the keynote of the life and ministry of Christ. The apostle John announced, "Grace and truth came by Jesus Christ" (John 1:17). Peter, at the historic Council in Jerusalem, declared, "We believe it is through the grace of our Lord Jesus that we are saved" (Acts 15:11). Grace is the unmerited favor of God toward us, through the atoning work of Christ on our behalf. Paul prays for that grace to be known by his readers.

"Love," the rich Greek word *agape,* is the very word John uses to define God in his epistle: "God is love" (1 John 4:8). No word or attribute denotes as meaningfully and assuringly his relationship to the world and the people he has created. Unlike the pagan gods — remote beings of caprice and vengeance — God, as taught by Jesus, is our loving heavenly Father. Paul's benediction prays for that love upon the lives of the believers.

Paul prays for the Christians in Corinth to know the very fellowship of the Holy Spirit. What a peerless privilege! Imagine — fellowship with the Holy Spirit! Herein is the supreme privilege and joy of the Christian life.

May we so live that the extravagance of this benediction will be upon us.

Remember the poor. (Galatians 2:10)

A practical note surfaces amid the major doctrinal dispute addressed in Paul's letter: "Remember the poor." This topic engendered no dispute, only consensus. From its earliest days, Christianity not only had its "heart to God" but also its "hand to man" as it reached out to aid the poor.

Our faith must never lead us to a withdrawal from the world of need around us, but must make us ever more sensitive and responsive to the cries of those who suffer. The true servant of God goes forth with the gospel in one hand and the cup of cold water in the other.

The gospel is like a pair of scissors. You cannot cut anything with just one blade; you must have two. And the two blades must be riveted together to be effective. The gospel has two components that must ever work in unison — evangelism and outreach to the desperate needs around us. God calls the church to be evangelical and justice-oriented at the same time.

E. Stanley Jones observed: "Evangelism without social action is like a soul without a body. Social action without evangelism is like a body without a soul. One is a ghost, and the other is a corpse." When evangelism and social action are joined, we have a living organism.

This text reminds us that we have a whole gospel for the whole person in the whole world.

I have been crucified with Christ and I no longer live, but Christ lives in me. (Galatians 2:20)

Paul's letter to the church in Galatia has been called the Magna Carta of the Christian faith. It proclaims his great declaration of freedom in Christ. The message of this epistle is contemporary for we are ever in danger of serving the system instead of the Savior, of adhering to creeds instead of to Christ. By God's grace, as demonstrated on Calvary, we are saved from the slavery of sin, liberated from legalism and its rigid rules.

The apostle Paul in our text makes a remarkable statement of our new life in Christ. He identifies with the crucifixion of Christ. Calvary was to him a very personal experience. Every believer comes to know this transforming power of Calvary, and like Paul, becomes a new person in Christ.

The late Robert G. Lee often told of his first visit to the Holy Land. When he saw the hill of Calvary, his excitement was so great that he started to run and soon outdistanced his party in climbing the hill. When the guide caught up with him, he asked, "Sir, have you been here before?" For a moment there was a throbbing silence. Then, in a whispered awe, Dr. Lee replied, "Yes, I was here, nearly two thousand years ago."

Indeed, we were all at Calvary some two thousand years ago. We were under the sentence of death, but in God's amazing grace, Jesus took our place and our judgment upon himself. With Paul, we identify with the crucifixion of our Lord. Our sinful self was nailed to that cross in his substitutionary death, and the life we now live has been transformed by Christ, whom we know not only as Savior but also as our living Lord.

When the time had fully come, God sent his Son. (Galatians 4:4)

The course of history up to the time of our text is incorporated in the pregnant phrase, "When the time had fully come." The coming of Christ into the world was the culmination to which all events were moving.

The timing of the Advent of Jesus Christ was not accidental, incidental, or coincidental. Christ came at the most auspicious moment of history.

Politically, the Mediterranean world was united under the *Pax Romana*, a period of universal peace. The Roman network of international highways provided the roads over which the gospel would travel throughout the world. The Greek language provided a universal medium for its proclamation. God's timing was perfectly synchronized for the Savior's birth.

"God sent his son" eloquently speaks of the preexistence of Christ. He is the Eternal Reality who became manifested in time and space at his Advent.

God, who through millennia guided the course of history for the perfect timing of the Advent of his Son upon earth, surely can guide our lives through their brief sojourn toward their eternal destiny. Let us, with the psalmist of old, be able to say, "My times are in your hands" (Psalm 31:15).

But the fruit of the Spirit is love, joy, peace, patience, kindness, goodness, faithfulness, gentleness and self-control.

(Galatians 5:22)

We have two great needs: forgiveness — that was met at Calvary; and goodness — that was met at Pentecost. We need both the atoning work of Christ and the attuning work of the Spirit. All creeds have to blossom into character.

Paul, in writing to the early church and to Christians of all ages, lists the character traits of the Christian life as the fruit of the Spirit, as a work of grace within the heart.

He gives three clusters of fruit, three in each. The first cluster has to do with our relationship to God, the second our relationship to others, and the third has to do with ourselves.

The first fruit is love, the superior and all-encompassing fruit, and the foundation for all the other graces. Joy is the runner-up virtue, a joy not dependent on circumstances or happenstances, but an abiding joy that transcends even the trials of life. Peace as the fruit of the Spirit surpasses all understanding (Philippians 4:7) and all misunderstanding.

Then there are the elusive virtues of patience and of kindness for which the world around us cries out; of goodness or integrity; of faithfulness; of gentleness; and finally, the mastery and discipline of self-control. All these are essential for our day-to-day relationships.

All this beautiful and bountiful harvest in the spiritual life can be ours through the nurturing husbandry of the Holy Spirit within the heart and life.

Brothers, if someone is caught in a sin, you who are spiritual should restore him gently.   (Galatians 6:1)

S ome years ago one of our daughters wrote a motto that her mother placed by our kitchen window, reminding us of a great truth: "We are responsible for one another." The apostle Paul preached that truth when he wrote: "Brothers, if someone is caught in a sin, you who are spiritual should restore him gently" (6:1).

What should be our response to those who falter and fail? The first word of Paul sums it up: "Brothers." Believers are brothers and sisters in Christ. Just as we would be compassionate and responsible for a brother or sister in the flesh who failed, so should we be for brothers and sisters in Christ.

There are two "John 3:16s" in the Bible. We tend to think of only one: "For God so loved the world that he gave his one and only Son, that whoever believes in him shall not perish but have eternal life." But 1 John 3:16 states: "This is how we know what love is: Jesus Christ laid down his life for us. And we ought to lay down our lives for our brothers." Both have the same theme, yet the latter is seldom quoted. Perhaps for the reason that in the first text God does everything and we have only to believe. In the second, God does his part, and then it says that we are to do our part — "to lay down our lives for our brothers."

As a remedy for self-confidence, or apathy towards the fallen, Paul warns: "But watch yourself, or you also may be tempted" (6:1). We are all vulnerable to the wiles of Satan. When we see someone slip and fall, we must say, "There, but for the grace of God, go I," and lend our encouragement and support to restore such a one in the faith.

Payday!

A man reaps what he sows. (Galatians 6:7)

Paul employs an agricultural metaphor to impress his message: "A man reaps what he sows. The one who sows to please his sinful nature, from that nature will reap destruction; the one who sows to please the Spirit, from the Spirit will reap eternal life" (Galatians 6:7-8).

This law of reaping what is sown is immutable, whether in the realm of nature or of the spirit. If a man sows wheat he will not expect to reap corn. If he plants bulbs for tulips he will not expect to grow roses. In the spiritual realm, if one plants seeds of sinfulness he should not expect to reap a harvest of good character and the blessings of God. The day of harvest will ultimately come and we shall reap from the seeds we have planted.

A mountain lad once left his log cabin home and traveled to a distant city to make his living, marry, and rear his family. After thirty-five years he returned to visit the old weathered home and to walk through misty memories of the past. As he sauntered slowly along, he saw a row of tall, stately walnut trees with branches spread in an amber path of sunlight. He remembered how as a young boy he had brought home from the woods a bag of walnuts and planted them, where now the trees silently witnessed to the lad's foresight.

But what had he done with the rest of those walnuts in the bag? He had not planted them all. Then he remembered. The remainder he had hidden in the attic of the cabin. He wondered, could they still be there? He walked into the old cabin, climbed a rickety ladder, pulled himself through the hole in the attic floor, and made his way into the far corner. There was the bag, musty and fragile, and within it the walnuts.

The walnuts he had collected as a boy once had equal chance to make good. But those stuck in the attic merely existed through wasted years, whereas those planted fulfilled their purpose for being.

Let us sow that we may reap God's bountiful harvest of beauty and blessing.

Let us not become weary in doing good.   (Galatians 6:9)

C hristians are not immune from depletion of energy and the danger of burnout. We can suffer fatigue in the work of God. Paul urges, "Let us not become weary in doing good," and adds a word of encouragement, "for at the proper time we will reap a harvest if we do not give up. Therefore, as we have opportunity, let us do good to all people, especially to those who belong to the family of believers" (6:9-10).

An unknown poet speaks to us of a perspective on life's fleeting opportunities:

> The bread that brings strength I want to give,
> The water pure that bids the thirsty live.
> I want to help the fainting day by day;
> I'm sure I shall not pass again this way.
>
> I want to give the oil of joy for tears,
> The faith to conquer doubts and fears.
> Beauty for ashes may I give always;
> I'm sure I shall not pass again this way.
>
> I want to give to others hope and faith,
> I want to do all that the Master saith;
> I want to live aright from day to day;
> I'm sure I shall not pass again this way.

Glorying in the Cross

May I never boast except in the cross of our Lord Jesus Christ.
(Galatians 6:14)

In the last heartbeat of his letter to the Galations, Paul affirms his devotion to the Christ of the cross: "May I never boast except in the cross of our Lord Jesus Christ." Reserved for the vilest of criminals, the cross was a cruel instrument of death, a symbol of shame and disgrace. But since the crucifixion of Christ it has come to symbolize salvation and life eternal.

How prone we may be to boast of ourselves and our achievements. But we only have been able to do what we may have done by the grace of God. We have no reason to boast of ourselves. May we with Paul only boast of what Christ has done for us.

When John Bowring visited Macao on the South China coast he was deeply impressed by the sight of a bronze cross towering on the summit of a massive wall that had formerly been a great cathedral. This cathedral, originally built by the early colonists, overlooked the harbor and had been destroyed by a typhoon. Only that one wall, topped by the huge metal cross, remained. The scene and its symbolic truth inspired Bowring to write the words we often have sung and to reflect on what should be our relationship to the cross:

> In the cross of Christ I glory,
> Towering o'er the wrecks of time;
> All the light of sacred story
> Gathers round its head sublime.
>
> Bane and blessing, pain and pleasure,
> By the cross are sanctified;
> Peace is there that knows no measure,
> Joys that through all time abide.

I bear on my body the marks of Jesus.   (Galatians 6:17)

Paul, in concluding his letter to the church in Galatia, cites his highest authority as an apostle, writing, "Finally, let no one cause me trouble, for I bear on my body the marks of Jesus." We cannot know what he specifically meant but in some way it refers to his suffering for the cause of Christ.

There are no bargain rates for Christian commitment. Our Lord still calls to a costly discipleship, to a vulnerable involvement amid the agonies of our world.

Amy Carmichael, who gave her life as a missionary in India and endured suffering, could identify with Paul's bearing the marks of Jesus on his body. Her powerful poem challenges us:

> Hast thou no scar?
> No hidden scar on foot, or side, or hand?
> I hear thee sung as mighty in the land,
> I hear them hail thy bright ascendant star,
> Hast thou no scar?
>
> No wound, no scar?
> Yet, as the Master shall the servant be,
> And, pierced are the feet that follow Me;
> But thine are whole: can he have followed far
> Who has no wound nor scar?

To the saints in Ephesus, the faithful in Christ Jesus.

(Ephesians 1:1)

"To the saints," writes Paul in this letter to the church in Ephesus, as well as similarly addressing his readers in Rome and Philippi. Who were the saints? What is a saint?

The word conjures up mental images of venerable patriarchs in stained-glass windows, or a dear aged Christian with sweet disposition, or someone who has been canonized. The Roman Catholic Church has over four thousand saints in the *Martyrologium Romanum,* the church's official list of universally recognized saints.

Also in our stereotypes, martyrdom has been equated with sainthood. So what is a saint? One either has to be canonized — recognized for extraordinary spiritual qualities — or cannonaded — martyred for the faith. It appears that we of the common ilk are safe from sainthood!

But wait. Whom is Paul addressing when he writes to the saints? The Greek word for "saints" is *hagios,* the same root word from which is derived "holiness," which essentially means set apart for God's use. This term never occurs in the singular, but always in the plural form. Paul is never addressing some singular Christian with extraordinary virtues, but rather the body of believers, the faithful in Christ Jesus.

To lose sight of the sainthood of all believers is to resign ourselves to spiritual mediocrity. The vocation of all believers is the life of holiness, being set apart for God's use.

A girl on her way to church with her mother asked, "What is a saint?" The mother replied, "I have to think about that one." Then during the church service she saw the sunlight illuminating a hero of faith in one of the stained-glass windows. The mother nudged her daughter, pointed to the illumined window, and said, "There, that is a saint." The girl replied, "Oh, I see. A saint is a person the light shines through."

As incredible as it may seem, God calls you and me to be saints, to be those whom the light of Jesus Christ will shine through in a darkened world.

*For he chose us in him before the creation of the world to be holy and
blameless in his sight.*   (Ephesians 1:4)

The book of Ephesians has been described with such superlatives as
"the Grand Canyon of Scripture," and the "Queen of the Epistles."
It lives up to those titles in sharing the highest and deepest spiritual
truths concerning the Christian life.

The towering truth Paul declares in this verse and its context is that
the cross was in the mind and heart of God even before the creation of
the world. God's plan and provision for us in Christ, which includes
Calvary, was made even before our world was created.

God's plan of salvation was not an afterthought. The cross was not
a divine expedient to meet an unforeseen emergency. It was conceived
in the eternal heart of God when planet Earth was merely a "blueprint"
in the divine mind. How inscrutable are the ways of God!

The fact of divine anticipation is written on all the pages of human
experience. God knew that we would be cold, so he put coal and gas in
the earth. He knew that we would dread the dark, so he put electricity
in the air. He knew that we would be hungry, so he put seeds in every
piece of food. He knew we would be thirsty, so he put water in the
clouds. He knew that we would be lonely, so he put family instinct
within us. And he knew that we would sin, so he provided a Savior. We
cannot help but sing in praise:

> Oh, the love that drew salvation's plan!
> Oh, the grace that brought it down to man!
> Oh, the mighty gulf that God did span
>   At Calvary!

Having believed, you were marked in him with a seal, the promised
Holy Spirit.   (Ephesians 1:13)

T he readers of Paul's letter to the Ephesians would immediately
have a picture of what Paul meant when he wrote that the believer
was "marked with a seal," that of the Holy Spirit. A seal was the personal sign of the owner or sender. The seal would be pressed into the
hot wax on a document, verifying the person to whom the seal belonged.

How do we know a person belongs to God? The true sign of a
Christian, that a person belongs to God, is not church denomination
or attendance, or religious customs, or good works, or even our profession of faith. The true mark of God's ownership is the seal of the
Holy Spirit upon the life. The fruit of the Spirit adorns the life and con-
firms God's work within. The Holy Spirit impresses the beauty and holiness of Christ upon the life.

A seal in the day of Paul was proof that a document was authentic.
What proves genuineness in our Christian life? How do we avoid role-
playing, going through empty ritual, and the sterility of a profession
without possession? We can only become authentic for God by the
work of the Holy Spirit within the life.

A Christian is the product of the work of the Trinity within the life.
God the Father purposed our salvation, God the Son provided our salvation, and God the Holy Spirit perfects our salvation. May the Holy
Spirit's presence and power give authenticity to our Christian profession.

For it is by grace you have been saved, through faith.

(Ephesians 2:8)

In this text Paul gives to us one of the premium words of the New Testament and of the Christian faith, the beautiful word "grace." It is the unmerited favor of God toward humankind, his incalculable generosity to every believer. Someone also has defined it with the acrostic: "Cod's Remedy At Christ's Expense."

In this text Paul equates grace with God's great provision of salvation. "By grace," he declares, we "have been saved." The word receives its most exalted meaning on Calvary as it sums up the sacrifice of the Son of God upon the cross for the sins of the world.

It was no surprise to find over three hundred entries on the word "grace" in the Song Book of our church, which witness to God's wonderful work in the life of the believer. The song of grace that has swept our land was written by a slave trader from his long struggle to be rid of the vicious self he had come increasingly to hate. John Newton knew that it was only by the grace of God that he had been saved from his great depths of sin, and he gave to the world his testimony:

> Amazing grace! How sweet the sound,
>   That saved a wretch like me!
> I once was lost, but now am found,
>   Was blind, but now I see.

> 'Twas grace that taught my heart to fear,
>   And grace my fears relieved;
> How precious did that grace appear
>   The hour I first believed!

I pray that out of his glorious riches he may strengthen you with power through his Spirit in your inner being.   (Ephesians 3:16)

For what do we pray, when we pray for ourselves and others? From the apostle Paul we can take a lesson on how to pray for God's highest and choicest gifts that will enrich our lives.

He first prays that his readers may have the power of the Holy Spirit — "he may strengthen you with power through his Spirit." Our needs argue the necessity of a power. My life — so frail, so fragile, so finite — has a great need for power outside of myself. My weakness, my temptations and testings — all require power to overcome. Paul identifies the source of power — the Holy Spirit. The Holy Spirit is the answer to weakness, defeat, and ineffectiveness.

The second great gift for which Paul prays is for the presence of Christ: "that Christ may dwell in your hearts through faith" (3:17). The word for "dwell" means to settle down and be at home. It speaks of a permanence and at-home-ness of Christ in the heart.

The third great gift for which Paul prays is for the priority of love: "being rooted and established in love" (3:17). From the roots of love will come the adorning fruit of the Spirit.

Paul further prays for his readers to "grasp how wide and long and high and deep is the love of Christ" (3:18). The dimensions of God's love are "greater far than tongue or pen can ever tell."

This great prayer concludes with the petition that "you may be filled to the measure of all the fullness of God" (3:19). A bold petition indeed!

Paul supports his bold petition with his unforgettable doxology, of a God able to do "immeasurably more than all we ask or imagine, according to his power that is at work within us" (3:20).

Do not let the sun go down while you are still angry.

(Ephesians 4:26)

S eneca called anger "a brief insanity." Anger can blast the flower of
friendship, destroy harmony in the home, lead to acts of hurt and
violence.

We take note that Paul does not tell us to avoid anger. Rather he
says just the opposite, "Be angry" (KJV). But of course the full text includes "and sin not."

Thomas Fuller called anger "one of the sinews of the soul." Martin
Luther King prayed, "Give me the indignations of Jesus Christ." It is
possible to commit the sin of not being angry. Injustice, man's inhu-
manity to man, the innocent victims of man's greed and violence — all
of these should make us angry.

Jesus demonstrated anger over the rigid orthodoxy of the religious
people who were against his healing the man with the withered hand
on the Sabbath (Mark 6:3). His blazing anger was again displayed in the
cleansing of the temple (Matthew 21:12). But when brutally treated at
the crucifixion, he never said a word of anger. His anger was never on
behalf of his own need, but in reaction to unloving acts toward others.

Paul further gives the sound advice: "Do not let the sun go down
while you are still angry." A quarrel or a breach should be mended immediately. He adds, "And do not give the devil a foothold."

The essence of our text is that we are to be "good and mad." There
is a rightful place for anger. But we must not allow anger to be sinful, or
nursed to become an opportunity for the devil in our lives. Self-
control comes through God's control of our lives.

And do not grieve the Holy Spirit of God.   (Ephesians 4:30)

The Holy Spirit is a divine person, and can be grieved, as Paul warns. "Grieve" is a love word. We grieve those we love. Because the Holy Spirit is our best friend who dwells within our heart, he is grieved by our wrongdoing.

Scripture relates the sad declension of the Holy Spirit in the Christian life, in three verses that should become watchwords to the Christian.

Besides the danger in our text of grieving the Spirit, Scripture tells us that it is possible to "resist" the Holy Spirit (Acts 7:51). The Holy Spirit woos us in tenderness and love. He does not force us to faith and discipleship. We can resist him. In Noah's day the people continually resisted God's Spirit, leading God to say: "My Spirit will not contend with man forever" (Genesis 6:3). To resist the Spirit, God's Evangelist in the world, is to oppose God's redemptive measures on our behalf.

The apostle further cautions, "Do not put out the Spirit's fire" (1 Thessalonians 5:19). The Authorized Version reads, "Quench not the Spirit." Everything that counteracts the work of grace in the soul quenches the Spirit of God — both sins of omission and sins of commission. Neglect of prayer and the Bible damps the sacred flame and leaves us to the foolish desires of our own heart. Continuing in sin quenches the Spirit.

Let us beware of the triad of dangers relative to the Holy Spirit in our lives: resist not, grieve not, quench not.

Be kind and compassionate to one another.   (Ephesians 4:32)

What is there more needed in life, in our relationships, in our world of hurts and heartaches, than kindness?

When the sons of Jacob were about to make their second trip to Egypt to buy corn during the famine, he counseled them to "carry a little honey." Jacob knew well the efficacy of gifts in a day when they served as peace offerings. The advice of Jacob is good for us, too, as we make our journey through life: "carry a little honey." We need to take a sweetening influence with us to all our human relationships. There is nothing that will be more telling of our walk with Christ than this quality of kindness. It is needed in our homes, our businesses, our churches, and our world.

It is not enough to be right and good. All of us know people who are morally correct but are disagreeable, unpleasant, and difficult to get along with. They may be religious but they lack a kindly spirit and a grace of character.

Paul adds in our selected verse, "forgiving each other, just as in Christ God forgave you." Someone has described forgiveness as "the fragrance that flowers give when trampled." God himself, through Christ, is the supreme exemplar of kindness and forgiveness. Charles Wesley has invited us to sing a prayer for this need:

Help us to help each other, Lord,
Each other's cross to bear;
Let each his friendly aid afford,
And feel his brother's care.

Imitators of God

Be imitators of God. (Ephesians 5:1)

Paul urges us, "Be imitators of God." What a bold and audacious command!

Imitation is a powerful motive in human behavior. It is the response of the will and life to that which one sees in another and esteems so highly as to want to incorporate it into one's own life. It may be a trait, a talent, a lifestyle, or the essential quality of a life.

To imitate God? Is not this an impossible command? But God in his Word does not ask the impossible. To imitate never implies coming up to the full quality or perfection of the original. Rather it implies having the essential qualities and features. In seeking to imitate God, we will of course not come to his perfection, but our lives can reflect the qualities of his love, kindness, purity, and power.

True, the God of the universe is too transcendent, too distant and unknowable to be imitated by frail and finite humans. But in Christ, he became incarnate — God understandable in human flesh. Thus we can sing the prayer chorus:

> To be like Jesus, this hope possesses me,
> In every thought and deed,
> This is my aim, my creed:
> To be like Jesus! This hope possesses me,
> His Spirit helping me, like him I'll be.

Redeeming the Time

Redeeming the time, because the days are evil.
(Ephesians 5:16 KJV)

"**D**o not squander time, for that's the stuff life is made of," was the sage advice of Benjamin Franklin. Time is life. When time has run out, life has gone.

Time is given to each person in minute fragments. A year is made up of 31,536,000 seconds, as the seconds, minutes, hours, and years make up life.

> Little drops of water, little grains of sand,
> Make the mighty ocean and the pleasant land.
> So the little minutes, humble though they be,
> Make the mighty ages of eternity.

Time can be the corrector of errors, the tester of truth, the healer of sorrow, and the one preacher to whom all must listen. Time can either be our friend or foe, depending on how we deal with it.

The apostle Paul urges us to redeem the time. Joseph Thayer, in his *Greek-English Lexicon of the New Testament*, interprets this text: "to make a wise and sacred use of every opportunity for doing good." Paul in our text is telling us to be master of our time. The spiritually effective person does not live under the tyranny of the clock or the calendar, but has learned to make time his servant rather than his master.

For the Christian, time is a sacred trust. The wasting of time can be a sin of neglect. Time is a great gift of God to us. Let us not abuse, but use it.

Be filled with the Spirit.   (Ephesians 5:18)

Paul writes to the Christians in Ephesus: "Be filled with the Spirit." The verb in the Greek is in the present imperative tense. This means that being filled with the Spirit is not a once-for-all experience, but rather a continuing experience.

The practical application of this in the Christian life is to be receptive to being filled repeatedly by the Holy Spirit. Although the Holy Spirit is a constant indwelling presence there are those times of special needs and blessing when we need to be filled to overflowing with the Spirit of God in our lives.

The imperative tense of the verb makes this a command. This is not an optional experience for the Christian, but one that God commands us to have. A human responsibility is entailed inasmuch as the command directs us to let the Spirit fill us.

We need to be filled with the Holy Spirit, as he is the antidote to weakness, helplessness, and ineffectiveness in Christian service. He is the divine Paraclete, the One called alongside to help us be adequate in our Christian life and service.

One man was known to pray, "Fill me, Lord." A person nearby was overheard to say, "You can't, Lord, he leaks." Many are not filled because of their undisciplined or unloving living.

A devotional chorus expresses the simple prayer:

With thy Spirit fill me;
Make me wholly thine, I pray,
With thy Spirit fill me.

Always giving thanks to God the Father for everything.
(Ephesians 5:20)

C an we really be thankful always? Are there not some circumstances where it would be impossible to be thankful?

What about if unjustly confined to prison, deprived of loved ones, basic comforts, and freedom? This was the situation of Corrie ten Boom. In her book *The Hiding Place*, she tells how in the German concentration camp during the war she even learned to thank God for fleas. When she was put in the cell that had fleas, she discovered that the guards stayed away from that cell, which enabled her and the other prisoners to have a time of devotions and Bible reading together.

Paul himself was a prisoner when he wrote this text. He praised God and sang hymns in a dungeon while his feet were in stocks and his back was lacerated.

Amy Carmichael, bedridden as a result of an accident some twenty years before her death, and in almost constant pain, yet shared a beautiful ministry through her devotional writings and poetry. She became a striking example of a Christian whose physical suffering enabled her to still reflect gratitude to God in the midst of suffering.

Gratitude is the memory of the heart, remembering the providence, goodness, and grace of God in all of life's situations. Let us heed Paul's counsel to always give thanks to God for everything.

Husbands and Wives

Wives, submit to your husbands as to the Lord. . . . Husbands, love your wives. (Ephesians 5:22, 25)

P aul in this passage was calling Christians to a revolutionary concept of marriage, a new fidelity, a new purity, a new partnership.

"Wives, submit to your husbands" is too often quoted in isolation from its context, wrongly suggesting passivity on the part of the wife. It is a teaching that must be contextually interpreted with women having equality (Galatians 3:28) and culturally conditioned in light of the major differences in the status of women in Paul's time and our own.

Paul does not tell husbands to treat their wives as subjects. But submission is the posture for all Christians because we follow the Lord of the universe who "emptied himself," submitting himself as the servant of all. Any attitude of superiority over another will be out of character for a Christian and will inhibit or fracture a relationship.

"Husbands, love your wives" must always be the companion verse with the one quoted for wives. Paul uses the great New Testament word for love, *agape*. He could have used *phileo* meaning an affectionate love, or *erao* referring to physical love. Classical writers would have employed these terms. But Paul uses the term that speaks of the love of God, love that strives and sacrifices for the highest good of the beloved. He gives the highest and holiest analogy possible in saying the husband is to love his wife "as Christ loved the church and gave himself up for her."

The hallmark and dominant note of this passage on marriage is not control, but love. Mutual love is the foundation that brings to marriage its true felicity and fulfillment.

Bring them up in the training and instruction of the Lord.

(Ephesians 6:4)

This text holds parents responsible for the religious education and training of their children. It is their most sacred duty. We cannot transfer this responsibility to the church or others. It has to be fulfilled by our own example, teaching, discipline, and training.

In the New Testament are four references to "the church in your house." They remind us of the sacred function of the home. In God's economy, the home and family are the primary and most sacred institutions of society. Our first school is the home. Our first place of prayer is the home. Our first learning of the Scriptures is in the home. Our first place of healing is the home. And the first church was a home.

Let us make our homes the places where our children first learn the name of Christ, and his love through our examples and teaching. Poet T. Yates expresses it poignantly:

I found a piece of plastic clay,
And idly fashioned it one day,
And as my fingers pressed it still,
It moved and yielded to my will.
I came again when days had passed.
The lump of clay was hard at last;
The form I gave it still it bore,
And I could change that form no more.

I took a piece of living clay,
And gently formed it day by day,
And molded with my power and art,
A young child's soft and yielding heart.
I came again when years had gone.
It was a man I looked upon;
He still that early impress bore,
And I could change him nevermore.

Put on the whole armor of God.   (Ephesians 6:11)

The warrior in Ephesians 6:10-18 is every Christian. The warfare is a spiritual one. C. S. Lewis warned: "There is no neutral ground in the universe: every square inch, every split second, is claimed by God and counterclaimed by Satan." Never trust the ceasefires of Satan.

The weapons of our warfare are described as "the whole armor of God" that we are to put on. As Paul in prison looked at the armor of the Roman soldier who guarded him, he drew an analogy with the Christian soldier. The Christian's armor includes the belt of truth, the breastplate of righteousness, the shield of faith, the helmet of salvation, and the sword of the Spirit which is the Word of God. The sword was used for both defense and offense. Dwight L. Moody wrote in the flyleaf of a Bible: "Either this Book will keep you from your sin, or your sin will keep you from this Book."

Paul culminates his listing of the Christian's armor with the most important of all: "Pray in the Spirit on all occasions." What good is the best weaponry or armor if the soldier is not in touch with and under proper direction of his commander? Prayer keeps our lines of communication open with Christ.

Who is the winner in this warfare? The text teaches that it is the Christian who takes to himself this whole armor of God, which makes him invincible.

I thank my God every time I remember you.   (Philippians 1:3)

Philippians is the most upbeat, personal and affectionate of all of Paul's thirteen letters. From his inventory of memories and blessings he starts out with personal words to his readers.

I, as others, have often referred to this text in writing to a loved one or friend: "I thank my God every time I remember you. In all my prayers for all of you, I always pray with joy because of your partnership in the gospel from the first day until now, being confident of this, that he who began a good work in you will carry it on to completion until the day of Christ Jesus" (1:3-6).

This four-verse text has three main components. First, Paul thanks God for those who have been a source of encouragement and blessing to him. There are parents, loved ones, friends, and Christian leaders whom God has used to encourage and bless us on our way. Let us thank God for them and let them know of our gratitude to them.

Secondly, Paul prays with joy for what his readers have meant to him. He prays that "your love may abound more and more . . . so that you may be able to discern what is best and may be pure and blameless until the day of Christ" (1:9-11). We should so remember in prayer those persons special to us in our spiritual journey.

Thirdly, Paul affirms that the Lord will continue to work in their lives for their spiritual growth and service. I'm reminded of a T-shirt with the letters BPWMBGINFWMY, which according to the person wearing it meant, "Be patient with me because God is not finished with me yet." As a sculptor polishes his work to refine and perfect the end result, so the Divine Sculptor continues to smooth out the rough places of our lives that we may conform more fully to the likeness of Christ.

A Matter of Life and Death

For to me, to live is Christ and to die is gain.   (Philippians 1:21)

Paul shares the innermost thoughts of his heart, confessing his am-bivalence about departing to have the joy of being with Christ, yet knowing the need to remain to help his readers in their pilgrimage of faith. This text may well express the highest point to which our faith can take us.

Dietrich Bonhoeffer, a German pastor, ministered during Hitler's oppressive regime. While activism formed the central focus of much of his short life, he also gave voice to his beliefs and actions through seminal writings and books. Executed at age 39, his life and writings continue to have a powerful impact upon Christian thinking today.

The doctor who attended prisoners to be executed, including Bonhoeffer, years later wrote: "Through the half-open door in one room of the huts I saw Pastor Bonhoeffer kneeling on the floor praying fervently to his God. I was most deeply moved by the way this lovable man prayed so devoutly and so certain that God heard his prayer. At the place of execution, he again said a short prayer and then climbed the steps to the gallows, brave and composed. In the almost fifty years that I worked as a doctor I have hardly ever seen a man die so entirely submissive to the will of God."

What was the secret of Bonhoeffer's courage in his hour of execu-tion? His biographers reveal that as he approached the gallows he drew a fellow prisoner aside, and in his last words said, "This is the end, for me the beginning of life."

For all who embrace the Christian faith, Christ has transformed both life and death, so that when the time of our departure comes, we know that we shall be with him forever.

But made himself nothing, taking the very nature of a servant.

(Philippians 2:7)

O ur text ushers us into this oceanic depiction of Christ where the fathoms and tides are measureless. Eminent biblical expositor F. B. Meyer states: "In the whole range of Scripture, this paragraph stands in almost unapproachable and unexampled majesty."

Christ was, declares Paul, by his "very nature" God. Divinity was intrinsic to him. Then comes the transition, "But made himself nothing, taking the very nature of a servant, being made in human likeness" (2:7). J. B. Phillips gives us a crystal translation: "For he who had always been God by nature, did not cling to his prerogatives as God's equal, but stripped himself of all privilege by consenting to be a slave by nature and being born as mortal man." C. S. Lewis calls the Incarnation "the central miracle" of our faith.

There was no evolution of these doctrines; these truths were believed about Christ from the beginning. The amazing Jesus, who "without him nothing was made that has been made" (John 1:3), in divine condescension stooped to mortality and to ignominy. He who was the master of death "became obedient to death — even death on a cross!" (2:8).

Why such condescension? Why such divine humiliation? It was all on our behalf. Charles Wesley has conveyed this marvel of the Incarnation in his refrain:

He left his Father's throne above,
So free, so infinite his grace,
Emptied himself of all but love,
And bled for Adam's helpless race.
'Tis mercy all, immense and free,
For, O my God, it found out me.

Therefore God exalted him to the highest place.

(Philippians 2:9)

T he exaltation of Christ was a divine act — *God* has highly exalted him. God entitles him to universal homage: "Every knee should bow, in heaven and on earth and under the earth, and every tongue confess that Jesus Christ is Lord" (Philippians 2:10-11).

The transitional word, "therefore," points to the fact that it was because of his earthly humiliation that God exalted him. As a member of the divine Trinity Christ needed no exaltation, he was already enthroned in heaven. But at his Incarnation, becoming clothed in human flesh, he abandoned his glory. Because he had stooped to degradation and death, God now "exalted him to the highest place." It was not from the heights of heaven, but from the depths of woe that he mounted up to glory, in one mighty step from the tomb to the throne. He stooped to conquer, and he conquered because he stooped.

The Christian, as an heir of heaven, shares in his exaltation. With Paul we affirm, "Now there is in store for me the crown of righteousness, which the Lord, the righteous Judge, will award to me on that day — and not only to me, but also to all who have longed for his appearing" (2 Timothy 4:8).

Thomas Kelly, in one of his verses, invites us to rhapsodize over this truth:

The head that once was crowned with thorns
Is crowned with glory now;
A royal diadem adorns
That mighty victor's brow.

And every tongue confess that Jesus Christ is Lord, to the glory of
God the Father. (Philippians 2:11)

"Lord" is one of the most common titles for Christ, found over two hundred times in the letters of Paul. It may well be the most theologically significant of all the titles of Christ.

The Greek, *kurios*, denoted the owner of possessions. As Lord of the universe, "He has the whole world in his hands." The imagination is staggered at the thought of his proprietorship in the cosmos. Yet, wonder of wonders, he holds our life in his mighty hands.

This title also speaks of the authority of Jesus. With the voice of authority, he commanded the raging wind and waves to be still. With the voice of authority, he brought forth Lazarus from his tomb. He demonstrated his authority over death and the grave by the mighty act of his resurrection. In the authority of Jesus Christ there is security for the believer.

Kurios was also applied to *deified rulers*, in particular, to later Roman emperors. But their glory was short-lived. Christ alone was great enough to fill this title.

Most important of all, *kurios* was a designation for God. It was the Greek translation of the sacred name Jehovah or Yahweh in the Old Testament. This title, following his resurrection, when applied to Christ is a recognition of his divinity.

"Jesus is *Kurios*" became the first creed and confession of the New Testament church: "That if you confess with your mouth, 'Jesus is Lord' ... you will be saved" (Romans 10:9). The earliest church creed was not a what, but a whom. We affirm the creed of this golden text, acknowledging Christ as Lord, Lord of the universe, and Lord of our life.

Do Not Complain

Do everything without complaining or arguing.

(Philippians 2:14)

Our words are always moral. They can transcend the moment — when written, they are not done with the writing; when spoken, they are not done with the speaking. They may have a separate life from the writer or speaker. Jesus said that we shall be held accountable for every idle word.

Paul here counsels us to avoid words of complaint and argument. "Murmurings," the word translated in the King James Version, is an onomatopoeic word, that is, a word whose sound resembles its meaning. The same is true of the Greek word Paul employs — *goggusmos*. People in the church were growling when they should have been glowing.

It's always much easier to be a critic on the sidelines than to be a combatant for God on the front lines. Our words, both in tone and selection, characterize our spirit. "Voiceprints" have been accepted as evidence in courts of law, with each word as a set of wavy lines that reflect the qualities of the speaker's voice. It has been suggested that most friction of daily life is caused by mere tone of voice. When a person speaks, his or her words convey the thoughts, but tone conveys the mood.

The word "everything" in our text covers a lot of ground in our daily life. It represents the dull routine and often onerous tasks of life, the hard work or even labors of love for which there may be no expression of gratitude. Nonetheless, let us heed the good advice of Paul: "Do everything without complaining or arguing."

I want to know Christ. (Philippians 3:10)

It is often said that knowledge is power. Paul aspires to the greatest and most powerful knowledge of all, that of knowing Christ.

There are different ways we may know someone. By hearsay or history we may know Luther, Churchill, or the President of the United States. The latter we may see and hear often on television and come to know him vicariously. We may also know persons by casual contact, but still not know them well. But then there are those few persons we know most intimately. We spend time with them, know their heart, mind, and thought. These same varied ways of knowing others apply to our knowing Christ.

Paul's aspiration was not a wistful sighing to become acquainted in some historic or casual way. He had already known Christ for some thirty years. All his discoveries of him only made him want to know more. For the word "know" he employed the Greek verb *ginoskein*, which means to know, not in theory, but in the most personal and intimate manner. "I want to know Christ" was the great longing of his soul.

Paul earlier in this passage speaks of "the surpassing greatness of knowing Christ Jesus my Lord" (3:8). Not merely the creeds, but Christ, not what but whom he believed. His was an unending quest for an enlarged and ever-expanding knowledge of his Lord.

Paul's longing is our heart's longing. We too want to know Christ better. How do we achieve that goal? Historically through the records of the Gospels, doctrinally through the teachings of the epistles, and personally through prayer and the illumination of the Holy Spirit, whose ministry is to reveal Jesus.

Pressing On

I press on toward the goal to win the prize for which God has called me heavenward in Christ Jesus. (Philippians 3:14)

None other than the apostle Paul writes the startling disclaimer, "Not that I have already obtained all this, or have already been made perfect, but I press on." In this passage he reminds us that the Christian race is not for sprinters; it is a marathon, requiring endurance over the long haul to the very end.

The National Archives building in Washington houses the priceless documents of our nation — the original Declaration of Independence, the Constitution, and other historic papers. Engraved over the front entrance of this monolithic edifice are the words, "Eternal vigilance is the price of liberty." These words are no less true of our spiritual liberty in Christ. We must, as the apostle Paul reminds us, never let down our guard or surrender to complacency, but ever "press on."

Paul shares his secret for pressing on: "But one thing I do: forgetting what is behind and straining toward what is ahead" (v. 13). His singleness of purpose and focus on his goal overcame a past that could otherwise haunt and hinder him.

We must leave behind our achievements as well as our failures, our past sins and our heartaches, and with Paul, say, "I press onward toward the goal." The goal of the Christian race? It is "the prize for which God has called me." That prize? Abundant life in Christ here on earth, and life eternal in the hereafter — surely worth our "pressing on."

Rejoice in the Lord always.   (Philippians 4:4)

I n Paul's "Epistle of Joy" he not only says, "Rejoice in the Lord," but adds, "I will say it again: Rejoice!" No fewer than eleven times in this brief letter he says to his readers, "rejoice." Five times he flings out his mirthful monosyllable, "joy."

"Rejoice always." The rejoicing of the Christian is not something reserved for special times, but it is "always" — incessant, uninterrupted, unbroken. "In the Lord" makes it independent of all circumstances. The Christian's joy is not dependent on happenstance, but its unfailing source is the Lord.

Someone has expressed it this way: "If you don't love God, you will be miserable in your happiness. If you love God, you will be happy in your misery." Another has written: "It's easy enough to be pleasant, when life flows by like a song, but the man worthwhile is the one who will smile, when everything goes dead wrong."

Bernard of Clairvaux, in the solitude of the monastery, found the source of unremitting joy, and composed a hymn that has been sung for over a thousand years:

Jesus, thou joy of loving hearts,
Thou fount of life, thou light of men,
From the best bliss that earth imparts
We turn unfilled to thee again.

The Peace of God

And the peace of God, which transcends all understanding, will guard your hearts and your minds in Christ Jesus.

(Philippians 4:7)

Paul's word for "guard" is a military word, as of a sentinel who mounts guard and protects that which is entrusted to him. Not the fragile peace of the world, but the impregnable peace of God, will like a sentinel stand guard over our heart's door, protecting us from those things that would rob us of our peace.

Two artists were once commissioned to paint a picture that would depict peace. One painted a landscape with a mountain lake — calm, tranquil, unperturbed, set in beautiful green hills, ringed by tall pine trees reflected in the mirror-like surface of the lake.

The second artist painted a turbulent scene with a violent waterfall crashing down on jagged rock. Alongside the waterfall was a slender birch tree, with its fragile branches reaching just above the crashing foam. In the fork of one of the branches was a bird's nest, in which lying serenely was a small bird fast asleep.

He had captured the feeling of peace that we can know in our troubled world amid the storms of life that may rage about us. There will always be problems, and even trials and tragedies. But God has promised that his peace, a peace that passes all human understanding, will guard our hearts in the midst of life and its strife.

The words of the chorus to Francis Blackmer's song give expression to this peace:

O the peace my Savior gives,
Peace I never knew before!
And my way has brighter grown
Since I learned to trust him more.

If anything is excellent or praiseworthy — think about such things.

(Philippians 4:8)

I n essence, we are not what we think we are, so much as what we think, we are. Emerson wrote, "A man is what he thinks about all day long." Long before he offered that aphorism, the sage of Proverbs taught, "For as he thinks in his heart, so is he" (23:7 NKJV).

There is a power in negative thinking. Unwholesome thoughts can shrivel the soul, distort perceptions, and actually make us ill. In contrast, praiseworthy thoughts as outlined by Paul are a dynamic power within the psyche and the soul. They can create an affirmative attitude, cultivate character, and bring wholeness and healing.

Our world has been revolutionized by the computer, which has multiplied human knowledge, enabling us to explore the reaches of outer space and to unravel some of the mysteries of the universe. But it has done nothing for us in exploring our inner space, the mystery of who we are and where we are going. In fact, science and technology have left us all hostages of the nuclear age.

Thoughts dye the mind. That is why the apostle Paul urges: "Whatever is true, whatever is noble, whatever is right, whatever is pure, whatever is lovely, whatever is admirable — if anything is excellent or praiseworthy — think about such things."

To follow the counsel of the apostle will invest the portfolios of our mind and heart with a wealth that will pay the highest dividends of enrichment.

I have learned to be content whatever the circumstances.

(Philippians 4:11)

The apostle Paul was not writing from a suite in the Holiday Inn but from a prison cell when he wrote, "I have learned to be content whatever the circumstances." His body was in chains, but his spirit was free, and his heart was glowing. His words witness to God's enabling grace for an inner peace in even the most untoward circumstances.

True contentment is not so much a state of circumstances as it is a state of mind and heart. This is illustrated in the story of a legally blind 92-year-old woman who moved to a nursing home after her husband of seventy years had passed away. She waited patiently in the lobby, and when her room was ready she maneuvered her walker to the elevator. As she did so she was provided a visual description of her tiny room. "I love it," she stated with enthusiasm. "But Mrs. Jones, you haven't seen the room yet." She replied, "That doesn't have anything to do with it. Happiness is something you decide on ahead of time. Whether I like my room or not doesn't depend on how the furniture is arranged, it's how I arrange my mind. It's a decision I make every morning when I wake up. I have a choice; I can spend the day in bed recounting the difficulty I have with the parts of my body that no longer work, or get out of bed and be thankful for the ones that do."

Thomas Kelly caught the spirit of contentment in the song he composed:

Happy we who trust in Jesus,
Sweet our portion is and sure;
When despair or doubt would seize us,
By his grace we shall endure.

I can do everything through him who gives me strength.

(Philippians 4:13)

This text has been called "the Mount Everest affirmation of Paul's life." The apostle, through Christ, was enabled to surmount the most formidable obstacles in his preachment of the gospel. The secret of his all-sufficiency was "through him" — the presence and power of Christ in his life.

We too can have victory through the strength imparted by Christ. He has bequeathed to us the Holy Spirit who is the source of power in the Christian life. Without him, we will fail; without him we are like a ship without a sail — no receiving of the silent power that can drive us to our destination and destiny. Ella Wheeler Wilcox in her poem reminds us that the sails of our life need to be set in the right direction:

> One ship drives east and another drives west
> With the selfsame winds that blow.
> 'Tis the set of the sails and not the gales
> Which tells us the way to go.
> Like the winds of the sea are the ways of fate,
> As we voyage along through life:
> 'Tis the set of a soul that decides its goal,
> And not the calm or the strife.

Let us set the sails of our life to catch the wind of the Spirit, and with his power we with Paul will affirm, "I can do everything through him who gives me strength."

A Blank Check

And my God will meet all your needs according to his glorious riches in Christ Jesus. (Philippians 4:19)

This golden text gives the believer one of the most extravagant promises in the Bible. It is as a blank check from God, for us to endorse personally, and to draw from it on the bank of heaven. The date on it is open-ended, its resource to be available at any and all times of need.

My God — It is personal, this blank check that comes to us from the God who loves us and knows us by name.

Will meet — No ambivalence, no doubt about the validity, the efficacy of this promise; we "can bank on it."

All your needs — The text does not say that this promise will supply all our wishes, but rather our needs, that which is essential to our spiritual life.

According to his glorious riches — The bank of heaven has inexhaustible riches, and God's extravagance is at our disposal.

In Christ Jesus — Without Christ, the glorious riches of God are beyond our reach. But when Paul adds "in Christ Jesus," that brings them down to us. The atoning work of Christ on our behalf brings to us the infinite bounty of God's blessings.

Some go through life and fail to place their endorsement on this check, to appropriate its riches, and they remain spiritually poor and destitute. God has given no pledge that he will not redeem, and encouraged no hope that he will not fulfill. Let us believe the promises of God and act upon them, knowing that God is more than adequate to meet every need we bring to him.

He is the image of the invisible God.   (Colossians 1:15)

Paul's letter to the Colossians contains the highest reach of the apostle's lofty statements on Christ. Elton Trueblood, who acknowledges that he had to come to "a Christocentric faith," counsels: "The best way to know what God is like is to study the life of Christ." Paul's definition of Christ in this passage (1:15-20) is one of the great Christological passages of Scripture.

Who is Jesus Christ, really? This is the central issue Paul addresses in this letter. He affirms: "He is the image of the invisible God." This statement calls to mind Jesus' revealing words to Philip, "He who has seen me has seen the Father." Paul here states that Christ is the exact likeness of God. He is God's authentic self-disclosure. In the blazing light of Christ's divine effulgence all shadows of false teaching retreat into the darkness from which they came.

Paul further makes the astonishing statement that Christ is "the firstborn over all creation" (1:15). The peasant carpenter who had died a felon's death just a half century earlier, had preexistence, was eternal, and "by him all things were created" (1:16).

Paul soars to the heights in his hymn on Christ: "In everything he might have the supremacy" (1:18). He culminates his magnificent doxology with reference to Christ having made "peace through his blood, shed on the cross" (1:20).

The sovereignty of Christ alone would merit his supremacy in our lives. But to also have shed his blood for us leads us to say with C. T. Studd, famed missionary, "If Jesus Christ be God, and died for me, then no sacrifice can be too great for me to make for him."

Our Rosetta Stone

In whom are hidden all the treasures of wisdom and knowledge.

(Colossians 2:3)

In 1799 Napoleon's soldiers found near Rosetta on the Nile a large piece of black basalt bearing an inscription in several languages. The writings provided the key to the deciphering of ancient Egyptian hieroglyphics. Today the Rosetta stone is in the British Museum as one of the greatest discoveries for the unlocking of ancient language.

Just as the Rosetta stone furnished the clue for deciphering all that ancient lore, so Jesus is the Rosetta stone that gives us the clue to the language of creation, to the hidden purpose running through all things. Wisdom is hidden, until found in Christ. He is God breaking through, unlocking for us the treasures of wisdom and knowledge.

Philosophers tell us that we must have a *Weltanschauung*, a worldview, a cosmic framework in which to live and work, to give validity and meaning to all we do. Paul declares, "Reality, however, is found in Christ" (Colossians 2:17). Otherwise life becomes a crazy quilt of happenstances and expediencies. Theologian Hans Küng writes, "The God of Jesus Christ is not enigmatic, like the Egyptian sphinx. He is Immanuel, God with us." Jesus is Reality, God in understandable terms, and our source of all wisdom and knowledge.

The hymn writer William Pearson has sought to convey this truth in his verse:

> Thou art love's unfathomed ocean,
> Wisdom's deepest, clearest sea,
> Heaven's and earth's salvation portion,
> Parent of eternity.

Set your hearts on things above.   (Colossians 3:1)

"**D**octrine is the seed of duty" is borne out in Paul's letter as he moves from doctrine to the realm of deeds, from creed to conduct. The false teachers in Colossae were caught up with rituals and regulations.

The apostle now gives his own rules for holy living. The tendency is to become preoccupied with the things of this earth. Paul adds this fundamental principle: "Set your minds on things above, not on earthly things" (3:2). Our heart and our mind, our affection and our intellect, our desires and our thoughts, need to be focused, not on the temporal things of this earth, but on the eternal things of God.

In order to do this the believer deals decisively with sin: "Put to death, therefore, whatever belongs to your earthly nature." Paul then identifies some of those things that defile (3:5-9). But the Christian's renunciation does not leave a vacuum. We are to "put on the new self, which is being renewed in knowledge in the image of its Creator" (3:10). He further enjoins, "Clothe yourselves with compassion, kindness, humility, gentleness and patience," along with a forgiving attitude toward others (3:12-14).

Paul writes his final trilogy of rules for holy living. First, "Let the peace of Christ rule in your hearts" (3:15). This divine peace "rules" — reigns, exercises control over all the emotions, actions, and reactions of the heart. Secondly, "Be thankful" — gratitude is a hallmark of a holy life. Finally, "Let the word of Christ dwell in you richly" (3:16).

Let us set our hearts and minds on things above, so that our deeds will be the fruit of our doctrine, and this holy conduct the outgrowth of our creed.

Christ Is All

Christ is All and in all. (Colossians 3:11 NKJV)

Paul seems to summarize his teaching on the Christian life with the sweeping statement "Christ is All and in all." In other words, he is saying, "Your Christian life cannot be a half-hearted, lukewarm, fickle, inconstant thing. It demands total commitment. Christ is not to be just a part of our lives, but he is to be our All."

To the Christian, Jesus is not something, he is everything; he is not in a part of the Christian's life, he is in all of his life — he is All in all.

In a sense this title is a summary of all the titles of our Lord. He is our All in all — our Savior, Peace, Teacher, Light, Friend, Hope, Lord, King, Guide, Shepherd, God.

"Give me a place to stand and I will move the universe," boasted Archimedes. Physically, of course, there is no such place. But spiritually, Christ is the fixed point from which all of life can be directed. The eternal Christ is the central point of reference, our source of life and meaning, our All in all.

Our golden text has been the theme of hymn writers, among them Herbert H. Booth, who composed this verse:

> I bring to Thee my heart to fill;
> I feel how weak I am, but still
> To Thee for help I call.
> In joy or grief, to live or die,
> For earth or heaven, this is my cry,
> Be Thou my All in all.

> *For the Lord himself will come down from heaven.*
>
> (1 Thessalonians 4:16)

In this epistle we have the earliest reference to the Second Coming of Christ. This tumultuous truth becomes the grand climax of this letter and the underlying theme that resonates through all Paul's letters to the churches. All prophecy of the Bible points toward this one grand event, the culmination of all history, the mighty and triumphant return of Jesus Christ.

In the fullest description of the Parousia — the Second Coming — in the New Testament, Paul in vivid language tries to describe the indescribable: "For the Lord himself will come down from heaven, with a loud command, with the voice of the archangel and with the trumpet call of God. . . . And we will be with the Lord forever" (4:16-17).

This awe-inspiring though brief description of Christ's return does not allow for undue dogmatism. The apostle disclaims the need to write "about times and dates" (5:1). Date setters, who will always be doomed to fiascos, would do well to take heed of this statement. There are obviously many details we wish we could know, but Paul gives us the essentials. The Lord is coming again, climaxing with the glorious fact that "we will be with the Lord forever."

Well might Paul call on believers to "Therefore encourage each other with these words" (5:18). There is no greater truth in all history than the fact that Christ is coming again! Surely the Lord's coming for each of us is no further away than the remaining span of our lifetime. May this glorious truth stir our own hearts and strengthen our faith. Let us, with Paul and the believers of old, stand on tiptoe. Someone is coming!

Pray continually.   (1 Thessalonians 5:17)

"He who has learned to pray," wrote William Law, "has learned the greatest secret of a holy and happy life." The apostle Paul gives priority to prayer in the final instructions of his first letter to the Thessalonians when he writes, "pray continually."

E. Stanley Jones witnessed to the priority of prayer: "Most of the casualties in the spiritual life are found at the place of a weakened prayer life. Prayer is pivotal. I find I am better or worse as I pray more or less. When I pray I'm like an electric bulb put into the socket, full of light and power. When I don't pray I'm like that same bulb pulled out of the socket — no light, no power."

This text calls us to live constantly in the spirit of prayer, realizing our dependence on God. "Pray continually" means to pray without great interruptions, to be faithful in our practice of prayer. Prayer need not be relegated to certain restrictive places and times. Any time throughout the day we can shoot "arrow prayers" to God — prayers of praise, thanksgiving, intercession, petition.

Our full-throttle lifestyle can all too easily crowd prayer out of our lives. In the words of a hymn expressing our constant dependence on God, "I need thee, every hour I need thee." Prayer links us with the infinite resources of God's power, wisdom, and guidance that we need to see us through each day.

Every Christian at some time has received the following widely circulated memo and will no doubt see it again: "When faced with a busy day, save time by skipping your devotions." Signed, "Satan."

Do not put out the Spirit's fire. (1 Thessalonians 5:19)

As Paul brings his letter to a close, he includes the warning, "Do not put out the Spirit's fire." He knew how absolutely essential was the Holy Spirit in the lives of his readers, and did not want them to forfeit his presence and power in their lives.

Fire is one of the major symbols of the Holy Spirit. John the Baptist said of Christ, "He will baptize you with the Holy Spirit and with fire." As fire, the Holy Spirit purges, removes the dross and undesirable elements in our lives. As fire, he purifies the deep recesses of our hearts. As fire, he illumines our understanding of God's Word and will, and reveals Jesus to us. As fire, he warms, leading John Wesley and generations of believers to have their hearts "strangely warmed" by the fire of the Spirit.

William Booth reminded his troops, "The tendency of fire is to go out." It is possible, as Paul elsewhere reminds us, to "grieve the Spirit," to lose his presence by disobedience and neglect. Let us tend the Spirit's fire within our hearts with the constant fuel of prayer, the Word, and obedience. In the words of Charles Wesley, we voice our prayer:

O Thou Who camest from above
The pure celestial fire to impart,
Kindle a flame of sacred love
On the mean altar of my heart.
There let it for thy glory burn
With inextinguishable blaze,
And trembling to its source return
In humble prayer and fervent praise.

May God himself, the God of peace, sanctify you through and through. (1 Thessalonians 5:23)

The final words of Paul, before his signoff in this epistle, express his heart's longing for his readers. It is a call to holiness, enclosed in his closing benediction: "May God himself, the God of peace, sanctify you through and through. May your whole spirit, soul and body be kept blameless at the coming of our Lord Jesus Christ. The one who calls you is faithful."

Paul yearns for the believers to have a full salvation, cleansed and empowered by the Spirit, with no part of life left untouched by grace. The salvation of God is thorough — the "whole spirit, soul and body." Sanctification is spiritual wholeness, being saved "through and through." William Pearson caught the strain of this truth and incorporated it in his verse:

> Jesus, save me through and through,
> Save me from self-mending;
> Self-salvation will not do,
> Pass me through the cleansing.

> Through my thoughts and through my heart,
> Through my flesh and spirit;
> Save me, Lord, through every part,
> Through thy saving merit.

The apostle Paul moves into a subject little heard today — the judgment of God (1:5-10). The Scriptures were not written just to tell us the things we want to hear. They must reveal the truth of the reality of God's righteous judgment, painful as it may be.

The alternative to divine retribution would be a world with no lasting consequences to our actions. Saddam Hussein and Billy Graham would receive the same rewards in the afterlife. Our character and actions do have eternal meaning and consequences. In a moral universe sin cannot go unpunished. The moral basis of judgment is based on the righteousness of God. Jesus emphasized this in his parable on the Last Judgment (Matthew 15:31-46).

Paul declares that those who do not know God "will be punished with everlasting destruction and shut out from the presence of the Lord and from the majesty of his power on the day he comes to be glorified" (2 Thessalonians 1:9-10). To be eternally banished from the Lord's presence and his glory will be the terrible fate of those who reject God in this life. The final horror of sin will be eternal separation from God.

But for the righteous there will be the grand reward "when the Lord Jesus is revealed from heaven" (1:7). The presence and glory of Christ will be a "breathtaking wonder to all who believe" (1:10 Phillips). No one need be overcome by the bad news of eternal punishment. We may all live by the good news of Christ's return in glory and eternal reward for the righteous.

Christ Jesus came into the world to save sinners. (1 Timothy 1:15)

"Christ Jesus came into the world to save sinners — of whom I am the worst" is the ringing testimony of the apostle Paul. This declares the Incarnation of our Lord. In order to come into the world, Jesus had to be outside of it. The coming of Christ, the Son of God, into the world, is the unparalleled event of human history.

God, clothed in the garb of humanity, is a staggering truth, a miracle beyond our comprehension. He did not come to start a religious movement, or to teach an ethical system, or to found a social order. Christ came to save sinners. The miracle of all miracles is that God in Christ came to save each of us.

"Of whom I am worst," says Paul of his sinful past. Paul himself was "Exhibit A" of the salvation of an undeserving sinner. God's grace transformed him from a persecutor into a preacher, from a murderer into a missionary for Christ.

As he ponders the wonderful grace of God in his life, Paul is overwhelmed and bursts into majestic phrases of praise, giving us one of the great benedictions of Scripture: "Now to the King eternal, immortal, invisible, the only God, be honor and glory for ever and ever. Amen" (1:17). Our hymnbooks echo this praise of our Creator and Savior:

> Immortal, invisible, God only wise,
> In light inaccessible hid from our eyes,
> Most blessed, most glorious, the Ancient of Days,
> Almighty, victorious, thy great name we praise.

Fight the good fight, holding on to faith and a good conscience.
(1 Timothy 1:18)

Paul's letters to Timothy vibrate with the fatherly affection and trust he held for him. His name occurs seventeen times in ten of Paul's letters, more than any other companion. He describes him as a son who served with him in the work of the gospel (Philippians 2:22).

"Stay where you are" (1:3 Moffatt), Paul counsels Timothy. It seems that he wanted to come to Paul, but Paul knew he was needed where he was. There are many situations in life where it would be easier to move on than to stay with a difficult task. The story is told of a farmer who, out in his field one day, looked up at the sky and saw the clouds in an unusual formation, appearing to be the initials "P. C." He thought it meant that he should leave his work and "preach Christ." But when he sought counsel from a wise Christian leader, he was told it meant to "plant corn."

"Fight the good fight" right in his present place was Paul's word to his son in the faith. The Christian is engaged in a warfare. The verb "fight" is in the present tense, indicating that Paul is not referring to an isolated battle, but to a lifetime conflict.

Christ calls us, not to a frolic, but to a fight, not to a picnic but to a pilgrimage, not to comfort but to the cross. Our text inspired John Monsell to write the hymn that echoes this truth:

> Fight the good fight with all thy might,
> Christ is thy strength, and Christ thy right;
> Lay hold on life, and it shall be
> Thy joy and crown eternally.

For there is one God and one mediator between God and men, the man Christ Jesus. (1 Timothy 2:5)

C hrist fulfilled two vital functions of a mediator, as perceived in his day. A mediator had to be able to *represent* both parties. Christ represented both God and man. He represented God as a member of the godhead. The miracle of the Incarnation, clothing him in the garb of humanity, qualified him to represent man. He was the infinite who had become the intimate, the divine Sovereign who became the human sufferer.

In the days of Ezekiel the prophet, the people to whom he spoke were exiles in Babylon, refugees of war, dispossessed of their country, their homes, their freedom. The prophet wanted to give them a message of comfort, of hope. Before he could encourage them with his vision, he had to know himself something of the depths of their despair. So he went down to Babylon to live with the captives, to feel himself their sorrows and humiliation. Then he could say, "I sat where they sat." Then his message had authority because it was forged in the fires his people were experiencing.

Our Lord is a mediator who has sat where we sit. He carried our burdens, endured our agony, was tested by our trials and temptations, lived as a man among men, and died a man's death. His message to us, and his mediating role, have infinite authority.

A mediator also had the task of *reconciliation.* Jesus' role as mediator is to bring human beings back into relationship with God. Our rebellion had stamped on it the penalty of eternal death. The way of the cross was the only way to reconciliation. The cross was the bridge from earth to heaven, spanning the deep chasm of sin. We are incalculably in debt to God's amazing love — that the Lord of the universe came to be our mediator, reconciling us to fellowship with our Creator.

A woman should learn in quietness and full submission.

(1 Timothy 2:11)

F ew texts in the Bible raise the temperature of some people more than this one. If taken literally, this passage would exclude women from all leadership in the church. Paul's teaching on the silence and submission of women does not go well in this day of feminist movements. His strictures seem terribly archaic and unfair.

Paul is writing in the context of the Jewish and Greek culture of his day when women were often treated as chattel, as personal property rather than persons.

This passage is dealing with a problem of disorder in the church. We need to distinguish between texts that describe events or practices in the culture of that time and those that teach principles for universal and timeless application. It does not seem reasonable that this passage should be used in isolation as a "proof text" to exclude women from leadership or relegate them to subservient roles in the church.

Historically, women have played a vital role in Christianity. To a woman was given the first glorious announcement of the resurrection and the privilege of being the first to herald the triumphant news. Dorcas and Lydia are mentioned prominently in the Acts of the Apostles. We find Phoebe and eight other women in Paul's greeting to the church at Rome, and it was Phoebe, a deaconess, who carried the great epistle to its destination. Paul elsewhere refers to "every woman who prays or prophesies" (1 Corinthians 11:5). Philip had four daughters who were prophetesses (Acts 21:9) and Priscilla is called by Paul "a fellow worker in Christ Jesus" (Romans 16:3).

Paul's classic statement expressed the transforming difference Christianity made in that era of male chauvinism: "There is neither male nor female; for you are all one in Christ Jesus" (Galatians 3:28). That is the great text of principle on the place of women in the Christian faith, for whom Jesus Christ was the great emancipator.

Don't let anyone look down on you because you are young.

(1 Timothy 4:12)

Paul gives to his young protégé in the faith a motto for youth of all time: "Don't let anyone look down on you because you are young, but set an example for the believers in speech, in life, in love, in faith and in purity" (4:12).

D. L. Moody was once asked, "How many converts did you have in the meeting?" "Two-and-a-half" he replied. "I suppose you mean two adults and a child," said the enquirer. "No, two children and one adult," responded Moody. The Christian faith and every Christian movement is always a generation away from extinction, unless youth takes up the cause. This text issues a clarion call to youth to be convincing examples of the highest qualities of the Christian life — in speech, in love, in faith, and in purity.

The following young person's prayer provides an apt response to Paul's advice.

Lord, let my life be like a light that shines in every way,
To show to those sunk in sin's night the road to perfect day.
Lord, let my life be like the sea that comes in wave on wave,
To show thy fullness, Lord, in me, through God's great power
    to save.
Lord, let my life be like a book, its pages all aglow
With words of life for all who look and want their Lord to know.
Lord, let my life be like thine own, pure, holy, undefiled,
And never let me from thee roam or be by sin beguiled.

Love of Money

The love of money is a root of all kinds of evil. (1 Timothy 6:10)

H ere is perhaps the most misquoted verse of the Bible. Paul did not say that "money is the root of all evil," but rather "the love of money is a root of all kinds of evil."

There are many things that money cannot buy. Money can buy medicine, but not health. Money can buy a house, but not a home. Money can buy companionship, but not friends. Money can buy entertainment, but not happiness. Money can buy a bed, but not sleep. Money can buy books, but not brains. Money can buy finery, but not beauty. Money can buy a crucifix, but not a Savior. Money can buy "the good life," but not eternal life. As Seneca, the Roman statesman, once said, "Money has never yet made anyone rich."

Money can be too high on our list of values, to the point even of idolatry. It can be put to good use, but it is the obsession for money that breeds evil. The love of money often leads people into wrong ways to obtain it and in the end to paths of remorse and destruction. "Keep your lives free from the love of money" is the Bible's advice, "and be content with what you have" (Hebrews 13:5).

"Content comes," writes William Barclay, "when we escape the servitude to things, when we find our wealth in the love and the friendship and the fellowship of men, and when we realize that our most precious possession is our friendship with God, made possible through Christ."

God, the blessed and only Ruler, the King of kings and Lord of lords.
(1 Timothy 6:15)

The poet Shelley, in one of his sonnets, speaks of meeting a traveler from Egypt. In the desert the traveler had found the remains of a statue, with two "trunkless legs," and near them a broken face. On the pedestal was the inscription: "My name is Ozymandias, king of kings: Look on my works, ye Mighty, and despair!" Ozymandias had the effrontery to style himself "king of kings," but left behind him only remnants of legs and a broken visage in stone. Jesus in his unapproachable glory as King of kings left behind an eternal kingdom.

Every king must have a *right to the title*. Earth's monarchies and dynasties have had a succession by royal lineage. Matthew, the genealogist, carefully traces the Davidic descent of Jesus to certify his credentials as the Messiah. However, it is not Christ's descent from Israel's illustrious king that bestows his divine right. Rather, this right is given him because he is the Son of God.

Every king has *power*. Jesus alone could make the claim, "All power is given unto me" (Matthew 28:18 KJV).

Every king has *subjects and a kingdom*. Jesus said, "My kingdom is not of this world" (John 18:36). While other kingdoms fade and vanish, the eternal kingdom of Jesus Christ continues to expand.

Every king has a *throne*. Scripture states: "Jesus is set down at the right hand of the throne of God" (Hebrews 12:2 KJV). Another throne needs to come under the lordship of Christ, a throne from which there issues all the orders of life — the throne of the human heart. May the King of kings reign without a rival on the throne of our heart.

I know whom I have believed, and am convinced that he is able to guard what I have entrusted to him for that day.

                     (2 Timothy 1:12)

This testimony of Paul has resonated across the centuries as a radiant affirmation of confidence in Christ. It is noteworthy that Paul did not say he knew "what" he believed, but rather "whom" he believed. The apostle's faith was not founded on a creed but on Christ, not in a system but in the Savior, not in a program but in a person.

Paul uses the vivid Greek word that means "deposit." He entrusted or "deposited" his life and work with Christ. A deposit was a sacred trust to keep for another. We too entrust our lives and work to Christ. We do not know what the future holds, but with Paul we may know the One who holds the future, and our life commitment is safely in his keeping.

Ptolemy, a second-century Egyptian astronomer, worked out a model of the universe in which the earth was the fixed center, with the sun and all the stars revolving around it. For more than a thousand years scientists embraced the Ptolemaic system. But they found the sums just did not come out right, until Copernicus, a sixteenth-century Polish astronomer, worked it out that the earth revolved around the sun. It was a complete reversal of the way people imagined the earth.

We live within a spiritual solar system that is as fixed as the one that fills our heavens. Christ is the center of this system, but many people wrongly think they are the center. This human-centered system has defects, just as the Ptolemaic system of astronomy had. The shift from a self-centered to a Christ-centered life is as radical spiritually as Ptolemy to Copernicus cosmologically. John Stott reminds us: "Christ is the center of Christianity; all else is circumference." And that makes all the sums of life come out right.

Faithful Steward of the Word

Do your best to present yourself to God as one approved.
(2 Timothy 2:15)

Paul's analogy of a workman is presented in one of the best-known verses of the Bible: "Do your best to present yourself to God as one approved, a workman who does not need to be ashamed and who correctly handles the word of truth" (2 Timothy 2:15). The handling of the Word of God — whether it be by teaching, preaching, witnessing, or personal devotions — is a serious and sacred matter. It requires both devotion and diligence.

Richard Foster has given us a prescription: "People don't care about our wonderful sermons. They want to know if we know God. They want to know if we have experienced Jesus Christ. They want to know if we know something of the life of righteousness, peace and joy in the Holy Spirit. Without the experience of the life of God, our exegesis may be impeccable, our rhetoric may be magnetic, but we will be dry, empty, hollow."

May we be faithful stewards of the priceless treasure of the Word and merit the approval of its author. A minister once prayed the following petition:

> I do not ask
> That crowds may throng the temple, that standing room
>   be priced;
> I only ask that, as I voice the message,
> They may see Christ.
> I do not ask
> That men may sound my praises or headlines spread
>   my name abroad;
> I only pray that, as I voice the message,
> Hearts may find God.

All Scripture is God-breathed.   (2 Timothy 3:16)

With this text Paul produces one of those gems of rhetorical and theological expressions for which his letters are justly famous: "All Scripture is God-breathed and is useful for teaching, rebuking, correcting and training in righteousness, so that the man of God may be thoroughly equipped for every good work" (3:16-17).

This verse has become a proof text for the inspiration of Scripture. The inspiration of the Bible is a foundation of our faith. If it is not true, then all it teaches can be spurious. The evidence of history, its own integrity, and the experience of God's people validate its divine inspiration. The Bible is "God-breathed," distinguishing it from all human utterance.

The apostle reminds Timothy and all modern-day disciples of Christ that no person is adequately prepared to serve Christ without being equipped with a sound knowledge of God's Word. He relates that the Scriptures will bring wisdom that leads to salvation, that they are useful for teaching and equipping us for God's work. Let us all be "people of the Word."

Other books are ephemeral; they will all give way to the passing of time. But the Word of God is eternal, always timely and timeless. There's a big difference between the books that people make, and the Book that makes people. In answer to the question, "How do you know the Bible is inspired?" someone has said simply, "I know the Bible is inspired because it inspires me."

Paul's Valedictory

I have finished the race, I have kept the faith.   (2 Timothy 4:7)

As Paul comes to the end of his letter to Timothy, he anticipates the executioner's axe that will bring to an end the thirty-year ministry that launched the Christian faith on its worldwide conquests. Having described the Christian as an athlete in a race, he now passes the baton to Timothy for the next lap of the race.

In these parting words to his son in the faith he charges him to keep the highest priorities. "Preach the Word. . . . Be prepared in season and out of season" (4:2). There are no closed seasons for the Christian. The apostle's mandate is, "Do the work of an evangelist" (4:5).

He does not describe his impending death as an execution but rather as an offering to God. "The time has come for my departure," he writes (4:6). The Greek word Paul uses for "departure" refers to the loosening of the mooring ropes of a ship. He viewed death as a sailing forth to a new and permanent haven. At the end of his earthly journey awaits the Savior to give to him the crown of eternal life.

Paul's final words of farewell comprise one of the most memorable statements in the Bible. A prisoner in chains, the shadow of the executioner's axe looming over him, he confidently affirms: "I have fought the good fight, I have finished the race, I have kept the faith. Now there is in store for me the crown of righteousness, which the Lord, the righteous judge, will award to me on that day."

Paul appended to the end of that statement, "and not only to me, but also to all who have longed for his appearing." We are included in that final word!

We wait for the blessed hope — the glorious appearing of our great God and Savior, Jesus Christ.   (Titus 2:13)

In the middle of this letter from Paul to Titus, his troubleshooter in Crete, we come upon a textual jewel, coruscating with radiant truths of our faith. The apostle acclaims the triumphant Second Coming: "We wait for the blessed hope — the glorious appearing of our great God and Savior, Jesus Christ, who gave himself for us to redeem us from all wickedness and to purify for himself a people that are his very own, eager to do what is good" (2:13-14).

"The blessed hope" has become a familiar designation for the Christian's belief and expectation for the Parousia — the Second Coming of Christ. It will be the crowning event of all history and for every believer. As the songwriter Bill Gaither has put it in our own day, "The King is coming. He's coming for you and for me."

The first advent of Jesus Christ was awesome — the marvel of God taking upon himself that mystical composite of "theanthropos" — the God-man. The event of that starlit night in the hamlet of Bethlehem is the most colossal event of history. But the apostle Paul in this text exultantly declares that there is yet a more awesome event to take place — "the glorious appearing of our great God and Savior, Jesus Christ."

When we hear the news of our day, we say, "The worst is yet to come." But when we read this and kindred texts in the Bible, we say, "The best is yet to be!"

From Slave to Sonship

No longer as a slave, but . . . as a dear brother. (Philemon 16)

Within the brief one-chapter letter to Philemon is one of the most fascinating stories of the New Testament. The church in Colossae met in the home of Philemon. His slave, Onesimus, ran away and apparently became a thief. Onesimus became converted during Paul's imprisonment in Rome and rendered valued service to the apostle. Legally, Onesimus was the property of Philemon. The unforgivable crime for a slave was an attempt to escape.

Paul warmly greets Philemon and his family, and then, remarkably, makes his plea for Onesimus to be taken back, not as a slave, but as a dear brother in the Lord. What a revolutionary concept and frontal assault on the entrenched institution of slavery in that time! When slaves become brothers, the system has lost its control. In Christ all are equal, and there is no slave or free (Colossians 3:11).

Paul made this letter into a promissory note with the force of an I.O.U. To Onesimus, Paul's letter was his charter of liberty. Why did this single papyrus sheet, alone of the many personal ones Paul had written, get preserved and published among Paul's epistles? It presents no great doctrine, addresses no threatening heresy.

In A.D. 110, Ignatius, on his way to execution, wrote a letter to the church at Ephesus, in which no fewer than fourteen times he refers by name to the bishop at Ephesus. The name of that bishop was none other than Onesimus. The epistle of Ignatius contains clear literary linkages to Philemon. This phenomenon suggests that Onesimus, the bishop at Ephesus, is the same Onesimus of Paul's letter. What better explanation of the inclusion of Philemon in the collection but that all might know what the grace of God had done for him.

In Onesimus we may see ourselves, our renegade status against the Master of the universe. By the grace of our Lord Jesus Christ, we can be ransomed, forgiven, restored as a very child of God. The spiritual biography of Onesimus, who went from slave to sonship can very well be our own. Let it be so.

But in these last days he has spoken to us by his Son.

(Hebrews 1:2)

The book of Hebrews presents one of the most revealing portraits of Christ found in the Bible. It deals with the very foundation of our faith — who Jesus Christ is. Christology is the heart of our theology, for without Christ we have no faith, no hope. The theme of the epistle is the superiority and supremacy of Christ.

"In the past God spoke . . . through the prophets" (1:1). Each prophet revealed a facet of God. Isaiah spoke of God's holiness, Hosea of his forgiveness, Amos of God's justice, and Micah of God's judgment. Each presented but a fragmentary revelation. Everything prior to Christ was partial and preparatory. God's past and progressive revelation prepared for his perfect revelation in Christ, who revealed God in understandable human terms.

The author of Hebrews flings out his thesis with the statement: "But in these last days he has spoken to us by his Son, whom he appointed heir of all things, and through whom he made the universe. The Son is the radiance of God's glory and the exact representation of his being" (1:2-3). His reference to Christ is reminiscent of Pauline and Johannine texts, which declare that all things were created by Christ (John 1:3; Colossians 1:16). In these simple words, "through whom he made the universe," lie all the mystery and secrets of creation.

This text declares that Jesus Christ, the sovereign God, is the supreme articulation of Deity to all humankind. By him we may know and draw near to God.

How shall we escape if we ignore such a great salvation?

(Hebrews 2:3)

O ur tutor poses the rhetorical question: "How shall we escape if we ignore such a great salvation?" Of course, there is no escape from a neglect of God's salvation.

The greatness of this salvation is that it comes direct from the Lord, cradled in supernatural signs and wonders, and mediated through the Holy Spirit (2:3-4).

Evangelist D. L. Moody said that he made the greatest mistake of his life on October 8, 1871. On that night in Chicago, addressing one of the largest crowds of his ministry, he preached on the text, "What shall I do then with Jesus?" As he concluded his message he said, "I wish you would seriously consider this subject, for next Sunday we will speak about the cross, and at that time I'll inquire, 'What will YOU do with Jesus?'" Ira Sankey sang the closing hymn, which included the lines, "Today the Savior calls; for refuge fly. The storm of justice falls, and death is nigh."

But the hymn was never finished, as there was the rush and roar of fire engines on the street outside. That was the night of the great Chicago fire that almost destroyed the entire city. And before the next day, Chicago lay in ashes. "I have never since dared," said Moody, "to give an audience a week to think of their salvation."

According to our text, what do we do about God's great salvation, in order to be lost? The answer: indecision, or nothing.

For the Word of God is living and active.   (Hebrews 4:12)

This golden text is one of the great verses on the Bible itself: "For the word of God is living and active. Sharper than any double-edged sword, it penetrates even to dividing soul and spirit, joints and marrow; it judges the thoughts and attitudes of the heart." Such a statement cannot be made of any other book in all of history. This text declares several transcendent attributes of the Word of God.

The Word of God is living. It is no dusty record of antiquity. Other words pass into oblivion or acquire an academic or antiquarian interest. But the Word of God is always contemporary, alive and dynamic. J. B. Phillips likened his work of translation to that of an electrician working on the wiring of a house with all the mains turned on.

The Word of God is powerful. It convicts us of our sin and leads us on to salvation, holiness, and service for God. Augustine, upon being led by the Spirit to "take up and read," turned to a passage, read it, and his life was utterly transformed. An innumerable company have given witness to the powerful impact of its dynamic truths upon their lives. While men make other books, the Word of God makes men.

The Word of God is penetrating. In figurative speech the writer says that the Word of God penetrates the very "joints and marrow." It is in the marrow that diseases may lurk long before their symptoms are known. A person may seem healthy but his marrow may be harboring a life-threatening disease. God's Word searches our inner life — "the thoughts and attitudes of the heart" — to reveal the spiritual condition not seen on the surface.

For each of us, the Bible is a bright candle of the Lord, a star of the heavens, guiding us to our eternal destiny.

Let us then approach the throne of grace with confidence.

(Hebrews 4:16)

O ur Lord's mediatorial role as our "great high priest" (4:14), and his having experienced the testings of our humanity (4:15), results in one of the great invitations to prayer presented in the Bible: "Let us then approach the throne of grace with confidence, so that we may receive mercy and find grace to help us in our time of need."

Prayer ushers us into our highest and holiest estate, the noblest exercise of the soul and most exalted use of our faculties. It brings us to an audience with the Sovereign of the universe.

Admiral Byrd, in his book *Alone*, tells how in 1934 he spent five months in an isolated hut in the Antarctic. Blizzards raged around his shack; the cold plunged to 82 degrees below zero; he was surrounded by endless night. And then he found to his horror that he was being slowly poisoned by carbon monoxide seeping from his stove. He was convinced he would die and be buried by perpetual snows.

One day, in the depths of his despair, he reached for his diary and set down his philosophy of life. "The human race," he wrote, "is not alone in the universe." This realization that he was not alone — not even in the ice at the end of the earth, was what saved Richard Byrd. "I know it pulled me through," he says.

When we pray to God, we acknowledge within our hearts that we are not alone in the universe. There is a God who created us, who loves us, who hears our prayer. John Newton, in his memorable verse, calls us to such confidence in prayer:

Thou art coming to a King,
Large petitions with thee bring,
For his grace and power are such
None can ever ask too much.

We have this hope as an anchor for the soul, firm and secure.

(Hebrews 6:19)

This text gives us one of the great metaphors of the New Testament. The author describes our hope in Christ as "an anchor for the soul, firm and secure."

As a boater, I well know how essential an anchor is when one ventures onto the waterways. An anchor is so vital the law requires that a boat include it among its safety equipment. No seafaring captain would ever venture out without one. An anchor serves the purpose of a holding power for a ship, without which a boat would drift helplessly at the mercy of the wind or tides.

The apostle Paul states that our hope is the anchor for our soul, holding us amid the forces that threaten to tear us from our moorings of faith. Hope is our confident expectation in Christ and the fulfillment of the promises of God.

Some time ago the Hope Diamond, considered the most beautiful blue diamond in the world, was on display in the Smithsonian Institution. A tourist, after gazing at it for awhile through the bulletproof glass, finally walked over to one of the guards in the room and asked, "What is the value of this jewel?" He was told that no price could be put upon it, that it was priceless and could never be sold.

The hope of the Christian is more priceless than any earthly jewel. It is the anchor that will hold our soul secure amid the testings and storms of life until we safely reach the port of heaven. Priscilla Owens has transposed this metaphor into the chorus:

We have an anchor that keeps the soul
Steadfast and sure while the billows roll;
Fastened to the rock which cannot move,
Grounded firm and deep in the Savior's love.

Destined to Die

Man is destined to die once, and after that to face judgment.
(Hebrews 9:27)

The writer of Hebrews utters this stern statement on death and the judgment. A little further on he gives the text made familiar by Jonathan Edwards's sermon on it: "It is a dreadful thing to fall into the hands of the living God" (10:31).

None of us will get out of this life alive (unless we are here when the Lord comes)! Death is the most democratic of all experiences. George Bernard Shaw wryly said: "The statistics on death are quite impressive. One out of one people die." The Greek playwright Euripides called death "the debt we all must pay."

According to an old middle-eastern legend, a wealthy merchant in Baghdad one day sent his servant to the marketplace to secure provisions for the household. In a little while the servant returned, his limbs trembling and his face pale with fright. "What is wrong?" asked the merchant. "Master," cried the servant, "I just now met Death in the marketplace, and when Death saw me, he raised his arm to strike me. I am afraid and I must escape. Let me, I pray, borrow your fastest horse, and I shall flee to Samara."

The merchant, being a kind-hearted man, gave his consent, and the servant rode swiftly away to the city of Samara. After the servant had departed, the merchant himself went to the market. He, too, saw Death, and going boldly up to him, said, "Death, why did you raise your hand to strike my servant here in the marketplace a little while ago?"

"I meant him no harm," answered Death, "that was a gesture of surprise for seeing him here in Baghdad, for I have an appointment with him tonight in the city of Samara."

As our text declares, we are all "destined to die." And he adds the stern warning that after that we will face judgment. That event will come to us as surely as death. Let us be sure to be ready for both ultimate and inescapable events.

Now faith is being sure of what we hope for and certain of what we do not see.   (Hebrews 11:1)

The writer of Hebrews in this text gives his classic definition of faith — being sure and certain of what we cannot see. The Greek word translated "being sure" means something that is firm, solid. The word for "certain" means tested for validity or reality.

Faith is much more than wishful thinking or wistful hoping. Faith is linked with an evidence and knowledge of that in which we have placed our hope. Elton Trueblood stated, "Faith is not a blind leap into the dark but a thoughtful walk in the light we have."

"By faith," the author writes, "we understand that the universe was formed at God's command" (11:3). By faith, we believe the world is a creation of God. Voltaire, the atheist, was constrained to say, "The world embarrasses me: I cannot believe that so beautiful a clock is without a maker." The design and order of the universe witness to a Creator.

This great chapter is famous for its Roll Call of Faith (vv. 4-38). The stories behind the names illustrate the linkage of obedience with faith. The illustrious roster roams through the history of Israel with names that evoke reminiscences of great heroes. Many had faced incredible odds for God. But these dauntless believers chose to be in God's minority rather than in the world's majority. They triumphed in faith even though God's promises in Christ were not realized in their time (v. 39).

No fewer than eighteen times in this chapter we come upon the phrase "by faith." Faith was the secret of victory for all who had gone before, both the illustrious and the unknown. Let us then go on, and "by faith" be triumphant.

The Race of Life

Let us run with perseverance the race marked out for us.

(Hebrews 12:1)

"The Christian life is a race," writes William Barclay, "along a course that is set out before us." The Christian is not an unconcerned stroller along the byways of life.

We each have a handicap in this race, the handicap of our sin. "Therefore," our spiritual coach challenges, "let us throw off everything that hinders and the sin that so easily entangles, and let us run with perseverance the race marked out for us." The Greek word for "race" is *agon*, from which we derive our word "agony." It speaks to us of the disciplines and endurance required in this great race of life.

In running a marathon, we have to follow to the letter the advice of this spiritual coach. We have to run as lightly as possible, with absolutely no extra encumbrance. Twenty-six miles is a long way to go and even the lightest items would become unbearably heavy and hinder our ability to finish.

And of course we have to "run with perseverance." The prize goes not to the good starters but to the good finishers. When the body feels almost exhausted, the muscles aching, and every stride a major effort, we have to keep going.

The testing times of life will surely come. Steep hills, obstacles, distractions, and rugged paths will require every bit of energy and endurance to go on. How will we be able to do it? What is the secret of success?

Our writer gives us the secret of success. "Let us fix our eyes on Jesus" (12:2). He will be our example, our guide, and our source of strength, enabling us to run successfully the race of life.

Jesus Christ is the same yesterday and today and forever.

(Hebrews 13:8)

O ur world is dominated by change. Economic situations alter. Relationships may change. Our health ultimately diminishes. Loved ones experience tragedy or depart from this life. Our world goes through the constant upheavals of war among nations. Eventually even the sun and the stars will grow dim.

But there is One who will always be the same. One of the brightest jewels of this epistle emerges in its final chapter, revealing the immutability of our Lord: "Jesus Christ is the same yesterday and today and forever." He is the One in whom there is no variableness or shadow of turning.

Jesus Christ will not change in any of his attributes. He is unchangeably omniscient, unchangeably omnipotent, unchangeably holy, unchangeably loving.

Let us then set our affections, not upon the things around us that will pass away, but upon this rock that will be immovably secure amid the rains, floods, and storms that may beat upon us. Let us hold fast to this unchanging Christ who has given us the promise: "Never will I leave you; never will I forsake you" (13:5). With the hymn writer Henry Lyte, we would pray:

> Swift to its close ebbs out life's little day;
> Earth's joys grow dim, its glories pass away;
> Change and decay in all around I see;
> O thou who changest not, abide with me!

If any of you lacks wisdom, he should ask God, who gives gener-
ously to all.   (James 1:5)

We have a dire need for wisdom for living. In our volatile and dangerous world, our very survival as a society and as individuals requires a God-endowed wisdom.

Wisdom from God is not an elective in the school of life. It is a required course if we are to live purposefully, triumphantly, and eternally. To miss out on the wisdom from God is to flunk life itself. Our text conveys the promise of wisdom available to the one who seeks it: "If any of you lacks wisdom, he should ask God, who gives generously to all."

All the learning of all the educational institutions in the world, and all the books of all the libraries of the world, and all the most brilliant minds in every profession, would be but a millimeter of intelligence compared to the fathomless mind of omniscient God. The promise of our text invites us to tap this wisdom for our own needs and living.

Wisdom, in the biblical sense, means more than knowledge — it means discernment for living. We desperately need wisdom to discern life's priorities. How reassuring to know that we can receive from God perception for our perplexities, discernment for our difficulties, and understanding for our undertakings. Let us then go forth to live both wisely and well.

Every good and perfect gift is from above. (James 1:17)

J ames tells us that the God who is the Creator of the celestial lights is also the source of our spiritual illumination and blessings: "Every good and perfect gift is from above, coming down from the Father of the heavenly lights."

God has given to us the gift of life itself, with all its bounty of blessings and rich potential. He has given us the amazing planet Earth, designed and ordered for our every need and for our enjoyment. He has given us the Bible, containing his love letters and wisdom for guidance. He has set us in the community of believers. Above all he has given us his Son as our Savior, and the Holy Spirit as our Helper.

Writers tend to avoid superlatives, which usually overstate the case. But when the writers of the Bible spoke of the blessings of God they called forth their most lavish vocabulary. They write of a "peace that passes understanding" (Philippians 4:7 NKJV), of a "joy inexpressible and full of glory" (1 Peter 1:8 NKJV), of "an inheritance incorruptible and undefiled and that does not fade away" (1 Peter 1:4 NKJV). When Paul wanted to express how God answers prayer he piled superlative upon superlative, writing that he will "do exceedingly abundantly above all that we ask or think" (Ephesians 3:20 NKJV).

God has lavished extravagant gifts upon us. In him we have a love that can never be fathomed, a life that will never die, a peace that can never be understood, a joy that can never be overcome, a hope that can never be disappointed, a glory that can never be faded, a strength that can never be diminished, a purity that can never be defiled, a wisdom that can never be baffled, and resources that can never be exhausted.

But be doers of the word, and not hearers only.

(James 1:22 NKJV)

"Do not merely listen to the word. . . . Do what it says" is the straightforward rendition of the NIV. The Word of God must not only be heard, it must be heeded; it must not only be presented, it must be practiced with its teachings lived out in daily life. This counsel from James leads us to apply ourselves wholly to the text, and to apply the text wholly to ourselves.

An anonymous poet challenges us about a "fifth gospel" that is needed:

> There's a sweet old story translated for man
> But writ in the long, long ago —
> The gospel, according to Mark, Luke and John —
> Of Christ and his mission below.

> Men read and admire the gospel of Christ,
> With its love so unfailing and true;
> But what do they say, and what do they think
> Of the gospel "according to you"?

> You are writing each day a letter to men,
> Take care that the writing is true,
> 'Tis the only Gospel that some men will read —
> That Gospel "according to you."

Faith by itself, if it does not have works, is dead.

(James 2:17 NKJV)

In this passage on faith and deeds (1:27–2:26), James does not contradict but rather complements the apostle Paul's teaching that we are saved by faith. In his letter on practical Christianity, James stresses that good deeds must result from our faith in Christ. His polemic does not argue for the priority of works over faith, but insists that there is no valid Christian faith apart from works of righteousness. Our practice needs to equal our profession, and our deeds need to reflect our creed.

James gives his definition of authentic religion: "Religion that God our Father accepts as pure and faultless is this: to look after orphans and widows in their distress and to keep oneself from being polluted by the world" (1:27). These words echo Micah's famous dictum: "And what does the LORD require of you? To act justly and to love mercy and to walk humbly with your God" (Micah 6:8).

In his emphasis on good deeds, James warns especially against the evils of prejudice and partiality (2:1-6). One of the great scandals in the history of the Christian church took place when Gandhi, early in his career, went to a Christian church in South Africa, only to be turned away at the door by an usher because his skin was not white. The great opponent of caste in the Hindu religion found caste at the door of a Christian church.

James gives his remedy, that of love, which he calls "the royal law found in Scripture" (2:8). The "royal law" comes to us from the King of kings, who himself taught that to love God and to love our neighbor is supreme among all the laws of God. Love for God is the expression of our faith, and love for others is the expression of our works.

The Untamable Tongue

But no man can tame the tongue. (James 3:8)

O ur words tell our world who we are. Every time we speak the world sees us. James in his epistle has some stern words about the power of the tongue.

The tongue, James contends, is the most difficult part of our body to control. He illustrates that a small bit in the mouth of a horse controls the whole animal, a very small rudder drives a large ship against strong winds, and a small spark can set a great forest fire. "Likewise," says James, "the tongue is a small part of the body, but it can corrupt the whole person." He further writes that all creatures of nature are brought under control by man, "but no man can tame the tongue" (3:2-8).

The tongue, James adds, can be a means of praise as well as of curse. It has great potential for destruction or for blessing. The tongue can inflame a mob to violence, destroy friendships, and instigate wars. But it can also inspire a nation to heroic action, strike a blow for justice, and bring comfort to those in despair.

James gives the remedy for an uncontrolled tongue. It is to have the wisdom of God, which he already told us can be ours for the asking. He now tells us that "the wisdom that comes from heaven is first of all pure; then peace-loving, considerate, submissive, full of mercy and good fruit, impartial and sincere" (3:17). These eight attributes will characterize our life and speech when we live in the wisdom of God. With the psalmist of old, we make our daily prayer: "Set a guard over my mouth, O LORD; keep watch over the door of my lips" (Psalm 141:3).

*When you ask, you do not receive, because you ask with the wrong
motives.* (James 4:3)

N o one can estimate the mighty power of prayer, or all the good
and great things that have been accomplished because of prayer.

James gives valued insight on prayer in his short epistle. In this
passage he identifies two problems in prayer. The first problem is simply that of neglect: "You do not have because you do not ask God" (4:2).
We miss many of God's blessings because we do not ask him to supply
our spiritual needs.

Secondly, we do not always receive answers to prayer, because we
ask amiss — out of selfish rather than pure motives. God knows best,
and answers prayer in different ways:

When the idea is not right, God says, "No!"
When the time is not right, God says, "Slow!"
When you are not right, God says, "Grow!"
When everything is right, God says, "Go!"

God does not look at the eloquence of our prayers to see how articulate they are. Nor does he look at the geometry of our prayers to see
how long they are. Nor does he look at the arithmetic of our prayers to
see how many they are. Nor does he look at the logic of our prayers to
see how clever they are. He looks at the sincerity of our prayers, to see
how authentic they are.

He Gives More Grace

But he gives us more grace. (James 4:6)

Tucked away amid the collection of proverbial sayings of this epistle is one of the Bible's greatest promises: "He gives us more
grace." How many times we have had to claim God's promise for more
grace to get through the testings and the trials that have beset us.

A friend of mine, going through a very trying period of his life, responded to a letter, affirming: "We feel upheld at this difficult time, and
are finding a new reality in the words: 'He giveth more grace as our
burdens grow greater.'" Indeed, Annie Johnson Flint's hymn, from
which he was quoting, has brought the refreshing truth of this text to
many hearts, serving as a companion verse to our text:

> He giveth more grace when the burden grows greater;
> He sendeth more strength when the labors increase.
> To added afflictions he addeth His mercy;
> To multiplied trials, his multiplied peace.

When the burden seems almost too much to bear, when the winds
of adversity beat relentlessly upon us, when our own strength would
fail — he gives more grace, grace sufficient for the need of the hour. In
such seasons of our souls, our Lord says to us, as he did to the apostle
Paul, "My grace is sufficient for you."

Resist the devil, and he will flee from you.   (James 4:7)

We are engaged in a spiritual warfare, a real life-and-death struggle, with our eternal destiny at stake. "Resist the devil," asserts James, "and he will flee from you."

We dare not flirt with the temptations of Satan, or entertain his overtures, or be passive to his influence. We must actively resist him. Then we will cause him to flee.

In Greek legend, two famous travelers, Odysseus and Orpheus, passed where the Sirens sat on rocks and sang with seductive sweetness to lure mariners to their doom. Odysseus took the strategy of plugging the sailors' ears so that they could not hear, and ordering them to bind him to the mast with ropes so that he would not be able to answer the Sirens' call. He resisted by compulsion. The other traveler, Orpheus, known as the sweetest musician of all, played and sang so beautifully as his ship passed the Sirens' rocks, the attraction of the song he sang was greater than that of the Sirens. His method was to answer the seduction with a still greater appeal.

God's method is the second way. "Submit yourselves, then, to God," is the other part of this text. God does not save us from temptation by forcible compulsion. Rather, his love and exceeding goodness and grace captivate our soul, enabling us to resist all allurements of the world that would lead us to doom.

Thomas Chalmers writes of "the expulsive powers of a new affection" — a master passion so strong that it can regulate all the lesser passions. God seeks to make us love him so much that his voice is more compelling than those that would call us away from him. Let us then listen to his voice, and follow where he beckons.

Near to God

Come near to God and he will come near to you. (James 4:8)

H ere we have another jewel of a prayer promise in this epistle: "Come near to God and he will come near to you." Just think of it! The God of the universe becomes intimate with us when our hearts reach out for him.

Prayer is not overcoming God's reluctance; it is laying hold of his highest willingness. When we throw out a boat hook to catch hold of the shore, we do not pull the shore to ourselves. Rather we pull ourselves to the shore. Prayer does not pull God to us, it pulls us to God. It aligns our will with his will. E. Stanley Jones wrote: "In prayer I seldom ask for things; more and more I ask God for himself, for the assurance that my will and his are not at cross-purposes."

Prayer is the nearest approach to God, and the highest enjoyment of him that we are capable of in this life. "When our hearts are full of God," wrote William Law, "sending up holy desires to the throne of grace, we are then in our highest state, we are upon the utmost heights of human greatness."

Prayer is the soul's pilgrimage from self to God. Albert Orsborn's words remind us that prayer ushers us into the secret of God's presence:

In the secret of thy presence,
Where the pure in heart may dwell,
Are the springs of sacred service,
And a power that none can tell.
There my love must bring its offering,
There my heart must yield its praise,
And the Lord will come,
Revealing all the secrets of his ways.

*Anyone, then, who knows the good he ought to do and doesn't do it,
sins.* (James 4:17)

The reader of this epistle keeps encountering seminal truths that we cannot afford to gloss over. Suddenly we come upon a rare and discomfiting definition of sin: "Anyone, then, who knows the good he ought to do and doesn't do it, sins." None of us can feel exempt from this condemnation; we confess our neglect and pray for grace to do better.

James warns us of the sins of omission as well as those of commission. Near the end of his letter he gives a reason to avoid the sin of omission as it relates to our spiritual responsibility to others: "Remember this: Whoever turns a sinner from the error of his way will save him from death and cover over a multitude of sins" (5:20).

In the words of the traditional prayer we need to confess our "having left undone those things we ought to have done" — our omitted duties and the blessing God would have had us bring to others.

Jesus in his parable on the Last Judgment warned that some will be condemned, not only for sins committed, but for acts of kindness left undone. Someone has written a reminder that we journey this way but once:

I shall pass through this world but once,
Any good thing, therefore, that I can do —
Or any kindness that I can show any human being,
Let me do it now.
Let me not defer nor neglect it —
For I shall not pass this way again.

The Power of Prayer

The prayer of a righteous man is powerful and effective.

(James 5:16)

This epistle draws near to its close with one of the greatest promises on prayer: "The prayer of a righteous man is powerful and effective."

There is no more significant involvement in another's life than authentic and consistent prayer. It is more helpful than a gift of money, more encouraging than a good sermon, more effective than a compliment, more reassuring than an embrace. Prayer is the best effort we can make on behalf of another.

"And why should the good of anyone depend on the prayer of another?" asked George MacDonald. "I can only answer," he said, "with the return question, 'Why should my love be powerless to help another?'"

Some years ago one of our granddaughters, then about 7 years of age, gave to Marjorie and me for Christmas a small framed note that read, "I will pray for you every day." It was no doubt the least expensive gift we received, but also our most cherished Christmas gift that year. Today, over a decade later, it graces my study shelf. Prayer is the greatest gift we can give another.

Prayer is pivotal in the Christian life. In the words of our text, it is "powerful and effective." C. S. Lewis's *Screwtape Letters* tell of Screwtape, a demon in hell's higher echelons, writing to his nephew Wormwood, a novice demon, with advice on how best to defeat human souls. In relation to prayer Screwtape warns his nephew to "interfere at any price" when people start to pray, for real prayer is lethal to the devil's cause.

Tennyson's words complement our text and serve as a call to prayer:

More things are wrought by prayer than this world dreams of.
Wherefore let thy voice rise like a fountain for me night and day.

Into an inheritance that can never perish, spoil or fade.

(1 Peter 1:4)

P eter breaks into a paean of praise to God for bringing us "into a living hope" (1:3). The hope of the Christian is alive, dynamic, and vital. It comes to us "through the resurrection of Jesus Christ from the dead." Peter himself was an eyewitness of the resurrected Lord and speaks here with an indisputable authority.

In the midst of the despair and violence all around us, our world needs hope. Pressed with the frustrations of today and the fears for tomorrow, we need hope. Christ is the hope of the world. It has been said, "Life with Christ is an endless hope, without him a hopeless end."

The apostle calls forth his superlatives to describe the inheritance God has for the believer. He describes it as "incorruptible" (KJV). In this life all eventually comes to decay. But our inheritance in heaven is imperishable.

Peter also defines our eternal inheritance as "undefiled" (KJV) — free from impurity. And it "can never fade" (NIV) — its brilliance and splendor will be undiminished through eternity.

This inheritance, says Peter, is "reserved in heaven for you" (KJV). When we make a hotel reservation we are often asked if it is to be a "guaranteed reservation," that is, a reservation kept regardless of how late we arrive. But it must be paid for in advance. Our inheritance in heaven comes with a guaranteed reservation. It has been paid for by the infinite sacrifice of Christ.

The Eternal Word

But the word of the Lord stands forever. (1 Peter 1:25)

L ife is very fragile and finite, as described by Peter: "All men are like grass, and all their glory is like flowers of the field; the grass withers and the flowers fall." In contrast, "the word of the Lord stands forever."

God's love letter to humankind, his priceless treasure to us — anthology of divine thought, guidebook for our salvation, index to eternal truths — endures forever. Other books, even the great classics, will eventually become archaic and outdated. But the Word of God will endure throughout eternal ages.

History has recorded what have been called the Seven Wonders of the World. But each of those "wonders" has passed into oblivion, now but ashes in the dustbin of history. But what we may call the Seven Wonders of the Word proclaims the enduring quality of the Word of God. First, there is the wonder of its formation — the way it grew and came together. Second, there is the wonder of its unification — a library of sixty-six books, yet one book. Third, there is the wonder of its age — the most ancient and enduring of all books. Fourth, it has been read by the most people of all time. Fifth, it was written by largely uneducated men, yet remains the world's quintessential literary classic. Sixth, its preservation is one of the great miracles of history, surviving the most ferocious persecution.

But of course the seventh great wonder of the Bible is its proclamation of the eternal love of God for humankind and the transformation its timeless truths create in our lives.

Your beauty should not come from outward adornment.

(1 Peter 3:3)

Marriage, a divine institution, has come on hard times. Half of all marriages in the U.S. end in divorce. Many become merely marriages of accommodation, "keeping up appearances" but lacking the love that should undergird a marriage. Apparently marriages were in trouble in Peter's time, and he provides some guidelines and principles to follow.

The apostle sets the standard for a wife to have chaste conduct coupled with reverence for God (3:3). "Chastity" is a word not in vogue in today's lexicon, or in general practice in our permissive society. God's Word calls marriage partners back to the standard of purity and fidelity to the marriage vow.

Today, many worship at the shrine of physical beauty, blatantly held up in advertisements that constantly impinge upon us. On this topic, Peter writes, "Your beauty should not come from outward adornment . . . instead, it should be that of your inner self, the unfading beauty of a gentle and quiet spirit." Peter says that true attractiveness is the winsomeness of a Christian character and pleads for the graces and spiritual beauty that cannot be obtained at a cosmetic counter.

Husbands are not exempt from Peter's marriage counsel: "Husbands, in the same way be considerate as you live with your wives, and treat them with respect" (3:7). Elsewhere, the apostle Paul says, "Husbands, love your wives, just as Christ loved the church" (Ephesians 5:25). This teaching was radical in that day when women had no rights and often were treated as chattel. Christianity became the great liberating and equalizing force for women.

These "Peter Principles" will promote domestic harmony and love in marriage.

Give the Reason

Give the reason for the hope that you have.   (1 Peter 3:15)

Peter here is not suggesting that everyone be ready with a scholarly answer but that we be able to tell clearly what Jesus Christ means to us. In this text he implies that we have a reason for our hope and should be prepared to share it. Our Christian faith is not wishful thinking, "an opiate of the people," or "a blind man searching in a dark room for a black cat that is not there." Our faith has unshakable foundations, and is based on the highest hypothesis and experience of which human reason is capable.

Too many Christians are content to remain at the childhood stage in their faith, finding anchorage only in the fallible formulas of time-worn clichés. What does it really mean to be a Christian? Theologian Hans Küng reminds us, "Today the question is thrust even on the Christian who has been institutionally sheltered and ideologically immunized in the churches. Compared with the world religions and modern humanisms, is Christianity something essentially different, really something special?"

We need to seriously consider and come to a conviction of what being a Christian really means, and what it is all about. Confronted with pluralism, with competing ideologies and trends, it behooves the Christian to heed the counsel of Peter, to discover the reason for our hope, what is decisive and distinctive about the Christian faith.

It has been said, "Because all we want is just to live, it has become impossible for us to truly live." The world around us desperately needs the hope we have found in Christ. Peter calls us not merely to a readiness but also to a reasonable and relevant witness of our faith.

Cast all your anxiety on him because he cares for you.

(1 Peter 5:7)

Fears and phobias have been categorized from A to Z, from acrophobia — fear of heights, to zoophobia — fear of animals. Whether it's fear of heights, crowds, spiders, thunder, flying, failure, disease, death, or children's fear of the dark, it seems that everyone is afraid of something. These can develop into the corrosive fears called phobias. Many today fear the future, and suffer anxiety that causes unrest and stress.

The Scripture's prescription is: "Cast all your anxiety on him because he cares for you." The God of the universe cares for you, and that should make a difference.

Søren Kierkegaard defined anxiety as "the next day." It is this unwritten chapter of our lives that can cause stress. We can become so concerned about tomorrow that we lose the meaning and joy of today. Jesus gives us the key when he tells us to let tomorrow take care of itself.

Peace is the legacy of Christ to his followers: "Peace I leave with you; my peace I give you" (John 14:27). When the risen Lord comes into our lives he stills the discord and gives us his peace. May we hear him speak his words to our hearts, "Peace be unto you."

A Roaring Lion

Your enemy the devil prowls around like a roaring lion looking for
someone to devour.   (1 Peter 5:8)

Peter knew all too well the powerful wiles of Satan. "Be self-controlled and alert," he warns, because "Your enemy the devil prowls around like a roaring lion looking for someone to devour." We all have this diabolical enemy of our soul with whom we are in a life-and-death struggle that requires our constant vigilance.

Let us put aside any image of Satan as the comic character of the Middle Ages, dressed in red, with horns, tail, and pitchfork. Satan is real and powerful, cunning and crafty, with many strategies to defeat and destroy the Christian.

An artist once painted a picture of a young man engaged in a chess game with Satan. Should the young man win he would be forever free from the power of evil; should the devil win, the young man was to be his slave forever. The artist pictured Satan on the verge of a checkmate that would make him the victor. The young man's face paled; there was not hope.

For years this picture hung in a great art gallery. Chess players who viewed it acquiesced to the artist's concept of a hopeless checkmate. But one day a master chess player and undefeated champion, Paul Morphy, was invited to view the painting. Morphy stood and viewed it for over thirty minutes, all concentration. He lifted and lowered his hands as, in imagination, he made moves. Suddenly, his hand paused, and he shouted: "Young man, make that move. That's the move!" To the amazement of all, the old master had discovered a combination the artist had not considered. The young man defeated the Devil.

After the fall of Adam and Eve, it may have seemed that Satan was the victor. But Jesus came, defeated Satan, and made victory within reach for each of us.

*After you have suffered a little while, [God] will himself restore you
and make you strong.*   (1 Peter 5:10)

The apostle Peter addressed this epistle to a suffering church. He refers to their suffering some sixteen times as he brings them comfort, counsel, and hope.

No doubt he also wants to prepare them for severe persecution yet
to come under Nero, the deranged and infamous emperor of Rome. Peter will himself pay the ultimate cost of discipleship, that of crucifixion, requesting to be crucified upside down because he was not worthy
to die in the same manner as his Lord.

Isaac Watts's hymn is like a glove thrown down at the Christian's
feet:

> Must I be carried to the skies,
> On flowery beds of ease,
> While others fight to win the prize,
> And sail through stormy seas?

Peter states that God uses suffering for our good: "After you have
suffered a little while, [God] will himself restore you and make you
strong, firm and steadfast." God never wastes the suffering of his people, but builds character and faith through it all.

In his book *The Gulag Archipelago*, Alexander Solzhenitsyn poignantly shares this truth in his life. "It was only when I lay there on rot-
ting prison straw that I sensed within myself the first stirring of good.
So, bless you, prison, for having been in my life."

When we walk along the shore of the ocean we notice that the
rocks are sharp in the quiet coves, but polished in those places where
the waves beat against them. God can use the "waves and billows" of
life to polish us, if we will allow him.

He has given us his very great and precious promises.

(2 Peter 1:4)

Peter gives two adjectives for the promises of God — they are "great" and they are "precious." To emphasize how great and precious they are, he adds the intensifier "very," indicating that the promises of God are of a high degree of greatness and preciousness.

The Greek word for "precious," meaning costly, is used extensively in Peter's letters. He writes of our faith as being "of greater worth than gold" (1 Peter 1:7) and "the precious blood of Christ" (1 Peter 1:19). The promises of God are in this upper echelon of spiritual blessings.

Peter identifies two blessings that can be ours through the promises of God. First, "through them you may participate in the divine nature." The Authorized Version renders this as "partakers of the divine nature." This is what takes place when the Holy Spirit comes to dwell within us. He cleanses, empowers, and indwells us. Through his gracious and mighty work we can partake of the very nature of Christ — his love, his joy, his holiness. No wonder Peter refers to God's promises as "very great and precious."

Furthermore, Peter says that through these promises we can "escape the corruption in the world." That, along with participating in the divine nature, is a rather bold assertion for finite and sinful humans. But a promise is an assurance given by someone who has the power to fulfill it. God's omnipotence and infinite love are our guarantee for the fulfillment of all the very great and precious promises to us.

Let us claim the ineffable blessings of these promises of God!

But the day of the Lord will come like a thief.   (2 Peter 3:10)

"The day of the Lord will come," declares Peter. Jesus is coming again! The Lord's Second Coming is more than a theological curiosity, more than a threat wielded by fire-and-brimstone evangelists or a sheer fiction of the imagination. It is a prophesied event recorded over three hundred times in Scripture. When God says something over three hundred times, we had better believe it!

Peter's description of the end time, with its great noise and the dissolution of the earth by fire (vv. 10-12), was written long before the atomic age. This generation has witnessed the awesome destruction by nuclear weapons and seen great cities melted with fervent heat. We now know that such a total destruction is not only possible but even probable. Peter's description fits all too strikingly the threat of nuclear holocaust that hangs like the sword of Damocles over our generation.

Peter is not preaching a fatalistic gospel, but one of hope in Christ. Because the Lord is returning, there is assurance and hope. His reward will be with him, "a new heaven and a new earth, the home of righteousness" (v. 13).

The end, warns Peter, will come upon us "like a thief." A thief comes unexpectedly, and woe to the person not prepared. Peter asks, "Since everything will be destroyed in this way, what kind of people ought you to be?" His answer is immediate and urgent for each of us: "You ought to live holy and godly lives."

*But grow in the grace and knowledge of our Lord and Savior Jesus
Christ.* (2 Peter 3:18)

Peter warns his readers to "Be on your guard so that you may not be
carried away" (3:17). To remain steadfast and victorious he directs
them to "grow in the grace and knowledge of our Lord and Savior Jesus
Christ."

There are no "static Christians." There is no steadfastness except by
progression. It is told that on his pocket Bible Oliver Cromwell had a
motto written in Latin which, when translated, read: "He who ceases to
be better ceases to be good." Growth is the norm for the Christian.

Our golden text intimately links growth in grace with growth in
the "knowledge of our Lord and Savior Jesus Christ." There can be no
grace apart from Christ, and there can be no growth in grace except as
we grow in our knowledge of Christ. It is not mere knowledge *about* Jesus, it is knowledge *of* Jesus, a personal knowledge of the Savior.

We may test our growth by asking, "Do I know more of Christ today than I did yesterday? Do I live nearer to him today than I did a little
while ago?" The more we know of the Savior, the deeper will be our love
of him; the more we discover of his beauty and virtues, the more we will
love him. Growth will be in proportion to our knowledge of him.

The following came to my attention in my teen years, and ever
since I have been trying to measure up to its wise counsel:

Good, better, best, never let it rest,
Until our good becomes better,
And our better becomes best.

This we proclaim concerning the Word of life. (1 John 1:1)

John, the one who on earth had been closer to our Lord than any other, is the last survivor of the company of disciples. He is the last eyewitness to the momentous events of our Lord, the last to have known the historical Jesus. Into this epistle John has poured the distillation of his soul and faith, making this letter uniquely rich and rewarding.

A group of historians, authors, and editors were once asked to choose one moment in American history they would most like to have witnessed. One said he would like to have been among the sailors in the moonlit predawn moment of October 12, 1492, when a lookout spotted the island shore of the New World. Another chose that moment in November 1805 when Lewis and Clark first glimpsed their long-sought goal of the Pacific Ocean, or the moment when Clark scribbled in his journal, "Ocean in view — oh the joy!"

But the author of this epistle goes beyond mere wish to announce that he was an eyewitness of the most significant event of all history — the coming to earth of "That which was from the beginning . . . the Word of Life." Eugene Peterson's *The Message* renders verse 2 this way: "The Word of Life appeared right before our eyes; we saw it happen! . . . The infinite Life of God himself took shape before us."

Christ is the Word (*Logos*), God's highest revelation of life both here and hereafter. He is our source of spiritual life and of our ultimate reward of life eternal.

> *But if we walk in the light, as he is in the light, we have fellowship with one another.* (1 John 1:7)

John quickly announces his purpose in writing "so that you also may have fellowship with us. And our fellowship is with the Father and with his Son, Jesus Christ" (1:3).

The New Testament word for "fellowship," *koinonia*, is one of the most beautiful words of the Bible, expressing the unique relationship that exists between brothers and sisters in the Lord. It has been my privilege on occasion to be in company with fellow believers from around the world, of varied races, nationalities, and languages. Though we had not previously met, yet there was manifested an instant bonding and love with one another. *Koinonia* is a gift of God and one of the rich heritages of the Christian.

The historian Luke records of the early church that they "devoted" themselves to fellowship, along with prayer and Scripture (Acts 2:42). For the fledgling church, fellowship was not an elective but an essential for spiritual growth and health.

Thomas Kelly in his classic, *Testament of Devotion*, writes rapturously of Christian fellowship: "In glad amazement and wonder we enter upon a relationship which we had not known the world contained for the sons of men." How immeasurably enriched our lives have been by Christian fellowship. God blesses, affirms, encourages, guides, comforts, and speaks to us through our brothers and sisters in the Lord.

The blood of Jesus, his Son, purifies us from all sin.   (1 John 1:7)

A group of tourists was being conducted through the home of Beethoven, the peerless German composer. As they came to the room where he had spent so many hours at the piano, the guide paused and said quietly, "And here is the master's instrument." A woman in the back of the group pushed her way forward, sat down at the bench, and began to play one of Beethoven's sonatas. She said, "I suppose many musicians love to play this piano." The guide replied, "Last summer Ignace Paderewski was here and several in the group wanted him to play. But he responded, 'Oh, no, I am not worthy to play the same keyboard as the great Beethoven.'"

There are texts in the Bible that seem too sacred to touch. They usher us into the Holy of Holies of God's redemptive work. The treasured truth of our text leads us to realize our unworthiness as John brings us to the cross, to the unspeakable sacrifice of Christ and what it means to us. Spiritually, we remove our shoes, for we are on holy ground.

The apostle gives us one of the most sacred phrases of the Bible, "the blood of Jesus." It is a kind of spiritual magnifying glass that brings into focus the unsearchable and unsurpassed love of God in the Lord's atoning sacrifice on Calvary. It speaks to us of the costliness of our forgiveness, which does not come to us from a courtroom but from a cross, not from a human decree but from a divine death, not by any merit of our own but by the grace of our Lord Jesus Christ. It cost the very lifeblood of the Son of God. Such an amazing and sacrificial divine love, as Isaac Watts has reminded us, "demands my soul, my life, my all."

And if anyone sins, we have an Advocate with the Father, Jesus Christ the Righteous. (1 John 2:1 NKJV)

We have all sinned and come under the sentence of death. Our deadly adversary, Satan, is described as "the accuser of our brothers" (Revelation 12:10). The moment we sin, Satan becomes the prosecuting attorney in the high court of heaven.

If a person sins, that does not immediately sever the link that binds the believer to Christ. If that were so we would all have a tenuous and short-lived union with our Lord. But when we sin and confess it, Christ our advocate pleads our cause on the merit of his blameless life and divine sacrifice for us. He intercedes on our behalf at the bar of divine justice.

In Rockefeller Center of New York City reposes a bronze statue of Prometheus. Greek legend tells that Prometheus took fire from heaven and gave it as a gift to men. Zeus, the king of the gods, was angry that men should receive this gift. So he took Prometheus and chained him to a rock in the middle of the Adriatic Sea. There he was tortured with the heat of the day and the cold of the night, and with a vulture to tear out his liver, which always grew again only to be torn out again. This legend represents the pagan concept of gods, a horde of jealous and vengeful deities.

How different is this concept of deity from Christ and the comforting message that he is our advocate, the One who pleads our cause and secures our pardon.

He is the atoning sacrifice for our sins.   (1 John 2:2)

An infinity of truth is flung into a great New Testament word as John declares, "He is the atoning sacrifice for our sins." Earlier generations of Christians were familiar with the theological term used in the Authorized Version, "propitiation," for the work of Christ on our behalf. But in deference to our understanding the NIV translates it "atoning sacrifice."

This word speaks of our plight: we were under the judgment and penalty of sin. As rebellious sinners against a holy God, we were helpless in the magnitude of our need for forgiveness and reconciliation.

This word also speaks of the price of our redemption. Christ by his shed blood atoned for our sin. The costliness of our salvation, the death on a felon's cross of the Son of God, surpasses our comprehension.

This word speaks of the Person — our Lord — who became "the atoning sacrifice." He is the Sovereign who became our Savior, who "emptied himself" (Philippians 2:7) and endured the cross that we may be saved and have eternal life. Isaac Watts has helped us to sing our response to such a sacrifice:

Dear Savior, I can ne'er repay
The debt of love I owe!
Here, Lord, I give myself away;
'Tis all that I can do.

Do not love the world or anything in the world.   (1 John 2:15)

The apostle in memorable words warns of the rivals for the human heart: "Do not love the world or anything in the world.... For everything in the world — the cravings of sinful man, the lust of the eyes and the boasting of what he has and does — comes not from the Father but from the world. The world and its desires pass away, but the man who does the will of God lives forever" (1 John 2:15-17).

We must all contend with the notorious triad John identifies — the lust of the flesh, the lust of the eyes, and the pride of life. By "the world" John does not mean the world of people or the created world, but the world's pagan values. Love for the world and love for the Father are mutually exclusive; they cannot coexist in the human heart.

D. L. Moody once said, "It is all right for the boat to be in the water but not for the water to be in the boat. And it is all right for the Christian to be in the world, but not for the world to be in the Christian." The Christian must live in the world, yet not be of the world. John in this letter tells his readers that our creeds must be matched by our deeds, our assertions by our actions, and our talk by our walk.

Let us beware of the world's allurements — its vain pleasures and tinsel treasures. John Wesley wisely counsels, "Anything that cools our love for Christ is the world." Only when Christ reigns without a rival upon our heart is he truly Lord of our life.

How great is the love the Father has lavished on us.   (1 John 3:1)

J ohn in this text rhapsodizes on the love of God: "How great is the love the Father has lavished on us, that we should be called children of God! And that is what we are!" (1 John 3:1). It is for all of us an exclamation of amazement and wonder.

The last statement, "And that is what we are," was not included in the King James Version. But it is found in the oldest and best Greek manuscripts and has been included in newer translations. It adds a note of blessed assurance.

"How great" comes from the word *potapen* that literally means, "from what country, race or tribe?" It speaks of something foreign. The translation could well read, "What foreign kind of love the Father has bestowed upon us." One translator suggests, "From what far realm? What unearthly love, how otherworldly."

The expression "the Father" puts this love in the relationship of father and children. For his children who have responded to his divine overture of love on Calvary, God is our Father, not only in the sense of paternity — he has created us — but also by adoption — "To those who believed in his name, he gave the right to become children of God."

The verb translated "lavished" speaks of the extravagance of God's love. God's love to humankind, "lavished on us," surpasses our understanding, but it woos and wins our hearts. Indeed, as the song reminds us,

> The love of God is greater far,
> Than tongue or pen can ever tell.
> It goes beyond the highest star,
> And reaches to the lowest hell.

But we know that when he appears, we shall be like him, for we shall see him as he is. (1 John 3:2)

G od has great plans for us. A threefold sequence of events excites our anticipation.

First, Christ will appear. The word for "appears" is the Greek *Parousia*, which has become a technical term for the return of Christ. It speaks of our Lord's glorious Second Coming, his mighty and triumphant return. It will be the culmination and the coronation of all history, a rapture beyond our most daring imaginings. It is the Christian's blessed hope.

Second, John tells us we shall see him as he is. Just think — we shall see Jesus! We shall see him in all his majesty, his might, his magnificence. In one of the last promises to us in the Bible, John describes the joys of heaven: "They will see his face" (Revelation 22:4). It will be the greatest blessing and deepest joy of the Christian.

Then, wonder of wonders — we shall be like him! Imagine, you and me like Jesus! Clothed in garments of glory! A body not subject to the limitations and infirmities of the flesh! Made pure and holy as our Lord. On earth we know his works of salvation and sanctification. In heaven we will know his work of glorification. We praise and thank God for the love and grace, in spite of our unworthiness, that he lavishes upon us.

Such a gift brings sacred responsibility: "Everyone who has this hope in him purifies himself, just as he is pure" (v. 3). May we aspire to purity of heart, not because it is our duty, but because it will be our deepest delight and highest privilege.

We know that we have passed from death to life. (1 John 3:14)

These words of John reverse the world's order of things. The world says that we go from life to death, but John says that we go from death to life. "We know," he says, leaving no room for uncertainty.

The apostle Paul echoes this truth, "For the perishable must clothe itself with the imperishable, and the mortal with immortality" (1 Corinthians 15:53). A child of the resurrection passes from death to life, from mortality to immortality, from the temporal to the eternal.

The One who is "the resurrection and the life" replaces fear of death with an expectant faith that sees dawn beyond dusk, star beyond mist, light beyond darkness. The empty tomb of the resurrected Christ eloquently proclaims that death is not destruction, but a metamorphosis.

This golden text eloquently proclaims that the believer at death does not leave the land of the living to go into the land of the dying. Rather, we leave the land of the dying to go into the land of the living.

Winston Churchill planned his own funeral service, conducted at St. Paul's Cathedral in London, to the final detail. At the end of the service Taps was played. Then a pause, and from another section of the cathedral, Reveille resonated throughout the cavernous domain!

When we shall no longer cast a shadow in the sun and when Taps is sounded at the end of our earthly pilgrimage, may it be followed with the Reveille of the resurrected Savior, heralding the new and eternal life for all who know him as Savior and Lord.

And we ought to lay down our lives for our brothers.

(1 John 3:16)

John crystallizes for the believer the meaning of this mighty word, love: "This is how we know what love is: Jesus Christ laid down his life for us." This is the second great "John 3:16" of the Bible. The first declares Christ's sacrifice on Calvary as the supreme expression of love.

John reminds us that we are conscripted by Christ's love to a vulnerable involvement amid the wounds and warfare of life. In the second half of our text, John expresses it in ultimate and unmistakable terms: "And we ought to lay down our lives for our brothers."

Amy Carmichael, who sacrificially gave her life in missionary service to India, wrote in reflection on this text: "How often I think of that *ought*. No sugary sentiment there. Just the stern, glorious trumpet call, *ought*." Her biographer, Elisabeth Elliot, shares the principle that governed both their lives: "Ask not how little but how much can love give."

The love of which John writes is sensitive and responsive to the needs of others: "If anyone has material possessions and sees his brother in need but has not pity on him, how can the love of God be in him?" (3:17). The apostle calls us to love in action: "Let us not love with words or tongue but with actions and in truth" (3:18).

The words of Albert Orsborn's hymn serve as a postscript to this text:

> Except I am moved with compassion,
> How dwells your spirit in me?
> In word and in deed, burning love is my need;
> I know I can find this in thee.

The one who is in you is greater than the one who is in the world.

(1 John 4:4)

The world as defined by John is human nature apart from, and in opposition to, God. The evil and influence of the world's rebellion against God are powerful, more powerful than we can overcome in our own strength. But the assuring word from John is, "The one who is in you is greater than the one who is in the world."

John was present in the Upper Room and had heard Jesus in his farewell message to the disciples give the promise of the Holy Spirit to his followers. At Pentecost he witnessed the dispensation of the Spirit in coming upon and dwelling within the believer. He knew from his own experience that the power of the Spirit within the Christian is greater than all the world's evil that might assault us.

The story is told of the famed Scottish hero, Robert Bruce, who when fleeing his enemies took refuge in a cave and there prayed for God's protection. While he was inside the cave a spider wove a web across its entrance. His pursuers came to the cave, but seeing the spider web across its opening thought he could not have entered without breaking the web, and went on their way. Later Bruce said, "Without God, a stone wall is as a spider web; with God a spider web is as a stone wall."

We have an invincibility by the indwelling presence and power of the Holy Spirit, bequeathed by Christ to his followers. By the mighty Holy Spirit in us we have a power greater than Satan and all his temptations, and we can be "more than conquerors through him who loves us" (Romans 8:37).

God Is Love

God is love. (1 John 4:8)

This golden text is one of the most profound statements in the Bible. John twice makes this pronouncement: "God is love" (4:8, 16). The word "love" or its equivalent is found fifty-one times in this letter. We could very well title this "The Epistle of Love."

John's statement, "God is love," is the highest conception of the divine nature that has ever been attained. Nowhere else in all the realm of literature, philosophy, or religion has such a bold assertion been made.

Thomas Kelly in his classic, *A Testament of Devotion,* states: "God's love isn't just a diffused benevolence. The Infinite Love is the ground of all creatures, the source of their existence, and also knows a tender concern for each."

All God's attributes and activities are grounded in love. The apostle goes on to give the amazing example of his assertion: "He loved us and sent his Son as an atoning sacrifice for our sins" (4:9-10). God becoming flesh in Christ, and his sacrifice on Calvary, is the supreme articulation of love in the history of humankind.

When the renowned theologian Karl Barth visited the U.S., a seminary student asked, "Dr. Barth, what is the single most important truth you have learned as a theologian?" Barth replied, "The most important thing I have learned is this: 'Jesus loves me, this I know, for the Bible tells me so.'" The amazing love of God for us is the cardinal and central affirmation of our faith as expressed by John in the immortal words of this text.

This is the victory that has overcome the world, even our faith.

(1 John 5:4)

A mong the treasures of truth in this epistle is this sparkling jewel: "For everyone born of God overcomes the world. This is the victory that has overcome the world, even our faith."

The word "overcome" is used three times in verses 4 and 5. In the first and third instance it is in the present tense and denotes a continual overcoming of the world by the Christian. Its second instance is in the Greek aorist tense, which denotes an action completed — the victory over the world that was ours when we first believed.

We are engaged in a spiritual life-and-death struggle. Our enemy the devil is powerful and subtle. But by faith we shall be triumphant, for as a chorus reminds us, "Faith is the victory that overcomes the world."

Jesus said, "Believing is seeing." Faith is believing what we cannot see. When we exercise faith, we will see the power of God overcoming what otherwise seemed impossible. Faith sees the invisible, believes the incredible, and receives the impossible.

Herbert Booth's hymn speaks to us of the overcoming power of faith:

O for trust that brings the triumph
When defeat seems strangely near!
O for faith that changes fighting
Into victory's ringing cheer;
Faith triumphant,
Knowing not defeat or fear!

If we ask anything according to his will, he hears us.

(1 John 5:14)

Before John comes to the end of his letter he leaves with us one of the great promises in the Bible on prayer: "If we ask anything according to his will, he hears us."

The conditional phrase "according to his will" is a prerequisite for all our praying. Jesus taught us to pray "Your will be done," and set the example in his deep struggle in Gethsemane when he prayed, "Not my will, but yours be done." We are too prone in prayer to tell God what we want of him rather than ask what he wants of us.

Assured that God hears the prayers that are in the divine purpose for us, we have confidence of his answer: "And if we know that he hears us — whatever we ask — we know that we have what we asked of him" (5:15). Paul Rees reminds us, "Nothing lies outside the reach of prayer except that which lies outside the will of God."

None of us have actually seen the Internet, yet as we communicate by its marvelous technology, we have faith that it exists. A poet poses a rhetorical question as it relates to melodies from a radio sent across continents:

> If radio's slim fingers can pluck a melody
> From night, and toss it over a continent or sea;
> If the petaled white notes of a violin
> Are blown across a mountain or a city's din;
> If songs, like crimson roses, are culled from the thin blue air —
> Why should mortals wonder if God hears prayer?

And this is love: that we walk in obedience to his commands.

(2 John 6)

J ohn opens this brief one-chapter letter with a somewhat anonymous designation of himself, simply as "the elder." He could have
put forth the highest credentials of apostleship, having been closer to
Christ than any other during our Lord's earthly ministry. We note also
that in John's magnificent Gospel and his incomparable book of Revelation the apostle's humility precluded his affixing his byline.

This brief letter by John gives insight into the early life of the
church, and to the apostle's pastoral concerns. "To the chosen lady and
her children" identifies the receiver of this letter. She was blessed with
children "walking in the truth." Here we see the second generation of
believers coming into the life of the Christian community.

The dominant theme of John's three epistles is love — love for God
and love for others. Here he states that the true evidence of our love is
that of obedience to God.

J. Wilbur Chapman on one occasion in London visited General
William Booth, founder of the Salvation Army. At the end of his visit,
the American evangelist asked the general if he would disclose his secret for his great success as an evangelist. Booth, now past 80 years of
age, responded: "I will tell you the secret. Early in my life I decided that
God would have all there was of William Booth." Dr. Chapman said he
went away from that meeting with General Booth knowing "that the
greatness of man's power is the measure of his surrender."

When we truly love God, we will be fully surrendered to him, and
obedient to his will and commands for us.

I have no greater joy than to hear that my children are walking in the truth. (3 John 4)

T he apostle John here is referring to his children in the faith, those who through his teaching came to know the living Christ. It is always a cause for great joy to see those whom the Lord may have used us to encourage on the Christian way, continuing and growing in their walk of faith.

But our text also can apply to the great joy of hearing that our children in the flesh are walking in the truth. Nothing reported by others about them warms the heart of a Christian parent as much as to hear from another of the quality of spiritual life of their children.

Some years ago our oldest daughter shared with us what she wrote of her aspiration and commitment for her family: "I want to help build a Christ-centered home, with the teaching of God's Word, the love for acquiring knowledge, and the example of living for Christ — those qualities that enriched my home as a child and teenager. The Lord has given me so much and he now requires me to give much in return. I want my home to be a place that stimulates creativity, that offers opportunity for the study of music, of books, of hobbies, where ideas can be shared and questions safely discussed. I want Christ's presence to permeate our home. God is obviously a lover of beauty, color, simplicity, and creativity. Our God is a God of serenity and refreshment. I want my home and my family to radiate this kind of God whom we serve."

We often hear from others that she and her children model that aspiration expressed at the start of her family life, and that brings us great joy!

To him who is able to keep you from falling. (Jude 24)

J ude, one of the five one-chapter books of the Bible and very brief, is
full of surprises and timeless truths. Its magnificent two-verse doxology at the end has often resonated as a benediction in our worship
experience: "To him who is able to keep you from falling and to present
you before his glorious presence without fault and with great joy — to
the only God our Savior be glory, majesty, power and authority,
through Jesus Christ our Lord, before all ages, now and forevermore!
Amen."

Three times in the New Testament the joyful note peals forth of the
God who is able. Paul gives praise "to him who is able to establish you"
(Romans 16:25). He writes of "him who is able to do immeasurably
more than all we ask or imagine" (Ephesians 3:20).

Jude declares two tremendous truths about what God is able to do
for us. He is able to keep us from falling. Mountaineers are roped together so that even if one climber should slip, the other will hold him se-
curely. When we bind ourselves to God, he keeps us from falling. And
wonder of wonders, because of Christ's work on our behalf, God is able
to bring us into his very presence without fault and with great joy.

Rory Noland and Greg Ferguson have given us the beautiful devotional chorus:

He is able, more than able
to accomplish what concerns me today.
He is able, more than able
to handle anything that comes my way.
He is able, more than able
to do much more than I could ever dream.
He is able, more than able
to make me what He wants me to be.

The revelation of Jesus Christ.   (Revelation 1:1)

R evelation is the book for the present hour, God's special word to our age. The Greek word for "revelation," *apokalupsis,* literally means, "unveiling." The great theme of this book is the unveiling, the disclosure of Jesus Christ.

The apostle John, exiled in his old age to a prison cave on an island, heard no fewer than twelve times the command, "Write." With only a stone slab or a piece of driftwood as his desk, and as his altar, he obeyed the command. The vision he received and that of which he wrote must have made him wish he could dip his pen in some iridescent ink. In obedience to that command he gave the world his magnificent Apocalypse, unmatched in its divine revelation, profound theology, and literary craftsmanship. The swords of the mighty Roman Empire have long since vanished, but the pen of John lives on and will last into eternity.

Revelation portrays Christ as does no other book of the Bible. It takes up where the Gospels leave off. It reveals Christ in his glory, his celestial majesty, the triumphant Christ enthroned in heaven and who will mightily return to earth and set up his eternal kingdom.

It was my privilege on one occasion to sit next to Dr. M. Scott Peck at a conference of Christian leaders. In the course of conversation I asked him of his experience with Jesus Christ when he wrote about grace in his best-seller, *The Road Less Traveled.* He responded with one of the most memorable statements I have heard, saying, "I was absolutely thunderstruck by the Christ I found in the Gospels. The Jesus of the Bible is the church's best kept secret, and I found myself beginning to fall in love with Jesus."

May the revelation of Jesus Christ in God's Word have that kind of impact upon us.

Blessed is the one who reads the words of this prophecy.
(Revelation 1:3)

There are seven Beatitudes in Revelation — seven chords of joy that form a symphony of blessing for the believer. The first comes to us in the opening paragraph of the book: "Blessed is the one who reads the words of this prophecy, and blessed are those who hear it and take to heart what is written in it, because the time is near."

This is the only book of the Bible that contains a direct promise of blessing for reading it, a special blessing attached to the reading of Revelation. Perhaps the reason is that no other book so exalts the Lord Jesus and portrays him in his glory, as does this one.

There is a threefold challenge for the blessing of this beatitude. First, one must make the investment of time to "read it." Secondly, we must "hear it," let it speak its message to us. Thirdly, we must "take to heart," apply and live by what it says.

The following six promises declare the blessings that will accrue from this first Beatitude. There is the Beatitude of comfort: "Blessed are the dead who die in the Lord from now on" (14:13). Next comes the Beatitude of caution, to keep alert for the Lord's coming: "Blessed is he who stays awake and keeps his clothes with him" (16:15). The third Beatitude celebrates the grand climax of history: "Blessed are those who are invited to the wedding supper of the Lamb" (19:9). Then comes the Beatitude of conquest: "Blessed and holy are those who have part in the first resurrection. The second death has no power over them" (20:6). Fifth is the Beatitude of commitment: "Blessed is he who keeps the words of the prophecy in this book" (22:7). Finally comes the Beatitude of cleansing: "Blessed are those who wash their robes" (22:14). What abundant blessings God has in store for us!

Look, he is coming with the clouds, and every eye will see him.

(Revelation 1:7)

S tand with me on the tiptoe of your mind and contemplate the awesome wonder of John's launching of his magnificent manuscript with the peerless proclamation, "Look, he is coming." That statement encapsulates the most awesome, colossal event of human history, the Second Coming of Jesus Christ.

Jesus, on the eve of his departure, said to his disciples, "I will come again and receive you unto myself" (John 14:3). Luke, the church historian, records the ascension of our Lord on the Mount of Olives before five hundred followers. Without the aid of booster rockets or computers, the Lord in miraculous liftoff defies the law of gravity and ascends into heaven. As the followers stand agape in wide-eyed wonder, the angel announces: "This same Jesus, who has been taken from you into heaven, will come back" (Acts 1:11).

Over three hundred verses, or one in every thirty in the New Testament, speak of the glorious Second Coming of Christ. It is prominent in seventeen Old Testament books, and all nine authors of the New Testament herald the event. Twenty-three of the twenty-seven New Testament books refer to our Lord's return, with three of the four books that omit it being single-chapter letters.

The Second Coming of Christ is not hinted at, it is highlighted as a dominant New Testament teaching. Let us be sure to be ready for this culminating event of history and of our lives. With Charles Wesley we raise our voices in acclamation:

> Lo! He comes with clouds descending,
> Once for favored sinners slain;
> Thousand thousand saints attending,
> Swell the triumph of his train;
> Hallelujah! God appears on earth to reign.

"You have forsaken your first love." (Revelation 2:4)

The church at Ephesus was the queen church of early Christendom. In the letters to the seven churches in the book of Revelation, the commendation to this church was extravagant. It was praised as a working church (2:2), a church with high standards (2:2), a persevering church (2:3), and as a church that kept itself pure from heretical practices (2:6).

But the seeds of corruption had started to appear. The Lord says to them, "Yet I hold this against you: You have forsaken your first love." It was a sin the average observer would not detect. The church would be viewed as being zealous in activity, gallant in endurance, unimpeachable in doctrine. But in the Lord's searching eyes, it lacked that which is most important of all, a deep, fervent, undying love for God.

The church at Ephesus had lost its spiritual sparkle, its glow of love. A once ardent love had now become prosaic, commonplace. It happens in marriages. It happens in human friendships. It can happen in our relationship with Christ.

What happened in Ephesus can all too easily become the epitaph over a modern church. We too can be known for zealous good works, strict orthodoxy, past endurance — but with the fire going out. An absorbing round of activity, empty ritual, and a subtle and sterile legalism that passes for loyalty to Christ can replace the passion for Christ. Perhaps in this text Christ speaks, not only to the church at ancient Ephesus, but to us too.

When we gave our heart to Jesus, we loved him for his infinite love that drew us to him. Let us never abandon our first love, but keep it ever growing and glowing.

> *"Be faithful, even to the point of death, and I will give you the crown*
> *of life."*   (Revelation 2:10)

This radiant promise was given to the faithful church of Smyrna that was enduring a fiery persecution. Christians were brought into the coliseum and amphitheaters of Rome to be fed to lions for entertainment. But out of tribulation would come triumph, out of persecution would come the ultimate prize — life eternal. The crown follows the cross.

True, the Christians in Smyrna might even face death. But the risen Christ assures them: "He who overcomes will not be hurt at all by the second death" (2:11). Four times, and only in this book, the "second death" is referred to (2:11; 20:6, 14; 21:8). Death holds no terror for those who are born of the Spirit. For to be born once is to die twice; to be born twice is to die once.

Christians may have to suffer the first death on this earth, they may even be persecuted unto death, but over them "the second death has no power." The final power is not the power of evil, but the reigning power of Jesus Christ.

"We have a proof in our religion that you haven't in yours," a Muslim once said, on hearing a Christian preacher. "When we go to Arabia we can find the tomb of the Prophet, so that we have a proof that he lived. But when you go to Jerusalem you cannot be sure you have the burial place of Jesus. You have no tomb as we have."

"True," replied the preacher, "we have no tomb in our religion because we have no corpse." Our gospel ends not in a corpse, but in a Conqueror, not in a tomb, but in a triumph.

"To him who overcomes, I will give . . . a new name."

(Revelation 2:17)

The Lord promises to the overcomer a new name in glory. When I came upon this text some years ago, I said to my wife that morning at the breakfast table, "I wonder what your new name will be in heaven?" But then I remembered the rest of the text and had to say, "I guess I will never know because the verse says it will be "known only to him (or her) who receives it."

Upon earth we usually have a bevy of names. I am often called Colonel by those who know me least, Henry by those who know me more closely, and Hank by my closest friends. My children call me Dad, my grandkids call me Grandpa, my nephews and nieces address me as Uncle. In my most intimate relationship with my loving wife of over fifty years, there is a place for endearing names that even our children don't know. In heaven we will be given a new name, known but to God alone.

In the Bible often a new name was bestowed to mark a new status. Thus Abram became Abraham as father of a great nation, Jacob's name change to Israel designated him a prince, Simon was turned into Peter the rock, and Saul's new nature transformed him into Paul.

The "new name" of our text can represent the glorified person we will become through the transforming grace of Christ. We will not be lost in the great corporate fellowship of heaven, but will eternally be an individual, prized by God.

May we be able to sing from our hearts the song of the redeemed found in hymnals: "There's a new name written down in glory! And it's mine! Oh yes, it's mine!"

Reputation versus Reality

"You have a reputation of being alive, but you are dead."

(Revelation 3:1)

S ardis was one of the most powerful cities in the world and known for its fabled luxury. To the church in Sardis the Lord says, "I know your deeds" (3:1). It was probably a beehive of activity. Statistics were up, and perhaps like some modern counterparts, their philosophy was "in numbers we trust." Our Christian subculture all too often focuses on statistics as the measure of church success. In such a context the question asked is "How many?" rather than "How deep?" In his messages to the seven churches, Jesus makes no reference whatsoever to numbers or material assets, but rather focuses on qualities of the spiritual life.

The believers in Sardis thought they were a thriving congregation. But the startling and terrible truth declared to them by the Lord is: "But you are dead." They had a rich tradition, but it was all behind them. They were living on a reputation rather than a reality.

We have all had the experience of admiring what appeared to be beautiful flowers, only on closer inspection to find they were artificial. They were but imitations. Outward appearance can be notoriously deceptive. The church in Sardis appeared to be alive, but under the searching illumination of our Lord, it was pronounced "dead."

But the Lord does not leave them without a divine prescription. "Wake up! Strengthen what remains and is about to die" (3:2). If "eternal vigilance is the price of liberty," then for each of us eternal watchfulness is the price of salvation. Our watchword must be, "Take care of the reality and the image will take care of itself."

"I have placed before you an open door that no one can shut."

(Revelation 3:8)

The church at Philadelphia ranks as the most faithful of the seven churches of Revelation. It is given the only one of the seven letters that has no condemnation. One of the greatest promises in the Bible is given to this church, the promise of an open door that no one can shut.

Philadelphia lay at a vital crossroads of the world. Caesar's armies marched on the road that led to it, and the great caravans of merchants made their way there. The risen Christ was giving to the church in that great city its most prized opportunity, to witness to a Victor that paled the conquests of Caesar, and of riches that could never be carried in the ancient caravans.

The door Christ opens to us is a door that "no one can shut." Roman emperors tried to shut that door as they threw Christians to the ravenous beasts for their entertainment. But "the blood of the martyrs became the seed of the Christian church," as it spread around the world. Josef Stalin tried to shut that door, believing as Karl Marx did that religion was "an opiate of the people." But atheistic communism crumbled, and now in former communist countries the gospel is bringing light and liberation to countless. Neither the mighty Roman Empire, nor communism, nor all the "isms" and heresies that have opposed the gospel through the centuries could close the door Christ opened.

Christ gives to each of his followers an open door for service, a priceless opportunity to be his witness. Others cannot close it, but we can forfeit its rich opportunity by neglect or by sin. May we be faithful to use the open door he sets before us.

"I know your deeds, that you are neither cold nor hot."

(Revelation 3:15)

The letter to Laodicea has the grim distinction of being the only one of the seven letters with no word of praise. The Lord addressed them with the indictment: "I know your deeds, that you are neither cold nor hot. I wish you were either one or the other! So, because you are lukewarm — neither hot nor cold — I am about to spit you out of my mouth."

Laodicea had no water supply of its own. A stone aqueduct system brought water from a hot spring six miles away. By the time this water reached Laodicea it was lukewarm and tepid. The Laodiceans knew firsthand the repugnance of lukewarmness.

The Greek word for "hot" is *zestos* from which we derive the English word "zest." The Laodicean church had no zest; it lacked enthusiasm. It had a doctrinal correctness without spiritual fervor. The Lord exposes their self-deception in dramatic contrast between their self-image and the reality of their condition. They no doubt had self-esteem, yet our Lord tells them they are "wretched, pitiful." They said, "I am rich," but he tells them they are poor. They thought themselves well clothed in religious garments, but he tells them they are naked.

It is all too easy for our ardor to cool through preoccupation with bigness, buildings, and budgets, to be concerned with quantity rather than quality, size rather than goodness, program rather than people. These seven letters to the churches warn us of progressive degeneracy, and call us to priorities. Let us heed the Lord's warning to the seven churches, and to us today: "He who has an ear, let him hear what the Spirit says to the churches" (3:22).

"Here I am! I stand at the door and knock."　　(Revelation 3:20)

To the church in Laodicea, although it had grown lukewarm and merited no praise from the Lord, is given one of the most beautiful verses in the Bible: "Here I am! I stand at the door and knock. If anyone hears my voice and opens the door, I will come in and eat with him, and he with me." What sublime condescension! To that church where there was nothing to commend, Christ extends his gracious invitation.

Some years ago we were privileged to view Holman Hunt's masterpiece painting, *The Light of the World,* in St. Paul's Cathedral in London. To contemplate its majestic blending of color, light, and shade is a devotional experience. It portrays the moment when human destiny hangs in the balance, when divine love waits upon human reluctance. The door at which Christ knocks represents the human heart. Its hinges are rusty and the threshold is overgrown with weeds. Christ knocks at the door; his look is expectant. The one inside has only to open the door to permit the radiance of the Light of the World to flood his life.

As Christ knocks at the door of our heart, may we invite him in as the honored guest. He will flood every corner of our life with his radiance and grace. And he will speak to us his great promise: "To him who overcomes, I will give the right to sit with me on my throne" (3:21).

The New Song

And they sang a new song. (Revelation 5:9)

A new song resonates around the throne of God, a symphony of praise to the One found worthy to open the scroll in heaven, "because you were slain, and with your blood you purchased men for God." Never has such music been heard by mortal ear. Never have so many voices intoned such a majestic anthem, the number being beyond count (v. 11).

The anthem consists of a sevenfold doxology to Christ, the Lamb of God:

Worthy is the Lamb, who was slain,
to receive power and wealth and wisdom and strength
and honor and glory and praise! (v. 12)

All nature joins in the symphony of praise: "Then I heard every creature in heaven and on earth and under the earth and on the sea, and all that is in them, singing: 'To him who sits on the throne and to the Lamb be praise and honor and glory and power, for ever and ever!'" (v. 13). No wonder the final word is a grand "amen" (v. 14).

A. Catherine Hankey's hymn has captured every Christian's cherished hope in Christ:

When in scenes of glory
I sing the new, new song;
'Twill be the old, old story
That I have loved so long.

May you and I someday join that magnificent universal choir in its symphony of praise to the One who became the Lamb, sacrificed for our sin.

"Blessed are the dead who die in the Lord from now on."
(Revelation 14:13)

Here we encounter one of the most luminous and beautiful verses in the Bible: "Blessed are the dead who die in the Lord from now on." The Spirit affirms this truth: "'Yes,' says the Spirit, 'they will rest from their labor, for their deeds will follow them.'" What a comforting and reassuring text in the midst of life's tribulation and testing!

The great evangelist D. L. Moody said in his buoyant way: "Some day you will read in the papers that D. L. Moody is dead. Don't you believe a word of it! At that moment I shall be more alive than I am now. I shall have gone up higher, out of this old clay tenement into a house that is immortal, a body that death cannot touch, that sin cannot taint, a body fashioned like unto his glorious body." Shortly before his departure he was heard to say: "Earth is receding, and heaven is opening."

This radiant verse is reason for all of us in Christ to have the certainty and blessed hope expressed by Moody. For the end of time is eternity and the last step we take on life's journey leads us into the presence of God and the joys of eternal life in heaven.

For many people, heaven is perceived as a kind of postscript, an appendix to a book of which life on earth constitutes the actual text. But the contrary is true. Our earthly life is merely the preface to the book that will be recorded in heaven, a text without end. And we can be sure it will be "with a happy ending," one that will exceed our most daring imaginings.

The Hallelujah Chorus

*I heard what sounded like the roar of a great multitude in heaven
shouting: "Hallelujah!"* (Revelation 19:1)

This chapter of Revelation ushers in the greatest event of history,
the climax of the ages — the Second Coming of Christ. After all
the sufferings and trials, the onslaughts of Satan and the fierce battles
of life, there comes victory in Jesus, a uniting with him in heaven and a
great shout of "Hallelujah!"

The four "hallelujahs" of this chapter are the only place in the New
Testament where this mighty word of praise occurs (vv. 1, 3, 4, 6). It literally means, "Praise God!"

This passage was the source of inspiration for the "Hallelujah Chorus" of Handel's *Messiah*, considered by many to be the finest expression of praise in music. Handel came under divine inspiration, took his
pen, and began to write. The music for the Scriptural text began to
flow through his mind with such swiftness he could hardly write fast
enough. For twenty-four days he secluded himself, the food brought to
him often going untouched. He is described as "jumping up and running to the harpsichord, waving his arms in the air, shouting aloud,
'Hallelujah! Hallelujah! Hallelujah!'" He said, "I think I did see all
heaven before me." In an early performance of the cantata in London,
as the "Hallelujah Chorus" was being sung, the king was so moved he
rose to his feet. The audience followed his example, standing until the
end, a practice that has continued to this day.

That magnificent paean of praise will be superlatively eclipsed by
the celestial chorus described in our text. Wonder of wonders, we may
in that day be part of the grand Hallelujah Chorus in heaven, our souls
pouring forth God's praise in tumultuous celebration.

"Blessed are those who are invited to the wedding supper of the Lamb!"   (Revelation 19:9)

An awesome wedding is to take place: "Let us rejoice and be glad and give him glory! For the wedding of the Lamb has come, and his bride has made herself ready" (19:7).

We know that the Lamb, or the Bridegroom, is Christ. But who is the bride of verses 7-8? The relationship of God and his people has been symbolized in the Bible by marriage. Hosea hears God say, "I will betroth you to me forever" (2:19). Isaiah proclaimed, "For your Maker is your husband" (54:5). Jesus employed this symbolism in his parable of the wedding banquet (Matthew 22:1-14). Paul's model for human marriage is of Christ and the church (Ephesians 5:25-27). This beautiful teaching is fulfilled in our text as Christ takes the church to himself as his bride.

"The bride has made herself ready." Heaven is a prepared place for a prepared people. Obedience to God upon earth becomes our "fine linen" in which we will be arrayed to meet the divine Groom. Perhaps at this heavenly wedding each of us may be wearing the wedding garment of our own making from our life on earth.

It is always an honor to receive a wedding invitation. The greatest honor or invitation that we will ever have is God's invitation to the marriage banquet of heaven. Indeed, "Blessed are those" invited to be a part of the great family of God that will gather at that magnificent banquet. On that momentous day the presence of Christ will bring unspeakable joy and indescribable ecstasy, and his wedding gift to us will be life eternal! Let us be sure to respond affirmatively to his RSVP!

The "No Mores" of Eternity

"There will be no more death or mourning or crying or pain."
(Revelation 21:4)

The penman of Patmos gives us ten great "no mores" of eternity. I confess the first one causes me regret, admittedly because of my lack of understanding God's plan. John writes, "There was no more sea" (21:1 NKJV). I have had a lifelong romance with the sea — its matchless beauty, invigorating ambiance, recreational opportunities, fascinating marine life, and its most delectable offerings. "No more sea" almost seems like an epitaph to us sea lovers. But God's plan and design is always vastly superior to our finite concepts.

One of the Bible's most beautiful promises declares: "He will wipe every tear from their eyes. There will be no more death or mourning or crying or pain, for the old order of things has passed away" (21:4).

"No more death" (v. 4) peals forth a triumphant note. No more funerals, cemeteries, graves, or obituaries. No more severance of the cords of loving relationships. Christ has vanquished this great foe.

"No more sorrow, nor crying" (NKJV). There will be no tears in heaven. "There shall be no more pain." No more suffering the ravages of disease, or the pain from violence and circumstance.

There shall be no more temple (v. 22) for the Lord himself will be with his people, with no need for religious systems and places. There shall be no more sun or moon (21:23) or night there (22:5). The darkness of time has passed into eternity's day, for the glory of the Lord gives it light, and the Lamb is its lamp (21:23). And there will be no more curse (22:3), for sin and its curse will be forever gone. Hallelujah!

The twelve gates were twelve pearls, each gate made of a single pearl.

(Revelation 21:21)

John tells us that in heaven are twelve gates, each gate a single pearl and the gates will never be shut. The apostle furthers tells his readers that "There were three gates on the east, three on the north, three on the south and three on the west" (21:13).

William Barclay, eminent Bible expositor, draws an analogy from the twelve gates of the city. He suggests the three gates on the east represent the dawn, for those who find Christ in the glad morning of their days. The three gates on the north could stand for those who find faith through "the cold land" of their intellect. The three gates on the south are "in the warm land" and can represent those who come to Christ through their emotions. The three gates on the west can stand for the way into the holy city of those who came to Christ in the evening of their days. Dr. Barclay suggests that there are many roads and times in life when a person may find the way into the holy city and into the presence of God.

John tells us that each gate was made of a single pearl. What fabulous size pearls! Their priceless value speaks of the preciousness of the kingdom of God.

The pearly gates speak to us of another sacred truth. A pearl comes from a wounding of the oyster. Without a wound there would be no pearl. The pearly gates remind us that the glory of heaven comes to us through the sacrifice of the One who was "wounded for our transgression" (Isaiah 53:5 KJV). The magnificent pearls, hung eternally at the access routes of glory, speak to us of the One who hung upon a tree to unlock for us the gates of heaven.

The Book of Life

Only those whose names are written in the Lamb's book of life.
(Revelation 21:27)

The apostle John, near to the end of his manuscript, describes the joys and events of heaven, and warns, "Nothing impure will ever enter it, nor will anyone who does what is shameful or deceitful, but only those whose names are written in the Lamb's book of life."

There is but one access to heaven — through salvation in Christ, who said, "No one comes to the Father except through me" (John 14:6). The psalmist declared that the one who enters into the holy city of God must have "clean hands and a pure heart" (Psalm 24:4).

Heaven will be a perfect environment in contrast to the centuries of human sin, sorrow, and violence upon earth. Its inhabitants will be heirs of eternal life and absolute moral purity. Only the saved will enter into it. Mary Kidder has bequeathed to us the old hymn that affirms our status in the Book of Life:

> Lord, I care not for riches, neither silver nor gold;
> I would make sure of heaven, I would enter the fold.
> In the book of thy kingdom with its pages so fair,
> Tell me, Jesus, my Savior, is my name written there?

> Oh, that beautiful city with its mansions of light,
> With its glorified beings in pure garments of white!
> Where no evil thing cometh to despoil what is fair,
> Where the angels are watching! Yes, my name's written there.

They will see his face. (Revelation 22:4)

J ohn learned well from his Master — he keeps the best wine till last. The culmination of all the glories of heaven, its crowning joy, will be that "They will see his face." John elsewhere wrote, "When he appears . . . we shall see him as he is" (1 John 3:2).

When we endure a long separation from a loved one on earth, we can hardly wait to see that person and eagerly anticipate the joy of re-union. Nothing brings greater joy than again to see our loved one face to face. To see our Savior and Lord, the One who bore our sin on the cross, who triumphed over death for us, who has gone to prepare a place for us in glory, will be our highest joy, the summit of all the un-imaginable felicity of heaven.

Our hymnals exult in anticipation of it. Grant Tullar's beloved hymn captures for us the wonder of this anticipation:

Face to face with Christ, my Savior,
Face to face — what will it be —
When with rapture I behold him,
Jesus Christ who died for me?

Face to face I shall behold him,
Far beyond the starry sky;
Face to face in all his glory,
I shall see him by and by.

The Alpha and Omega

"I am the Alpha and the Omega." (Revelation 22:13)

Alpha and *Omega* are words for the first and last letters of the Greek alphabet. Their meaning is explicit in the amplification Jesus himself gives: "The First and the Last, the Beginning and the End."

Christ is the *Alpha*, the Beginning, the First. What a staggering claim! First — before the empires of Egypt, Babylon, Greece, Rome. First — before the solar system, the Milky Way, the Pleiades.

He is *Omega*, the End, the Last. What a blessed assurance. Although Dante's great work was filled with tragedy, he titled it *The Divine Comedy*, because of his belief that in the end God would give happiness to his people. Because Christ is the End as well as the Beginning, *Omega* as well as *Alpha*, eternal joy will be the reward for his people.

As the Alpha, Christ is Lord of our beginnings. He is there at the thresholds of our lives — at birth, at the marriage altar, at the start of a career, at the outset of new undertakings, at all our important beginnings.

As the Omega, he is Lord of our endings — when we leave home, at the completion of a task, the end of a stay, loss of a loved one, retirement, death.

We take comfort and courage from this title, with its assurance that our times are in the hands of the Eternal — the Lord of our beginnings and endings.

"I am . . . the bright Morning Star."   (Revelation 22:16)

Immanuel Kant wrote: "Two things fill the mind with ever new and increasing wonder and awe . . . the starry heaven above me and the moral law within me." My favorite sight in nature is the spectacle of a star-bejeweled sky on a dark night. It fills the soul with reverence to contemplate their majesty, their fathomless distance, their titanic size.

As dawn breaks, the stars of the sky gradually give way until only one star remains. All others fade from view except for the morning star. Christ, as the bright Morning Star, shines brightly when all other stars of our life fade away. Things that now shine so brightly on the horizon of our lives will someday fade and vanish away. The stars of prestige, position, possessions, of persons dear to us, will one by one grow dim and fade away. But after everything else has vanished, Christ will still shine brightly.

Every person of Christ's day had a picture in mind when Christ said, "I am the bright Morning Star." For centuries people charted their journeys by the stars. Travelers made their way over the trackless wilderness and sailors navigated the seas with their eyes on the stars. Stars were the roadmaps, the directional signs for their times.

An artist once drew a picture of a lone man rowing his little boat on a dark night. The wind is fierce, and waves crest and rage around his frail bark. But one star shines through the dark and angry sky above. On that star the voyager fixes his eyes and keeps on rowing through the storm. Beneath the picture are the words, "If I lose that I'm lost."

Our boat is small, the sea wide. Storms will come. But when we reckon our directions from the bright Morning Star we will safely reach heaven's harbor.

"Yes, I am coming soon!"   (Revelation 22:20)

John commenced his mighty manuscript with the glorious announcement, "Look, he is coming with the clouds, and every eye will see him" (1:7), and now no fewer than three times he repeats this glorious truth in his final chapter (vv. 7, 12, 20). The very last words of Jesus recorded in the Bible are, "Yes, I am coming soon" (22:20), followed by the final prayer that closes and culminates the Word of God, "Amen. Come, Lord Jesus" (22:20).

President Richard Nixon declared July 20, 1969, "the greatest day in history" when astronaut Neil Armstrong walked on the moon. Momentous as that day was, a far greater day occurred on an April morning some two thousand years earlier when the crucified Savior rose from the dead. The inspired seer declares an even greater, grander, and more glorious day — the day of his return.

During the First World War, a soldier in the trenches saw his friend wounded out in No Man's Land — that ground between his trench and that of the enemy. The man asked his officer, "May I go and bring him back?" The officer refused, "If you go I would lose you as well. I have to say no." But disobeying the officer, he went out to save his friend. He managed to bring him back, only to fall mortally wounded as he staggered to his trench. The officer was angry, "I told you not to go. Now I have lost two good men. It was not worth it." With his dying breath the man said, "But it was worth it, sir, because when I got to him he said, 'Jim, I knew you'd come.'"

Infinite love brought Christ from heaven to earth and led him to go to the No Man's Land of Calvary, there to be wounded to the death that he might bring us back from death to life. The glorious message of the Bible is that in the midst of the world's greatest battle Jesus will come, to bring us safely to himself. May we then be able to look up into his face, and knowing him as Savior and Friend, say, "I knew you'd come!"

About the Author

Colonel Henry Gariepy served for fifteen years as National Editor-in-Chief and Literary Secretary for The Salvation Army prior to his retirement in 1995. He now serves as a literary consultant, adjunct college faculty, adult Bible teacher, and Corps Sergeant Major — the Army's chief lay leader — in Toms River, New Jersey.

He is the author of more than twenty books and numerous articles. His *Portraits of Christ* has had a circulation of over 200,000 copies, and, like his *Portraits of Perseverance*, has been published in several editions and languages. His commissioned writings have included the authorized biography of General Eva Burrows (with a foreword by Billy Graham) and Volume 8 of the International History of The Salvation Army.

The author is an outdoor enthusiast and has completed three twenty-six-mile marathons. He earned his Bachelor of Arts and Master of Science degrees in Urban Studies and was honored by his alma mater with its 1994 Alumni Lifetime Leadership Award. He and his wife, Marjorie, take great delight in their four children and twelve grandchildren.